Screen Future

The Future of Entertainment, Computing,
and the Devices We Love

Brian David Johnson

ISBN 978-1934053263

This publication is designed to provide accurate and authoritative information in regard to the subject matter covered. It is sold with the understanding that the publisher is not engaged in professional services. If professional advice or other expert assistance is required, the services of a competent professional person should be sought.

Intel Corporation may have patents or pending patent applications, trademarks, copyrights, or other intellectual property rights that relate to the presented subject matter. The furnishing of documents and other materials and information does not provide any license, express or implied, by estoppel or otherwise, to any such patents, trademarks, copyrights, or other intellectual property rights.

Intel may make changes to specifications, product descriptions, and plans at any time, without notice. Fictitious names of companies, products, people, characters, and/or data mentioned herein are not intended to represent any real individual, company, product, or event.

Intel products are not intended for use in medical, life saving, life sustaining, critical control or safety systems, or in nuclear facility applications.

† Other names and brands may be claimed as the property of others.

This book is printed on acid-free paper. ∞

Publisher: Richard Bowles
Executive Director: Bill Boyle
Editor: David J. Clark
Text Design & Composition: Jim Stovall, Vincent A Caminiti - STI Certified Products, Inc
Graphic Art: Ted Cyrek

Library of Congress Cataloging in Publication Data:

Printed in the United States of America

10 9 8 7 6 5 4 3 2

First printing June 2010

IMPORTANT

You can access the companion Web site for this book on the Internet at:

www.intel.com/intelpress/tv30

Use the serial number located in the upper-right hand corner of the last page to register your book and access additional material, including the Digital Edition of the book.

Contents

Chapter 7 - The Implications of our Digital Future - A Conversation with Senator Stephen Conroy   157

Chapter 8 -Social TV   169

Chapter 9 - Being Bullish on TV - A Conversation with Jeffrey Cole   201

Conclusion - What is the Future of the Future?   211

215

To Bill Boyle
Who should have known better.
Thank you

ACKNOWLEDGEMENTS

This book could have never been written without the brilliant research and development efforts of my colleagues at the Intel Corporation: Dave Anderson, Ashwini Asokan, Cory Booth, Francoise Bourdonnec, Harlene Conley, Kevin Cornelius, Alan Crouch, Brad Daniels, Michael Espig, Jeff Foerster, Susan Faulkner, Robert Ferreira, Sharad Garg, Delia Grenville, Ousmane Diallo, Todd Harple, Horst Haussecker, John Hengeveld, Minnie Ho, Susan Kenney, Eric Kim, Lance Koenders, Lakshman Krishnamurthy, Andy Kuzma, Bill Leszinske, Daria Loi, Wilfred Martis, Jay Melican, Barry O'Mahony, Suri Medapati, Arjun Metre, Molly Mccall, Dina Papagiannaki, Steve Patzer, Sasanka Prabhala, Malinda Reese, KC Rich, Nina Taft, Ticky Thakkar, Steve Tolopka, Brendan Traw, Keith Wehmeyer, Sharon Wong, Rita Wouhaybi, Mark Yarvis, and Alex Zafiroglu. These pages would have been lost in an unintelligible sea of statistics, predictions and trends without the clarity and diligence of Tawny Schlieski.

Over the last few years while I was developing the material for *Screen Future* I would have surely gone under without the support and collaboration with my colleagues, friends, and partners in crime: Michael Payne and Genevieve Bell.

It was my intention to make sure this book was a mix of technology, history, culture, and economics. I could never have captured these without the hours of conversation and discussion with these industry experts who gave me so much of their time and honest opinions: Xavier Bringué, Carri Bugbee, Jeffrey Cole, Senator Stephen Conroy, Jim Denney, Stephanie Gaines, Erin Flood, Marcelino Ford-Livene, Mark Francisco, Irwin Gotlieb, Brian Seth Hurst, Henry Jenkins, Kevin Kahn, Rick Mandler, Malachy Moynihan, Elizabeth Mynatt, David Poltrack, Amy Reinhard, Arlo Rose, Shigeki Mori, John Slack-Smith, George Schweitzer, Ian Weightman, and Gary Wheelhouse.

I am grateful for the patience and humor of my editor David Clark and the hard work and flexibility of our illustrators Ted Cyrek and Jim Stovall. Thank you to the crew at Omedia—Jim Olsen, Dave Williams, April Miller, and Antonio Tatum—for their constant support no matter what the hour. This project was propelled forward by the optimism and positive support of my publisher Richard Bowles and Executive Director Bill Boyle. These pages are filled with references to other authors and works too numerous to list here—I am humbled by such intelligent and thoughtful writing.

From the very beginning this project was supported and guided by Justin Rattner—thank you for your insights and the hard questions.

Thanks to James Frenkel for telling me that my goal was to be *mundane*, not a cliché, and to Sandy Winkelman for being our secret Creative Director.25.

Preface

JUSTIN RATTNER
CTO AND SENIOR FELLOW - INTEL CORPORATION

Growing up in the fifties and sixties, I lived through what is now known as the Golden Age of Television. As a kid, I was fascinated and enchanted by the box. My oldest memory is sitting in front of our Hoffman TV at around the age of three or four, eating applesauce and looking at my mother standing at the stove in the kitchen. I don't know why this is my first memory, but I do know it involved television.

When I was ten or eleven, I badgered my parents into getting a Zenith color TV for our living room. While the color was far from perfect, it was amazing to watch the Rose Parade in "living color" as NBC called it in those days. The Zenith TV also had an ultrasonic remote control that let you turn it off and on as well as change the channel up or down. To a twelve-year-old, The Zenith remote was nothing short of magic.

As a teenager, I experimented with closed circuit television and built my own black and white camera using vacuum tubes. Transistor-based TV sets were just coming to market, and again I convinced my parents to buy a 9-inch Sony for the kitchen. On a long driving trip to Canada and the Northwest, we bought a cool-looking antenna so we could watch TV in the car as we drove down the highway. The TV wedged perfectly between the front bucket seats of my dad's Lincoln Continental and allowed my sister and me to be entertained for hours on end as we crossed the great expanse of the West.

TV was then on a very long plateau technologically. Set design improved, of course, but the basic standards had been set in the 1940s and '50s and remained static for decades. Tubes were replaced with transistors and cathode-ray tubes (CRTs) got better largely due to Sony's breakthrough development of the Trinitron picture tube. Integrated circuits helped make TVs smaller and more energy efficient, although CRTs remained the major challenge to portability. The 1970s and '80s proved to be a relatively quiet period for television although big changes were in the works.

Television began to reawaken in the late 1980s as developments began to take place across a wide range of technologies that would come to redefine TV as we knew it. Cable television began to transform the way television signals were delivered to our homes. Liquid crystal display began to get large enough to be more than a tradeshow curiosity. Perhaps most significantly, people began to think about something other than simply broadcasting television. The first video-on-demand systems, built in conjunction with the cable television providers, were developed and tested often to the frustration of their early customers.

By the early 1990s, the press was full of articles about the Information Superhighway with 500 channels of television. It was a pre-Web view of how information of all kinds would get delivered and consumed. Cable and later satellite television did ultimately provide a few hundred broadcast channels and an every growing number of pay-per-view channels. The World Wide Web emerged as the true information highway only slightly later, but had a far more profound impact on global society. It empowered individuals, not just governments or corporations, to make every possible kind of information available at almost no cost. As the downstream bandwidth to the home grew into the megabits per second, new kinds of television service began to emerge. YouTube is an important example in that, much like the Web, it allowed anyone to upload a video, no matter how amateurish or insipid, to be viewed by millions of people around the world.

Other experiments that attempted to combine the Web and television were not nearly so successful, but all played a role in the chaotic process of innovation that paved the way to the future vision of television described in this book. For me the glimpse of what television could be came in the summer of 2008 when NBC decided to make thousands of hours of television from the Beijing Olympics available on the Web. No matter how obscure the sport, you could find most, if not all, of the competition captured in these online video clips. I came into the office one morning, having just watched some of the equestrian competition on NBC's 2008 Olympic Web site, to proclaim that I had seen the future of television. Watching what I wanted, when I wanted, and where I wanted was a profound and, in a real sense, liberating experience.

The timing of those Olympics was just about perfect as we were starting our annual strategic technology planning cycle at Intel. As chief technology officer, it was my job to act as grown-up, overseer, and father-confessor to the various technologists who are chosen to participate in the process. After a broad solicitation to all Intel employees, the Technology Council at Intel, made up of Fellows and senior engineering managers, selects about a half-dozen topics for further development. For three months, cross-corporate teams propose, debate, and prepare each topic for senior management review. It was early in this process that I first met Brian David Johnson and began to encounter his ideas for the third generation of television or TV 3.0 as we came to call it.

At first I wasn't sure whether Brian and I were on the same page when it came to the future of TV. I shared my NBC Olympic experience with him, and got a few half-hearted nods, but quickly realized that he was thinking about a much bigger vision than just being able to click on an icon to choose a video to view. He was talking about reshaping the fundamentals of television in ways that I hadn't begun to imagine.

As the technology strategy process moved ahead, I began to realize that Brian's vision of television was consistent with a phenomenon I had observed taking place in a number of other fields and was following a familiar pattern.

If you look at certain fields, such as photography, over its several hundred year history, you find that it began as very much an analog process. Early pinhole cameras gave way to cameras with optical lenses and photosensitive emulsion on transparent film stock. The analog foundation held fast until well into the late twentieth century, when part of the camera, namely the film, was replaced by a electro-optical imaging chip, and the viewfinder was replaced by a small liquid-crystal display. A tiny microprocessor controlled all the electronics which translated the light readings from the imager to something that made sense to the a human eye looking at the screen. Digital cameras proved wildly popular given their "instant camera" characteristic, but were digital in only a limited sense.

A true digital camera views the capture and generation of an image as a computational problem, not merely one of replacing a few analog camera elements with their digital equivalents. Computational photography, as it's known in the technical community, considers the possibility of replacing most, if not all, of the analog elements of a camera. In the process of doing so, it opens up entirely new ways to think about photography. What if you could capture the entire light field of a given scene and store it for subsequent processing by the computer? What could you do? For one thing, you could compute focus and depth of field after the fact. You could also deal with camera shake and vibration. You could even change camera angles, within the limits of the captured light field, to reveal something otherwise hidden in a scene. No more cutting off half of your mother-in-law's face in the wedding pictures. Just tell the computer to shift the angle of view slightly to reveal her face in full view. Today's bulky optical lenses could also be dramatically simplified by replacing much of the optics with algorithms that perform the same functions in your laptop computer.

The evolution of photography from analog to digitally-assisted to fully digital obeys the same evolutionary pattern as is now taking place in radio design. Radios are a classic analog technology that is well into in its digitally-assisted phase and is just beginning to be rendered as a fully digital technology. As with photography, fully digital radios have been waiting for the underlying integrated electronic technology to advance to the point where it is practical and efficient to use digital means to replace the traditional analog circuit blocks. Once those challenges are met, we will begin to think about radio in entirely different ways. No longer will we allocate spectrum at major international conferences, the way we do today. In place of that human process, radios will negotiate for spectrum use on the fly, in real time, to use only what they need when they need it.

Television is currently at the height of its digitally-assisted phase. We have built analog equivalents for most of the familiar analog television elements, but we really haven't turned to the question about moving it to a fully computational footing. Yes, we have digital transmission standards such as HDTV, digital video compression standards such as H.264, and a host of digital consumer devices including DVRs and flat-screen television displays. What we have yet to do is bring large amounts of computation to be bear on the experience of television. The belief of this book is that by doing so we will enable vast new opportunities to create, distributed, and consume television content.

Let me describe just one way that future of television could fundamentally depend on computation. Various studies predict an exponential increase in the number of hours of television content. By 2015 estimates suggest there will be upwards of 500 billion hours of television content available for digital distribution. Simply put, that's a humanly unknowable amount on information. The Web also contains a humanly unknowable number of viewable pages, but we solve the problem of finding any particular page with powerful, text-oriented search engines such as Google and Bing.

While we are all familiar with the query side of these search services, what goes largely unnoticed is their indexing side which quite literally searches or "crawls" every reachable page on the Web to discover what's new and to collect information about each page, so-called metadata, to construct an index, which is a highly compressed and more searchable view of the Web. Just as we might look at the index of a book to find a particular topic, the index of the Web is examined in parallel by thousands of processors to find the pages that represent the most probable matches. Results are typically returned in less than half a second despite the fact that the Web contains billions of pages.

Making television content searchable in the same way will require computers to watch every frame of those 500 billion hours of television in order to create an index of the video content they contain that can, in turn, be searched by billions of television viewers whenever they're looking for something to watch.

It should be obvious that programming a computer to watch television is far more difficult than directing it to read lines of text and links on a Web page, but it can be done and, in fact, has been done in some restricted settings. A team at Intel Labs China created a program to watch football (what we in America call soccer) matches and construct a searchable index of these videos. The program identifies the players, the ball, the goals, and the field markers. It can even determine when a player makes a shot on goal and when a players scores. With the metadata the program constructs, you can ask to see all the shots on goal, all the shots by your favorite player, the steals, and the penalty kicks. You can ask to see these clips for a particular game or for a set of games. It's as if you're the producer for ESPN's Sports Center except that you get to assemble the highlight reel according to your own interests and watch it on your own schedule. It is television customized to the preferences of the individual viewer, which is just part of the power of computational television. As you are about to learn, there is much, much more to the story of what happens when television and computing comes together. Just as I marveled at the magic of my parents' Zenith TV with its ultrasonic remote control, our sons and daughters will soon marvel at the way computing has transformed television.

No longer will TV be a strictly linear experience. The time-driven program guide will be replaced by powerful visual search engines continually discovering new and potentially interesting television content

No longer will our viewing choices be determined by network executives programming for the 18 to 24 year-old demographic. Our choices will be guided by our individual interests and behaviors captured and managed in a secure way to preserve or privacy, but elevate our experience.

No longer will our viewing experience be captive to one type of display or service provider. Whatever we want to watch will seamlessly move between screens of all sizes in every imaginable location at any time and in any place.

And, finally, no longer will the social experience of television be limited to a family unit or a set of roommates. Our physical television spaces will have given way to virtual, 3-dimensional viewing spaces, as familiar to us as any room in our homes, and shared amongst our various social networks scattered around the planet.

The endless possibilities for our screen future take me back to that early memory of eating applesauce in front of the TV. I find it amazing that more than fifty years later, I'm still captivated and motivated by television. Let me recommend you serve yourself a big dish of applesauce and start your own exploration of our screen future.

Isaac Asimov and the Future of TV

Predicting the future is a hopeless, thankless task, with ridicule to begin with and, all too often, scorn to end with.

—Isaac Asimov "The World of 1990," written in 1965

Predicting the future is a losing game. Legendary writer Isaac Asimov knew this fact all too well. Most people know Asimov for his groundbreaking science fiction works like *I, Robot* and the *Foundation* series. What some may not know is that in his time Asimov was considered the twentieth century's greatest *popularizer* of science. Of his 500 books a great many are about science fact; exploring everything from astronomy and the solar system to biology and physics. He was so widely respected that at one point another literary legend Kurt Vonnegut asked him, "How does it feel to know everything?" (Isaac Asimov, *In Joy Still Felt*, 1980)

For Asimov's uncanny vision and intellect, forecasting the future was only natural. In January of 1965 Asimov wrote an article for *Diners' Club Magazine* called "The World of 1990" where he envisioned what our planet might be like 25 years into the future. It's wonderful to read now both for the accuracy of some of his predictions and for the things he simply got wrong.

He wrote that "the greatest single problem introduced by automation (and progress) will be surplus time. The large majority (of people) will only be working 30 hours a week at most, and will therefore be more subject than ever

1

to the dangerous disease of boredom. There will have to be a great emphasis on recreation and entertainment, and never in the history of man will so great an importance be attached to the general profession of 'people-amusing.'" (Isaac Asimov, *Is Anyone There?*, 1967)

Throughout this book we're going to talk about and investigate this general profession of "people-amusing." For most people their daily recreation, entertainment, and escape comes from TV. TV is a wonderful term that encompasses a wide range of activities, technologies, and content. TV is broadcast TV, the big networks: ABC, CBS, and NBC. TV is cable, extended cable, the premium channels, and on-demand. But this is just the beginning. For most people TV is also their DVD player, which means it's movies, extras, whole seasons of TV shows, 3D, kids entertainment, and even workout videos. TV is gaming, Xbox[†], Nintendo[†], PlayStation[†] or to be more specific Rock Band, Guitar Hero, Madden Football, Halo and the Nintendo Wii[†]. In the past few years TV has come to the Internet and the Internet has come to the TV. People are now using their TV to check Web sites and using Web sites to watch TV. Today TV and the entertainment experience now includes applications as well as social networking. The lovely thing about TV is that it is a catch-all for how each individual person wants to be entertained.

Isaac Asimov went on to write that "the television set will be, more than ever, the center of the home" (Isaac Asimov, *Is Anyone There?*, 1967). This of course we all know to be spot on. A 2009 Nielsen study showed that the average American spends 153 hours a month watching or interacting with their TV (Nielsen, 2009). Compare this to only 29 hours spent using the Internet and it's clear that the TV is the single most-used consumer electronics device in the home. Not only is it the most used device but it also shapes how homes across the world are designed and where we place our couches, beds, and easy chairs. When was the last time you saw a living room not centered around a TV? When was the last time you saw the furniture in a TV room arranged in front of a window? TV is such a powerful device it gets its own room as though it were a member of the family. Don't get me wrong, I don't think this is a bad thing. There's a good reason for this dominance of the TV. The television and the entertainment experience people all over the world get from it is knit deeply into their everyday lives.

Let me give you an example. Imagine waking up one Tuesday morning and turning on your television to get the morning news, traffic, and weather. It's a simple enough task and something we can all do without even thinking about it. Now imagine if when you flipped on the TV, your morning show wasn't on. The channel was dead and most channels but not all of them weren't working. What would be the first thing you thought? Would it be rational? Or would you be terribly worried that something was wrong—*deeply* wrong?

Now what if you went to your favorite Web site or even local newsstand to get your news and found the site was offline or the paper hadn't arrived yet— Would you be filled with the same sense of panic? When people are cut off from their TVs they do experience an overwhelming feeling that something in the world has gone terribly wrong. TV has that affect on people. It not only entertains us and our family but is also a trusted friend. When we're alone, it's our company. It's many things to many people: a babysitter, background chatter, and a constant and dependable lifeline to the outside world. TV goes far more deeply into our daily lives than most other technologies. TV and the experience of watching TV throughout our day is rich with meaning and personal importance.

Now in his many years of forecasting and writing, Asimov didn't always get it all right. He predicted the explosion of personal helicopters and hovercrafts "running on jets of compressed air rather than wheels" (Isaac Asimov, *Is Anyone There?*, 1967). He also foresaw that civilization would move away from its obsession with the skyscraper and migrate to living underground. He went on to imagine that "the ground above the city may be devoted to park and recreation and in part to farming and grazing" (Isaac Asimov, *Is Anyone There?*, 1967).

Asimov's successes and failures prove that predicting the future is a tricky business. He used an incredibly logical approach to envisioning the future. He knew that to look into the future with any accuracy that he "must guess as little as possible and confine myself as much as possible to conditions that will certainly exist in the future and then try to analyze the possible consequences" (Isaac Asimov, *Is Anyone There?*, 1967). When we use science more than imagination, the results can be more than just right or wrong. These predictions and the vision they give us can help make decisions and make sense of the technologies and changes going on around us today as well.

By the way, in another article in the *New York Times Magazine* called "Visit to the World's Fair of 2014" from August 16, 1964, Asimov predicted that "walls will have replaced the ordinary [TV] set by 2014, and transparent cubes will be making their appearance. In the videocubes, with the help of holography, three dimensional viewing will be possible. In fact one popular exhibit at the 2014 World's Fair will be such a 3D TV, built life size, in which ballet performances will be seen. The cube will slowly revolve for viewing from all angles" (Isaac Asimov, *Is Anyone There?*, 1967). If we look at current trends, Mr. Asimov may not be too far off on this one.

"Television Gaming Apparatus"

No technology before TV ever integrated faster into American life. Television took only ten years to reach a penetration of thirty-five million house holds, while the telephone required eighty years, the automobile took fifty, and even the radio needed twenty-five (Gary Edgerton, *The Columbia History of American Television*, 2007).

By the middle of the 1960s, 52.6 million American homes were watching on average 6 hours, 48 minutes of TV a day (*Broadcasting Yearbook 1965*). In 1966 a chief engineer and manager of equipment design for Saunders Associates, a large military electronic firm, came up with the idea of using all those televisions for something more than just watching broadcast TV. On September 1, 1966, Ralph H. Baer, a German immigrant, jotted down four pages of notes that outlined his idea of how to use an ordinary TV set to play games. His original idea was to sell his "game box" for around USD 25 (Van Burnham, *Supercade*, 2001).

The first game that Baer and a technician Bob Tremblay built was called Fox & Hound. "The game was to pretend that one spot was a fox and the other a hound. The object was to have the hound chase the fox until he was 'caught' by way of simply touching the spot. It was primitive all right, but it was a videogame—and it was fun" (Van Burnham, *Supercade*, 2001). Ultimately Baer's four page idea became Magnavox's Odyssey[†], released in 1972 for USD 100.

The history of home video games can draw a direct line from Baer's idea for using the TV for doing something other than watching TV. All of today's game consoles from Microsoft[†] (Xbox[†]), Sony[†] (PlayStation[†]), and Nintendo[†] (Wii[†]) are descended from this single visionary idea. Baer and team's first game Fox & Hound can be seen as very similar to games like Madden 10[†]—they are both played on a TV set, they are both social, and they are both designed to be fun.

The idea of using a television screen to do something other than watch TV, using the TV to play a game controlled by a computer for one or two players, is an excellent example not only of engineering but also of the evolution of the TV experience. Baer's idea decoupled the television hardware from the television broadcast. The television hardware was now being used to play games. For Baer, games, once the sole domain of cards, boards, and toys, became a task for a computer. Before Baer the most popular screen in the home had been used for one thing and for one thing only; watching broadcast TV programs. With his shifting of gaming via the TV screen to a computing based entertainment experience he not only began what would become a projected USD 63 billion industry by 2013 (*Game Daily* 2008) but he changed the very definition of TV.

Baer's "Television Gaming Apparatus" turned gaming in the home into a compute task. Baer had always envisioned his game system being sold directly to people and used with TVs in their living rooms. It was truly a consumer electronics based innovation and it built off an existing device that was ubiquitous with a well-developed infrastructure due to its popularity: the television set.

> *Interviewer:* 40 years ago you came up with the idea for using TV sets for playing games. Did you ever imagine things would get as far as they have?
>
> *Ralph Baer:* Could Thomas Edison have predicted that everyone would be walking around the street with portable telephones? No, I had no idea (Matthew Hawkins, The Father of Home Video Games: Ralph Baer, *Gamasutra,* 2006).

A Shock to the System

People have been writing and predicting the future of TV for about as long as TV has been around. As long as the Internet has been around people have been writing about how it will conquer the TV in the battle for our eyeballs and attention. But the reports of TV's death have been greatly exaggerated. Still others have said that the Internet will never grow up, never garner enough audience share to matter and basically remain the playground for geeks and kids. These folks sound a bit like Rex Lambert, editor of the *Radio Times* that proclaimed in 1936 that "Television won't matter in your lifetime or mine." Or even the legendary American inventor Thomas Edison who, in 1922, was sure that "the radio craze will die out in time" (Bob Seidensticker, *Future Hype,* 2006).

The Internet as a personalized information and content delivery system has changed where, when, and how people are entertained. Likewise good old-fashioned TV remains the center of people's homes and the center of their entertainment lives. People are not watching less TV. In 2009 people watched more TV than ever before. They watched it in more places, and they watched wider variety of programming.

In 2009 Apple Inc sold nearly 9 million iPhones (Apple) and in 2010 FutureSource has forecasted that nearly 10 million Internet connected TVs will be sold. Much like Baer's "Television Gaming Apparatus" these devices have the ability to radically change how, where and when people are entertained. The introduction of millions of these devices that offer substantially new entertainment experiences has had a tremendous affect on every industry they touch. From the entertainment industry to high-tech manufacturers and even service providers; no one has been unaffected. There has been a kind of shock to the system that has produced an interesting moment in time. The entire future of entertainment it seems is up in the air.

This shock to the system is not only affecting consumers' entertainment habits but their social habits as well. Dr. Alex Zafiroglu is a cultural anthropologist at Intel. She has spent the last few years observing this change from inside people's homes all over the world. Zafiroglu studies how people engage with technology so that we have a better understanding of what people will actually want to do with these new computing devices. She has observed something truly remarkable in her field studies and conversations with consumers. "As more and more people adopt new internet-enabled devices, services and interfaces that offer mobile, continuously updated, personalized, and rich media experiences," she explained. "People's daily entertainment consumption is extending far beyond the reach of the stationary, shared and less personalized television set. We are witnessing a period of flux in personal practices and social rules for engaging with these devices and services, as people work out how to fit the possibilities these devices offer into their daily lives. I think we can expect the use of these devices and services to be sources of tension within and beyond the home, and to be topics for public debate for a few more years before they, too, become as unremarkable as sitting on your couch watching a syndicated sitcom on your TV set on a weekday afternoon."

Looking to the future, by 2015 there should be about 500 billion hours of content available online, as shown in Figure I.1 (iSupply, YouTube. 2008). This includes mainstream content like TV shows and movies as well as non-mainstream content like Internet videos and user generated content. To go along with this, it looks like there will be about 15 billion devices that will have the ability to connect to the Internet by 2015 (Euromonitor, iSupply, IDC. 2008). So this means that you have 15 billion devices that have the ability to watch 500 billion hours of content. The network, distribution, and device implications of these numbers lead us towards a significant shift in *how* we imagine people being entertained and *where* they are enjoying that entertainment.

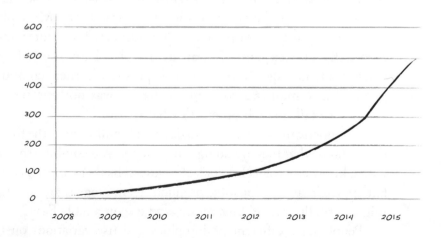

Figure I.1   Billions of Hours of Content

Design for Humans: Consumer Experience Architecture

> Change is the process by which the future invades our lives, and it is important to look at it closely, not merely from the grand perspective of history but also from the vantage point of the living breathing individuals that experience it (Alvin, Toffler, *Future Shock*, 1970).

With his book *Future Shock*, the American writer Alvin Toffler popularized futurism in the 1970s and 80s. In his following works he examined revolutions in technology, communications, and even corporations. His name may not have become a household word, but it has come to represent innovative explorations of the future. The *Financial Times* even went so far as to call him the "world's most famous futurologist."

Understanding the *living breathing individuals* is essential as we imagine and develop the future of TV. We need to understand what people will do with new technology. I think we can take this further and say we must not only understand what people will do with future technologies but we must also understand what they will *want* to do with them.

Being a Consumer Experience Architect with a focus on future technologies I was once asked at a press event if I could have predicted the popularity of e-mail. If by using my process of research and development I could have seen the remarkable shift from what was essentially a business application to the killer application for home users. My reply was simple, "Yes." For centuries people have communicated via notes and letters, and eventually via telegram. E-mail as a technology allowed for the digital delivery of messages from person to person via their computer or mobile phone. But e-mail as a consumer behavior was nothing new at all. People just like to talk to each other. It's what we do.

To understand what technologies people will want in the future you have to understand what they are doing today. When you combine this understanding with a knowledge of technological innovations then you can come away with a fair approximation of possible products, technologies, and services that people might actually want to buy, set up, and use on a daily basis.

People have different philosophies and use variations on this approach. The process we have used with some success at Intel Corporation over the past few years is called consumer experience architecture.

In brief, consumer experience architecture allows you to take multiple inputs and sources of information such as ethnographic research, emerging scientific theory, technology and infrastructure trends, innovation, even public opinion or science fiction, and gather them into a holistic description of the technical and experiential requirements that are needed to deliver a product or service that consumers would want to use. Additionally, the framework allows you to test and validate that the experiences you want to build are actually being developed into the product. This architectural framework is both repeatable and traceable. A more detailed exploration of Consumer Experience Architecture as a framework for design can be found in Appendix A.

We have used this framework and over a decade worth of research and development to guide our vision for the future of entertainment and computing.

Throughout this book, in conversations with industry and technical experts we've looked to quantify and understand the technological, economic, and experiential changes to the entertainment and computing experience as it migrates across all of the devices we love. In this vision all consumer devices can be seen as a vast and varied array of screens that can be personal and shared, mobile and fixed, local and mainstream. Whatever manifestation these screens take, they all have the ability to radically change people's entertainment and computing habits.

The Future of TV Is about Experiences

TV or the experience of watching TV is moving off the wall, moving from that flat screen on your wall or the traditional TV in your media cabinet and spreading across a wide variety and number of consumer electronic devices. (Remember that 15 billion by 2015 number?) So, now when we look at the good old-fashioned TV, we're really looking at a dynamic entertainment experience distributed across multiple devices, locations and consumers.

Over the past few years we've begun to think of the future of entertainment as groupings of experiences: Informative TV, Ubiquitous TV, Personal TV, and Social TV. Each of these experiences was formed by what consumers are currently doing in their lives today as well as what they would like to do in the future.

In the following chapters each of these experiences is broken down and examined in depth for both consumer and technical implications.

Informative TV

The foundation of this experience begins by thinking of TV, movies, games, and applications not as linear entertainment, files, or even digital signals but as raw data. This is not a revolutionary idea. In 1995 Nicolas Negroponte, founder of Massachusetts Institute of Technology's Media Lab, famously wrote in his book *Being Digital* that, "The key to the future of television is to stop thinking about television as television. TV benefits most from thinking of it in terms of bits" (Nicolas Negroponte, *Being Digital*, 1995). But the actual application of this has dynamic compute, infrastructure, and architectural infrastructure implications.

Imagine being able to recognize and track multiple people and objects in a piece of entertainment content then being able to get more information, search, shop, and personalize that media to your specific tastes. Once we see TV as data, an interesting shift begins. We begin to see entertainment quite clearly as a compute task. The important thing is to not only understand the technical efficiencies this brings about but also we need to understand what new experiences can be developed as well.

Ubiquitous TV

The experience of Ubiquitous TV gives you the ability to get your entertainment wherever and whenever you want it. This includes the full breadth of TV, movies, games, applications, and social networking. By no means is ubiquity a new concept for computing and technology. It has been called ubicomp, pervasive computing, and ambient intelligence; those who think about ubiquity generally envision a world where all computing devices are connected together seamlessly. In 1988 Mark Weiser pioneered the concept of ubiquitous computing when he was chief technologist of the Xerox Palo Alto Research Center (PARC).

There are even limited examples today of a spotty and sometimes fractured ubiquitous consumer experience, but for entertainment in particular to actually deliver on the promise of this experience it's going to take a good amount of work. Now some of this work is for the technologists, developers, and engineers, but there's also a large amount that needs to be done by the entertainment and service provider industries as well. Cooperation between everyone is going to be needed if TV is to reach its greatest potential.

Personalized TV

Bruce Springsteen sang it and people have been quoting and misquoting it for decades: "Fifty-seven channels and nothin' on" (Bruce Springsteen, "57 Channels [And Nothin' On]," *Human Touch,* 1992). The song tells about a man who buys his dream house and hooks up his cable only to find that there is nothing to watch. Frustrated, he gets satellite but still there are fifty-seven channels and nothing on. Ultimately he loses his wife and shoots his TV. Time has certainly shown us that more channels do not mean more entertainment. Imagine now the mess when you have 500 billion hours of content and there's no way to find something on.

> Television, therefore, may still be homogenizing taste; but the other media have already passed beyond the technical state at which standardization is necessary. When technological breakthroughs alter the economics of television by providing more channels and lower the cost of production, we can anticipate that that medium, too, will begin to fragment its output and cater to, rather than counter, the increasing diversity of the consuming public (Alvin Toffler, *Future Shock,* 1970).

When Toffler wrote this quote at the beginning of the 1970s he was surely envisioning the coming age of cable and satellite. Today we have food channels, history channels, and even an entire TV channel devoted to speed. Most consumers assume that there should be this sort of content specialization available to them on via their TVs.

But technological breakthroughs in television, communication, and entertainment have not stopped. This trend of the increasing diversity continues when you marry the TV with the Internet. The expanded access to a humanly unknowable amount of content is both promising and overwhelming. When the consumer is confronted with 500 billion hours of content how do they find something to watch? How is new content discovered for them?

The technologies that enable the two previous experiences (Informative TV and Ubiquitous TV) allow us to create experiences that are personalized not only for you but your entire family and social network too. When you can take your entertainment with you anywhere and watch whatever you want and you have vastly more detailed information about the entertainment then it's possible to personalize your entertainment in some pretty interesting ways.

One key component of how we personalize someone's experience with their entertainment and devices is also about how we personalize how it is paid for and delivered in a way that works for everyone.

Social TV

The act of watching TV and often the act of being entertained is a completely social act. As we develop these new technologies we must always remember that people are inherently social beings. It only makes sense that the technology, devices, or service that are developed for them needs to enable this social nature. Make no bones about it—people like to talk to each other. Just as e-mail did for the personal computer, social activity and communication will be key components for any entertainment device in the future.

Don't Get Hysterical

Superficial press plus technology myopia cause us to see today's change as more important than it really is while simultaneously minimizing the significance of past technologies. The result is that society sees technology from a warped vantage point. The comparison of today's developments against those of the past is not fair. On one hand we have marching bands trumpeting today's shiny new technology plus those exciting products-to-be from the cover of *Popular Science*. On the other hand, we have those few old and familiar technologies that manage to break through the mist of time—hardly an equal comparison. When looking at the products that affect our daily lives, it is difficult to see beyond the new veneer to appropriate the substantial laid during the previous centuries (Bob Seidensticker, *Future Hype,* 2001).

It is human nature to be fascinated with the next new thing. Here in the first half of the twenty-first century how can we not be excited by the possibilities that lay just around the corner—the next innovation, the game changer, the paradigm shift? There's certainly nothing wrong with a heaping helping of optimism and the hope for technologies and devices that will soon be apart of our lives. But we must not let that excitement cloud the sober eyes of technology development.

The chapters of this book can be seen as a collection of visions for the future of entertainment and computing. They do not all agree and many are filled with just as many questions as they have answers. But they are all pointed in the same general direction, with that sober eye towards the real hurdles and implications that separate our lives of today with those amazing new experiences of the future.

Chapter 1

Space Aliens, Pop Culture and What Happens after Convergence

A CONVERSATION WITH HENRY JENKINS

Henry Jenkins has been called the Marshall McLuhan of the twenty-first century. In the 1960s McLuhan changed the way we thought and talked about media, advertising, and TV. Over the last decade, Jenkins has reshaped how we think about the culture that surrounds media and technology. He is a media scholar and founder of the Comparative edia Studies program at Massachusetts Institute of Technology. In his many books *Fans, Bloggers, and Gamers: Exploring Participatory Culture* and *Textual Poachers: Television Fans and Participatory Culture* Jenkins investigates technology and media with an eye towards how real people use it, watch it, and change it into something that is more meaningful for them.

For years Jenkins has written in great depth about convergence, but his take on the subject is different from what most people are used to hearing in the high tech industry. Jenkins doesn't see convergence as a technological event or the coming together of devices into a single "black box" device. Quite the opposite: he sees convergence as a change in the way that entertainment is produced, marketed, and consumed. The convergence is not on the device side of the equation; it is the consumption part of this process that is of keen interest to Jenkins. He believes that the world is in the middle of a massive and ongoing convergence that is constantly changing and adapting to people's personal and collective interests and needs. Jenkins' books and writings provide us with a unique and functional perspective on the technological and cultural changes that are taking place at this very moment. I've included some quotes from these writings throughout our conversation.

Recently Jenkins moved to a joint professorship at the School of Cinematic Arts at the University of Southern California and the Annenberg School for Communication. On a broiling hot California day I sat down with him in his new office to talk about the future of TV and entertainment. I was a little bit late and he had a class to teach right after. To kick things off we started talking about the future of entertainment and what the media and technological landscape might look like five to ten years from today.

HENRY JENKINS: I think we are evolving toward a world where every story is going to be told across every available media platform. So, as we expand the number of media platforms, we expand the opportunities for stories to circulate. In particular you can see this with the entertainment industry as they engage with consumers across multiple touch points. They are broadening outward the reach of their marketing and their storytelling to tap into this emerging and expanding landscape.

It is also the case that consumers are demanding the media they want, when they want it, where they want it, and taking it illegally if it's not available legally. Piracy on the part of consumers represents the failure of the entertainment industry and the market. People are trying to cobble together an entertainment solution that makes it fairly easy for them to transmit and collect content across multiple media channels. One of my basic positions is that we can understand the future if we understand what people are doing when it is hard. If we can understand what people are working really hard to do, like piracy, then we have a better sense of what more people will do when it becomes easy. Usually what happens in this early experimental phase of the technology and media takes root and shapes what consumer expectations and habits will be in the future.

It is going to be really interesting to see what consumers and industries build on top of the new convergence culture. If we are living in a world where information is flying at us through every media channel and device and we have the tools to bring that media information together to reconfigure and organize it, then what kinds of social activities will emerge around sharing entertainment and organizing information? We have seen early signs of how people are going to be pooling information and working through problems together. We are seeing the emergence of large systems for evaluating and annotating information and for distanced collaboration between fans and other consumers. We can see Wikipedia[†] as an example of what this kind of collective intelligence might look like in practice.

So much of the talk of the first decade of the digital revolution was about personalization, but clearly personal media has given way to the social media and social media will give way to even more collective ways of navigating and organizing information.

> Convergence does not depend on any specific delivery mechanism. Rather, convergence represents a paradigm shift —a move from medium-specific content toward content that flows across multiple media channels, toward the increased interdependence of communications systems, toward multiple ways of accessing media content, and toward ever more complex relations between top-down corporate media and bottom-up participatory culture (Henry Jenkins, *Convergence Culture, 2008*).

***

In his writings Jenkins has highlighted the importance of looking specifically at the *bottom-up participatory culture* of fans when trying to understand the future of entertainment. In recent years, fan culture has had an increasingly greater affect on the entertainment industry. From *American Idol*'s voting to the vast numbers of entertainment blogs, average everyday people are asserting more control over their entertainment experience

I asked Jenkins if people are increasing their power over the industries that are creating entertainment then couldn't they also assert control over the hardware, devices, services, and networks that are delivering this entertainment?

HENRY JENKINS: When technology goes too far off course, away from social and cultural drivers, away from what people actually want it tends to fail. Technology can drive social change and people's behavior to a degree. We gravitate toward the affordances of the technologies we have access to. If it is easy to do we will probably do it more than we would do it when it is hard to do. I mean that's a basic rule of technology, but that law doesn't really work when the technology is used in a radically different way by people. When you have a real mismatch between what a technology is designed to do and what people actually want it to do then that technology is going to be negotiated or changed. It would be better if this happened before the product was released instead of after. Actually, when you think about it, the ideal situation would be for people to be able to influence changes both during the design and after the release.

I would say if designers are not paying attention to the social and cultural patterns, the desires of people, then they are going to create more work for themselves in the long term because there are going to be more adjustments that have to take place on a technological platform as people and markets renegotiate and realign with each other. So, it is not that culture and social forces simply drive technology. Technology can make a difference, but it is not the case that technology completely overrides every other consideration.

BDJ: I think you're right. Ultimately people will bend technology to meet their needs either by hook or by crook.

HENRY JENKINS: Yeah, literally by hook or crook. In the sense that you know they will steal it or they will mod it. They will break it through illegal practices or by perfectly legal reprogramming. But either way they are going to transform what they are given if it does not match their needs. If they can't do this then they will simply walk away and ignore it.

We've seen this happen plenty of times with technological innovations. Technological innovation that was dead in the water in the early days of digital media might thrive now. Companies walk away from ideas because they propose them far too soon. I think the first phase of the digital revolution was driven by that myth that it was a revolution and therefore change was going to take place overnight. The technology industry started believing its own prophecies. It is a kind of mental loop that technologists are prone to go into when they imagine their ideal consumer and then map it to reality.

But what we find out is that the consumers are resistant, they are recalcitrant, they refuse to go at the pace that the industry wants. People have to go through a cultural evolution. They have to acquire the skills, they have to develop a familiarity, and technology companies have to develop support for any new technology as it emerges. Technological change pushed by technology is always slower than technologists imagine.

What's interesting is that this happens in reverse from the bottom-up perspective. Often people are pushing forward demanding new things and the technologists are lagging behind because they are not paying sufficient attention to the social and cultural changes that are taking place around them.

BDJ: Do you think there's a way people could have a direct affect on technologies that are mismatched to their needs? I'm thinking of the moding and hacking culture—that literally remake devices once they have been released. Can you see or have you seen any evidence recently of that happening. How do you think technologists might be able to use these examples to better design devices?

HENRY JENKINS: I am trying to think about what that would look like. I think we are finding that people are very comfortable with code; they are comfortable with changing software at this point. We've seen all the open source ware movements and so forth, which have reshaped the design of the code today. It is the hardware that I think people have a greater difficulty hacking and putting together.

I did have a productive exchange with Jonathan Zittrain (an American professor of Internet law at Harvard Law School) who talks about technologies as generative or not generative. He and I have an interesting difference of perspective. He says the iPod† is not generative because people don't have access to the code and we can't transform the hardware. That's the way technologists look at it. When I look at the iPod I say it's socially generative. You can look at podcasting as a platform or a programming language that has enabled massive numbers of groups to communicate and get their message out. It has really reinvented radio over the last handful of years. The distribution channel that has emerged is totally different than the one that existed before. We're at a point where *Harry Potter* podcasts by an amateur have reached half a million subscribers. So I think that makes the iPod highly generative socially and culturally.

But, this really hasn't had much of an impact on the design and the development of the technology. The technology may still be closed in the sense that Zittrain is talking about. So the question would be how we get people to be able to rebuild hardware; something like *Make Magazine* and the people who are teaching themselves to rebuild and redesign things. They want to bring technology back under their control.

But the hardware is what's hardest to get at. Zittrain says that certain hardware makes it really difficult to access the code. If the code isn't transparent then it can't be manipulated. His distinction, and it's an important one, is that we should be concerned with the hard coding of certain options into technology because if certain social and cultural practices are designed into it then it becomes literally impossible to do certain things. It is going to be much harder for people and groups to change it when they need to.

The real problem this reveals is that if technology is developed in this way then all people are left with is an up or down vote. We accept the technology or we reject it. That's why the hardware designers need to be much more grounded in the social and cultural moment than they typically are. They are making an approximation of what people are going to want to have the capacity to do. Even a simple decision about memory has huge implications. Think about TiVo[†]. The memory limitations, the size of the hard drive in the TiVo[†] box, set limits on how people relate to television programming. I felt constantly dictated to by my TiVo because it won't let me store as much programming as I want to have. It means I can't record and collect a box set of a bunch of shows, store them up, and watch them in marathon session mid-season. With the smaller hard drive this type of thing is not an option. If I'm not managing the memory capacity of the TiVo that means it is going to constantly be dumping the content. It is determining the sequence in which I watch my television shows. Just by picking a smaller hard drive TiVo isn't allowing me to do something that I love doing; having a mini-marathon.

The idea that people only want to record 100 hours of TV grows out of the notion of media content as disposable, of television as a constant and irreversible flow, and of consumers only wanting to watch episodes once and then tossing them away like yesterday's newspaper. The best contemporary programs, from *The Wire* to *Lost*, assume a viewer who is archiving and rewatching content on an ongoing basis. For anyone who grew up with VHS and DVD the idea that you could keep your favorite shows for as long as you like has become the norm. So, the cultural model of TiVo's limiting memory capacity makes all kinds of assumptions about how we watch TV that simply aren't borne out by what people actually do. I should point out that recently I noticed that TiVo starting to sell the ability to upgrade the memory on your TiVo. You can actually buy as much memory as you want. This is going to be a much better way of dealing with that technology I think. It's flexible like we were talking about; people can change it to fit their needs.

BDJ: What if we combine your points about podcasting as a programming language and the TiVo hard drive requirements needing to be flexible. I believe you can think about media, the entertainment that is played on consumer devices as a kind of new programming language, a new kind of code. This changes the device requirements. It's no longer just the ability to *play* a piece of content or *launch* an application of social media connection but the combination of these things; the holistic consumer experience with all these pieces of entertainment.

Really you can say that it is the consumer's dynamic and changing experience with their entertainment that is the ultimate code, the driving requirement that needs to drive the development of consumer technology.

HENRY JENKINS: Maybe it's the humanist in me, but I am not sure that consumer behavior is anywhere near predictable enough to get classified as a code but it is indeed a driving force which should shape the future design of entertainment and information technologies.

We certainly know that people are going to be connecting to a broad range of media from many different platforms and sources and will be seeking ways to exert greater control over that media content and the experiences it enables. We also know that there is going to be increased integration between entertainment and information, between mass media and participatory culture, between media content and social networks, that need to be accommodated in the development of tools and platforms. We even know that people are going to be authoring rather than simply consuming culture and are going to need to be able to upload as well as simply download content in the most robust way possible. So that tells us we need to support the socialization of media. By that I mean its insertion into a range of social networks and niche communities—brand communities, fan communities, communities of practice—at the global as well as the local scale. We also need to support the personalization of media; the ability to quickly adjust parameters to reflect individual needs of consumes.

There is going to be constant change; people are going to want to be able to appropriate, adapt, and retrofit their tools and platforms once they have launched and released into the market. Developers and companies will need to engage with these lead users to better understand consumer demands. It is precisely because of my starting premise—that consumer behavior is less predictable than code—that we need to make that last requirement—people need to be able to retrofit their technologies to changing needs and desires.

People and culture will always set new demands on technology, often racing ahead of the visions of the engineers and designers. But we also know that emerging technology often reveals new cultural potentials, making some things easier to do, and thus creates new and unanticipated demands once it starts to enter into larger cultural circulation. We will not be able to predict the unintended uses and developments as culture meets technology so you need to create a context where both people and technology can be quickly adapted to each other.

> Who would have predicted that reality television series, such as *Survivor* (2000) and *American Idol* (2002), would turn out to be the first killer application of media convergence—the big new thing that demonstrated the power that lies at the intersection between old and new media? Initial experiments with interactive television in the mid-1990s were largely written off as failures. Few can argue with *American Idol*'s success. By the final weeks of its second 2003 season, Fox Broadcasting Company was receiving more than 20 million telephone calls or text messages per episode casting verdicts on the *American Idol* contestants (Henry Jenkins, *Convergence Culture, 2008).*

***

Jenkins has written that it is not technology that is driving the convergence of media. He believes that it is actually pop culture that is driving the technology convergence. I asked him why he thought that was true.

HENRY JENKINS: Pop culture lowers the risk of trying things. We learn skills through play that we later apply through work. There is nothing radical about this. In a hunting society, kids grow up playing with bows and arrows. Gradually they apply those skills to killing their food. In an information society, people grow up playing with information and in that process acquire skills that they are going to apply for more serious purposes.

A great example of this is text messaging. People learned how to text message on their mobile phones by watching *American Idol.* That was a hurdle that they were willing to get over in that case. Electing an American Idol[†] wasn't terribly urgent or important but this goal was something that led many Americans to lower their anxiety level enough to embrace the new technology.

More people are learning to do collective intelligence to solve problems when watching the TV series *Lost* than have done so working through complex algorithms of the sort that the visionaries of collective intelligence thought it was going to be. But, we are also seeing that social networks sites or Twitter[†] can be used to political ends having been the first acquired through social means. Ethan Zuckerman from Global Voices Online[†] says that any technology sufficiently robust to allow the sharing of cute cat pictures can bring down a government. He is absolutely right. For a year or so the world played around with Twitter; telling their friends what we had for breakfast. This paved the way in summer 2009 for us to get information out of Iran. It connected us in a vital way to political change that was taking place on the ground, and routed around the totalitarian regimes and centralized media coverage.

I think we see this again and again and again, that pop culture is the motivator. It creates the occasion and it lowers the anxiety level to allow people to embrace new technical practices, new social practices and then those get rerouted having been learned through play. Then these new technologies and practices get reapplied to more serious concerns of the society. In so far as we can close the gap between playful and applied deployments of technology, we may speed along the transition and adoption process.

A transmedia story unfolds across multiple media platforms, with each new text making a distinctive and valuable contribution to the whole. In the ideal form of transmedia storytelling each medium does what it does best—so that a story might be introduced in a film, extended through television, novels and comics; it's world might be explored through game play or experienced as an amusement part attraction. Each franchise entry needs to be self-contained so you don't need to have seen the film to enjoy the game, and vice versa. Any given product is a point of entry into the franchise as a whole. Reading across the media sustains a depth of experience that motivates more consumption (Henry Jenkins, *Convergence Culture, 2008).*

***

Jenkins has said that telling stories across multiple mediums and devices is a response to convergence. In fact, he points out that this type of transmedia storytelling is a sign that convergence is already happening. In 2009 Jenkins started teaching a class at USC about this very subject. I asked him how he prepared his students for thinking about this type of communications across devices.

HENRY JENKINS: I think the best way to tell you about the class is to describe the first day. I began with a picture of a park bench with "no aliens allowed" sign on it. It was from the movie *District 9,* but I didn't tell them that. I then asked them what the bench was.

Instantly, many of then recognized it as a promotion for a film. But, I pointed out that as a promotion for a film it operates in a radically different way than a poster. It does this on a number of different levels. When we look hard at the bench we see that it isn't simply an advertisement for the film. The only direct mention of the title *District 9* comes if a person goes to the Web site listed on the bench (D-9.com). With no obvious tie to the film, the bench is thrust into our own reality as an extension of the film's fictional world. The fun question is: Can a park bench be a narrative extension into our world? The answer is clearly yes in this case.

The bench makes the reality of *District 9* seem closer to our world, much closer than other science fiction films. That's part of what *District 9* is trying to create as a transmedia entertainment experience. It uses content in hyper-documentary style that is spread across multiple mediums and devices. It's trying to be topical and feed off issues of race in our world and it does this by placing a complex collection of information and video specifically produced outside of the theatrical film to get across this message. *District 9* as an experience is trying to erase the difference between the world of the film and the world we live in. The park bench takes the reality of *District 9* and gives people a way to literally sit in the world of the film, immersing them in that world, blurring the lines between reality and fiction. Yes, it is a marketing tool but it is also something else, something more complex and interesting.

Then I took the students to the Web and said: Alright, what has *District 9* done on the Web? Are they doing anything else to give us this same type of experience? Suddenly, the students begin to see dozens and dozens of videos and mock Web sites that are doing the same thing as the park bench but in a much more elaborate way. The creative team behind *District 9* have created separate videos and designed them to look like things that would circulate on the Web. They aren't identified as fiction at all. They are simply dispersed across our environment. What's really interesting is these videos provide information that is not in the actual theatrical feature film. There is stuff about alien biology, stuff about political organizations; things that really aren't a part of the traditional film's narrative. The affect of all is this is that my holistic experience of *District 9* is much deeper if I interact with this material; much more complex and engaging than watching the film alone.

As you dig into it, you find an even more interesting kind of layering that goes on. If you go to the *MNU Spreads Lies* Web site (www.mnuspreadslies.com), which is for alien rights activists in the world of *District 9*, you can see they have appropriated videos produced by MNU, the multinational organization in the film, and critiqued them. So, you have the video and you have the critique of the video right there. That Web site represents a voice that is almost entirely absent from the film. It provides a totally different narrative perspective of what is taking place on the film.

All of this feeds into the potential experience of watching *District 9*, and depending on whether you saw the benches or not or if you went to the Web sites or not you're going to experience *District 9* in some fundamentally different ways. It's exposition that's not contained in the film itself. It is an elaboration of the experience in the film that is dispersed across media platforms. *District 9* gives you a really powerful example of convergence as it is happening in summer 2009.

That first day in class the students could follow the *District 9* example pretty quickly because they grew up with Pokemon[†] and Yugio[†], and all of that stuff. But many of them know only some pieces of it because it's still just beneath the threshold of awareness for most people. But students are further along that route than adults today. My students have grown up in a world where they know that media is out there and dispersed. Its stories are spread across multiple media platforms. The line between branding and storytelling is blurred hopelessly. Creative teams and producers today assume this type of multiple medium or device activity as a pre-condition. The consumer is no longer passive in the world. Engagement comes by actively participating. Marketing comes by tapping the willingness of consumers to be evangelists for the brand. The satisfaction of a narrative experience comes in stitching together pieces of information you and I have gotten across multiple media platforms.

To be marketable new cultural works will have to provoke and reward collective meaning production through elaborate back stories, unresolved enigmas, excess information, and extratextual expansions of the program universe. The past decade has seen a marked increase in the serialization of American television, the emergence of more complex appeals to program history, and the development of more intricate story arcs and cliffhangers. To some degree, these aesthetic shifts can be linked to new reception practices enabled by the home-archiving of videos, net discussion lists, and web program guides. These new technologies provide the information infrastructure necessary to sustain a richer form of television content, while these programs reward the enhanced competencies of fan communities (Henry Jenkins, *Fans, Gamers, Bloggers*, 2006).

***

As we wrapped up the conversation and Jenkins prepared to go teach his class I asked him what he was excited about when he looked into the future. What did he think would be cool in five to ten years?

HENRY JENKINS: I am so excited about what is going on now; it's hard to imagine five years from now. You know when I wrote *Convergence Culture* three years ago, there was almost no mention of YouTube[†], no mention of Twitter, and Wikipedia came at the very end. Second Life[†] was not yet on the horizon and it has already now come and largely passed. The term *Web 2.0* was still being formulated. So, you cannot possibly envision five years out, given the horizon of change that we are talking about.

But even envisioning two or three years out, I am really excited about what happens when we become more adept at managing the interfaces and the social structure that enable us to augment our reality and expand collective intelligence. This will enable us to process information in a way that we are just learning to do right now. The narrative experiments like *District 9* that move freely across mediums and will become institutionalized. We will move from playing with these technologies in pop culture to using them creatively to communicate much richer truths and deeper experiences than we have experienced seen before.

Welcome to convergence culture, where old and new media collide, where grassroots and corporate media intersect, where the power of the media producer and the power of the media consumer interact in unpredictable ways. Convergence culture is the future, but it is taking shape now. Consumers will be more powerful within convergence culture—but only if they recognize and use that power as both consumers and citizens, as full participants in our culture (Henry Jenkins, *Convergence Culture,* 2008).

Chapter 2

Informative TV

I think I was born a geek. Ever since I was a kid I have always been fascinated by science and technology. My father was a radar tracking engineer and my mother was an IT specialist, so I pretty much grew up surrounded by electronic schematics and computers. Like most kids of my generation, I was introduced to the world of personal computers by the TI99/4A. Texas Instruments released the TI99/4A in 1981 and it cost around USD 525. Along with playing games like TI Invaders, Munch Man, and Car Wars on the "wired remote controller" I also did a good amount of computer programming in BASIC. One of the really neat things about the TI99/4A was that you could save your programs to the Texas Instruments Program Recorder. This was a tape deck that you plugged into the main unit via a dedicated port. Now here comes the geeky part. At night when I was done saving off my newest BASIC programming masterpiece, I would take the cassette tape up to my room and listen to it on my cassette player. As the tape screeched and bleeped along I used to imagine the code I had just written, trying to see if I could recognize the lines and commands in the noise. I used to imagine the complex collection of 1s and 0s on the tape flowing from my code onto the cassette tape. It fascinated me. It was almost as if I could see the glowing 1s and 0s floating in the air of my darkened bedroom.

Flash forward several decades and I'm working at the Intel Corporation. Intel's Jones Farm Campus is located in Hillsboro, Oregon. It's a massive facility consisting of five multistory buildings situated in a ring, all connected together with walkways and sky bridges. Jones Farm is full of research labs where engineers and computer scientists are developing the new technologies that will eventually make their way into Intel's various computing platforms. It was in one of these labs, in Jones Farm Building 5 to be specific, I saw something quite incredible.

If you have never seen a research lab I have to tell you the reality is a bit of a letdown. They are cold, loud, and kind of bland. Bright florescent lights beam down onto long rows of cluttered work benches. There are computers everywhere; some sit blinking silently in racks while others are torn apart yet still functioning like little alien beings made only of circuits and processors and cables. I had come to the lab to see some work from China that had just been completed in our Beijing lab. When the engineer brought up the picture on the flat screen TV on the wall I was amazed. The TV showed a European football match, soccer to us in the United States. While the two teams battled it out dribbling, passing, and making shots on goal, the computer was tracking them. Around each of the players was a small box, color coded to match the team. There was even a small circle around the ball as it zipped across the screen. The system was analyzing each frame of the match, identifying the players and keeping track of their movements. When one team scored a goal the entire net lit up, showing that the computer had recognized that the ball had gone into the net. It was incredible to see for the first time.

On the TV, next to the video of the match was a black dialog box that showed what was going on behind the scenes. Inside the little box I could see the frame-by-frame readout of the computer as it tracked each player, mapping their coordinates in the frame. Video moves at 30 frames per second so the data was flying past at an incredible rate but I could still recognize what the computer was doing. It was watching TV, analyzing the picture and turning that information into data. Instantly I was filled with the same wonder that I had experienced as a kid listening to the TI99/4A code in my bedroom at night. The computer was turning television into data. TV could be a computational task. This changed everything.

This idea is the foundation both conceptually and technically as we think about the future of television and entertainment. When we can transform TV from its current disparate digital states to a more pure form of data then we can do some really lovely things with it. In this chapter we're going to explore just how a computer system goes about analyzing video and identifying the objects of interest in the frame. Then we'll look into how we can make this information actionable so that we can do something with it. Can this information be both inside the video content and also connected to other information outside of the original piece of entertainment? What does this mean for the future of entertainment?

This transformation from an analog task to data is not entirely new. To better understand what we mean when we say Informative TV, let's take a quick look at a similar progression that has already taken place: the printed word. To track this progression let's use one of the foundational works of modern science: Sir Isaac Newton's *Principia*.

Sir Isaac Newton Is on the Kindle†

In 1665 Cambridge University was closed down due to a nasty outbreak of the plague. During the two years that it was closed, a twenty-three-year-old natural philosopher and alchemist named Isaac Newton began exploring a new approach to mathematics on his own in his country house called Woolsthorpe Manor in the village of Woolsthorpe-by-Colsterworth in Lincolnshire. Newton did this work in secret, keeping the progress away from the scientific community in handwritten notebooks. During these plague years, Newton developed the core of his thinking on calculus, gravity, and planetary motion.

In November of 1684, still working in complete isolation, Newton finished a nine-page handwritten tract called *On Motion* in which he explained what force would cause a planet to move in an elliptical orbit. Recognized as significant, the single copy became an object of desire in London. The English astronomer Edmond Halley begged Newton to publish the work but he refused. Over the next two and a half years, *On Motion* would be improved and expanded into Newton's groundbreaking work *Philosophiæ Naturalis Principia Mathematica* (*Mathematical Principles of Natural Philosophy*), known as the *Principia* for short.

The *Encyclopedia Britiannica Guide to the 100 Most Influential Scientists* calls the *Principia* "Newton's masterpiece (and) also the fundamental work for the whole of modern science" (p. 93).

Newton's work outlines his three laws of motion:

1. A body at rest will remain at rest unless compelled to change by force.
2. A body's change in motion is proportional to the force impressed upon that body.
3. For every action there is an equal and opposite reaction.

The power and genius of these three laws changed history and gave birth to science as we know it today. But the three laws were not the only significant contribution to be found in the *Principia*. Newton's methodical scientific style of neutral and plain writing complimented with mathematical calculations and figures was quite new when the book was first published. Even the language he uses to get across his ideas was an innovation. The use of terms like Motion, Force, Mass, and Weight as scientific terms, the almost mathematical quantification of the language into terms is still used today. Bestselling science writer and biographer James Gleick called Newton the "chief architect of the modern world" (*Isaac Newton*. James Gleick. p. 3) "He pushed open the door that lead to a new universe; set in absolute time and space, at once measureless and measurable, furnished with science and machines, ruled by industry and natural law" (p. 8).

In the mid seventeenth century when Newton was writing the *Principia* the art and industry of publishing was already quite sophisticated. The first movable type systems came out of China around 1041–1048. This printing process uses separate components, letters, or characters to reproduce text and was the foundation for the printing press. Invented around 1440 by the German goldsmith Johannes Gutenberg, the printing press, shown in Figure 2.1, brought about our modern understanding of printing and print reproduction.

Figure 2.1 An early printing press.

In 1687 less than 400 copies of the *Principia* were published by Halley and the Royal Society using these techniques. The first leather-bound edition was 511 pages and cost nine shillings. Later versions of the *Principia* were revised and updated by Newton and published in 1687, 1713, and 1726. The ongoing importance of Newton's work was summed up by the British biographer Peter Ackroyd "the value of his calculations became evident in the fact that Newtonianism had become by the eighteenth century the English orthodoxy" (*Newton,* p. 91). Essentially, Newton and the *Principia* had changed the way people thought about themselves and the planet they lived on.

The printing process evolved over the centuries, improving its technology with offset printing, lithography, and screen printing until the twentieth century, when photosetting was invented around 1940 but first came into wide use in the 1980s. The process of photosetting turned the manual printing and inking process to a chemical process where film was used to capture the printed work. In the 1970s photosetting machines made it economically feasible for small companies to set up their own printing departments.

Late in the twentieth century Xerox invented xerographic printing, giving birth to, among other devices, the photocopier and the laser printer. With this new printing technique, copies of the *Principia* could be made on a photoconductive drum that was charged with electricity. This increased the efficiency and volume for the printing process. The entire text of the *Principia* could now be printed on demand in a matter of minutes.

In the late 1970s electronic paper and ink were invented. Over the next thirty years the technology was refined and improved, allowing an electrophoretic display to be used as a way to present information on a screen. This meant that pigment could be rearranged using an applied electronic field and presented to a reader as text. This was the final step that took text and the printed word from a physical or chemical task to one that was completely accomplishable by a computer. No longer did we need massive presses, ink, and chemicals to deliver the *Principia* to a screen so that it could be read; we just needed 1s and 0s.

Figure 2.2 shows us how an electrophoretic display works. The positive and negative electronic charges can turn the pigment on and off. The positive charged "ink" moves away from or is attracted to a changing electronic charge. This attraction or repulsion creates tiny black or white dots on the reading surface of the electronic paper. These dots are called pixels and these pixels can be arranged and rearranged into text for the reader. Using this process a single page of electronic paper can be changed and updated to show all 551 pages of Newton's *Principia*.

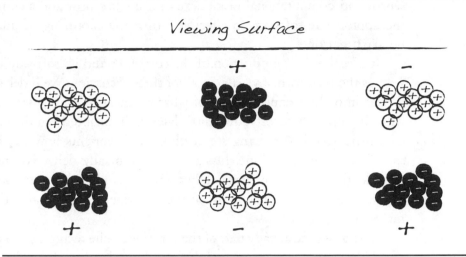

Figure 2.2 Detail of electronic ink

In November of 2007 Amazon introduced the Kindle[†] e-book reader and the product quickly sold out. The *Principia* can be wirelessly downloaded for free from the amazon.com Web site. Amazon's Kindle is by no means the first or only e-book reader. Others such as Sony, Samsung, Apple, iRex, and Bookeen have developed models.

This nearly 400-year journey from Newton's handwritten notebooks to the Kindle's digitally and computationally presented text provides an excellent example of how a manual task can be transformed into a computational task.

This transformation of text to data brings greater efficiency and portability (wireless transmission) as well as freedom from previous printing materials (no more paper, press, ink, and so on). Granted the e-readers have material and manufacturing costs but the physical materials needed to print each book has been removed.

The *Principia* and other printed works are just a short example of this process. We could have traced the evolution of phone switching from manual operators to mechanical switching to switched in time (TDMA) to switched in space (packetized). Another interesting and emerging example is photography. Recent developments have seen photography move from the physical and chemical realm of lenses, flashes, and film developing to a wholly sensor and computational task that uses a single sensor and a computer with the appropriate software to effectively turn the capturing of images into a binary function.

It is really the introduction of the computer and its software that can be seen as the transformative step in all of these scenarios. We'll delve a little bit deeper into the technical detail of what we mean when we say "a computer with the appropriate software" a little later in the chapter. But the introduction of this powerful pair changes everything and reorients how we think about specific tasks getting done. Just as an electronically delivered and rendered text like the *Principia* differs wildly from the handwritten *On Motion*, so too can we see the difference between the traditional TV signal and where the future will take us.

In fact, we are already part of the way there. The recoding and production of TV has jumped forward by leaps and bounds from the early days of live TV transmitted via a network of broadcasting towers. We now have high definition digital cameras as well as fiber optic and satellite delivery systems. The twentieth century saw TV and the video signal go from analog to digital. Now we want to look to the future where that digital signal or digital file becomes data.

When we think about video and entertainment as data we begin to decouple the information about the entertainment from the entertainment itself. This is a subtle point but an important one. Previously there was a one-to-one correlation between media and its method of delivery; the media, and the information about the media were inextricably linked. But by turning entertainment into data and making it a compute task, we are opening up new ways to present that entertainment and its accompanying information that uniquely separates the two and allows us to create completely new experiences.

And *data* is the key here. Turning the physical print block to e-ink brought about the ability to search every page, word, and letter in the *Principia*. This transformation to data will afford the same level of intelligence about the TV and video we all enjoy. But it doesn't end with just knowing what's contained in the file or the frames, this increased intelligence opens up the ability to do more, combine and mash up our TV to the point that the entertainment we watch in the future will make our early twenty-first century TV look as exotic as Newton's handwritten manuscripts.

When a Computer Watches a Movie, What Does It See?

As we start to dive into the particulars and details of what it means to turn TV into a computational take and make it more informative, I want to make sure that we understand these concepts in a specific and detailed way. I don't want to be vague and general just to be understood. To make sure this doesn't happen, let's use examples from science fiction movies as illustrations for our discussion. Science fiction is constantly imagining our future. The accuracy of these visions have varied wildly but there are some stand-out examples that can help us along in our discussion. Let's use an example from a movie to illustrate computer vision and image analysis. From this we can get into the details of the science and the implications.

***

Imagine it's the middle of the twenty-first century and we're in Washington, DC. A man frantically rushes into the Gap clothing store. As he comes into the store his retinas are scanned. The man's name is John Anderton but the store's holographic greeter calls him Mr. Yakamoto and asks him if he liked the assorted tanks tops he had purchased before.

John Anderton has had his eyes replaced to evade detection by the police. The store's computer and retinal scanner have identified him correctly—those are Mr. Yakamoto's eyes but they just happen to be in John Anderston's head.

***

This is of course science fiction. It's a scene from the 2002 Steve Spielberg movie *Minority Report* based on the short story by Philip K. Dick. The vision of the future expressed in the movie is not pure fiction. When Spielberg and the rest of the production team set out to design this future world they gathered together scientists and experts from crime fighting, healthcare, social services, transportation, and computer technology. At a three day summit in Vienna they worked with the assembled brain trust to explore what the world might look like in fifty years. The goal was to portray the future as accurately as possible. In an interview about the film director Spielberg said that "the future look of the story came from their best prognosticating."(Minority Report Interview DVD).

I like using this scene to kick off our exploration of Informative TV because it plays with the concepts of information and vision. Spielberg's scene illustrates that computer vision, no matter how precise and accurate, can get its information wrong. A computer system's understanding is limited to the information it can pull in through its sensors, cameras, and scanners. Just as our understanding of the mystery and plot of *Minority Report* is limited to how Spielberg unfolds the drama, a computer has its limits as well. You can really think of it this way: when a computer and its software are harvesting information from its sensors it's just watching TV. To a computer, the outside world is just TV. We are just TV.

The *Minority Report* example also illustrates some of the prime difficulties of computer vision, image recognition, and analytics. As we watch John Anderton race into the Gap, we know it's John Anderton the character from the movie. We also know it's Tom Cruise playing Anderton. Additionally we know that Mr. Yakamoto's eyes are in John Anderston's head. The smart, spooky computer with only its retinal scanner gets it wrong and we silly dumb humans get it right.

To be fair we have quite an advantage over the computer in this example. We have an incredible capacity to recognize what we are seeing based upon years of cultural learning. Humans have the ability to make huge assumptions based on our knowledge. When we see the upper torso and head of Tom Cruise as John Anderton we make the correct assumption that Cruise also has a lower torso, legs, and complete arms. We assume and pretty much know that Cruise is also three-dimensional with sides and a back. But to a computer the image of Cruise in that frame, taken in isolation, is just an image. It is devoid of any broad cultural knowledge and assumptions that humans possess. Humans have a keen temporal knowledge that allows us to make these assumptions and suspend our disbelief in case of minor inaccuracies. Computers today don't make these assumptions; they can't suspend their disbelief. Currently image recognition software isn't as fortunate. There is still a good bit of work to be done in this area.

Let's look at what happens when a computer watches a movie like *Minority Report*. For a computer to understand what it is watching it needs to identify and break down the images it's seeing from its video and audio sensors.

A computer has a number of ways it can go about doing this.

First, a computer can know what it's watching because just like us it's been told. We learn through the movie poster, DVD art, or title listed on the TV. A computer learns through a collection of unique and identifying information that is delivered along with the movie or video file. This information is sometimes called metadata and it provides basic information about the movie.

Using this simple metadata the computer knows that it's watching *Minority Report*. It knows that is was directed by Steven Spielberg and released in 2002. The movie is based on a short story of the same name by Phillip K. Dick and was adapted into a screenplay by Scott Frank. The movie stars Tom Cruise, Max von Sydow, and Colin Farrell. This is all pretty simple stuff that you could get from the credits, the DVD box, or any number of Web sites but it's important information for us to go to the next step.

For our next step we'll use our own scene from a fictitious movie called *Visage*. The scene follows Bill Character (our heroic lead) as he escapes from the police. Accused of a crime has hasn't committed, Bill Character must hide out in a local restaurant. The part of Bill Character is being played by Frank Actor. Let's dive into the action! Bill Character races into Vinsanto's Italian Restaurant to hide from the police. Let's stop on one of the first frames of the scene, shown in Figure 2.3. Using scene detection in the video file we know that we have started a new scene, section, or chapter. According to the DVD we are in Chapter 2 about 00:42 seconds in. This is helpful because it give us a beginning point for this particular scene and allows us to begin to collect information and keep track of it.

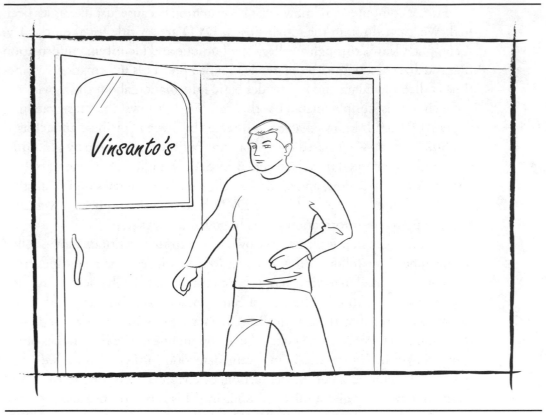

Figure 2.3   The opening frame of our fictional scene: Bill Character rushes into the restaurant.

As our scene continues forward Bill Character rushes into the restaurant. When his identity is scanned by the electronic hostess, we see that Bill Character has cleverly hidden his true name using a stolen identity card. As the scene progresses we begin to identify all of the objects in the frame, as shown in Figure 2.4.

Figure 2.4   Objects are identified in the frame

We don't know who or what these things are just yet but we do know that they are in the frame and in the Chapter 2 of the DVD. Now we can now start tracking them. Here we can take advantage of the computer's processing power to index the objects, estimate their motion, or where they might move to in the frames. We can even use some image restoration if we are not quite sure what we are seeing. In fact, there are many more objects in this scene that we could identify and track. There are steps, background actors and retail display pedestals. Here we have to be careful because many of these objects are critical to the authenticity of the scene but don't really need to be identified and tracked. The computer will need to determine if the time on screen and perceptual gap is small enough to ignore that object.

As we move through the scene the computer can watch the pixels that we have identified as Object A in Figure 2.4. Our next step is to identify what Object A is. This type of recognition, can be easy for a human but currently it's tricky for computers.

A number of people are working on solutions for this type of identification. As you can imagine this is a massive problem with implications and applications outside of just watching movies. Technically this is known as computer vision and video analytics. Both governments and companies are working on security, medical, and navigation applications for this type computer vision, each working to solve their specific flavor of the problem. But for us, let's just stick with the movies.

To identify Object A as Bill Character and Frank Actor we could access the metadata that came along with the movie. We could also do an image search on the Web and come up with a pretty close mathematical probability and identification. We could even use our own vast web of social networks and science fiction enthusiasts that could easily tag Object A and share the appropriate information. Any number of these solutions could get us our desired identification and in fact it would be best to use a combination of all of them to get us the links needed to not only identify Object A but also Objects B through E as well.

To recap: we have now identified a specific collection of pixels, we are now tracking them throughout the scene, and we have created the link that Object A = Bill Character = Frank Actor. By this process we have succeeded in taking Chapter 2 (Figure 2.3 and 2.4) of *Visage* from a video sequence to a data set, shown in Figure 2.5.

Figure 2.5   Chapter 2 has been transformed into a collection of data objects

This collection of data could include the actors, characters, as well as scene and location information; anything that's taking places in the scene. This data set will grow and change as the movie plays. It is at this point that a computer watching a move can do much more than a human watching a movie.

Now when I say a computer can do a lot more, I really mean it can receive, store, and send information as well as make connections between elements within that information. Now that we know that Object A = Bill Character = Frank Actor we can begin to make connections to other data sources and Internet sites that could offer up more information like:

- In the original John Q. Writer short story of *Visage* Bill Character was fat, balding, and nearing retirement.

- Frank Actor's recent movies have been *Mission into Night*, *The Runner* and *Our House*.

- Frank Actor's first onscreen appearance was in the 1981 movie *All for Love* where he played the part of Jay.

As you can imagine, the uses of this information and data goes far beyond trivia and linkages. Simple commerce connections would allow you to buy or rent *All for Love* or watch the trailer for *Mission into Night*. You could watch other films by director or films based upon the writings of John Q. Writer. We can identify places (Object C = Washington, DC) and brands (Object D = Vinsanto's) within the movie. You could buy the clothes that Frank Actor is wearing in the scene or purchase a gift certificate for the restaurant (Object E). The truth is at this point in the process the computer can identify more information about the scene than we'd know what to do with today.

But the real power of the transition of a movie like *Visage* to a collection of data comes from what the computer can do behind the scenes. One simple example could be when you buy that copy of *All for Love* it can take you directly to the scenes where Jay (Frank Actor) is shown. More complex examples populate the chapters that follow in this book concerning usages and experiences like ubiquity, personalization, and social interactions.

Having more information about your entertainment allows you to ask questions and make connections that you might not have been able to make before. Granted you could have done this research all on your own but it would have taken a little digging and would have involved more than just sitting in front of your TV.

All of this new information allows your TV to offer up hooks. *Hook* is a software term that allows other applications to make use of the information provided by a program or piece of entertainment. With this added intelligence the frame-by-frame video can be populated by these hooks giving you the ability to connect the hooks to other information, movies, TV shows, and applications. These types of interconnections are not new. We see this type of contextual linking all the time on the Internet. What is new however are the experiences that these types of interconnections open up when combined with TV shows, movies, games, and applications.

So How Does It Work?

I'm going to assume that most of you reading this book have a pretty good working knowledge of a computer; how it works and what it can do. But for the sake of detail and illustration let's do a basic overview as it relates to what we need for our computer to watch a movie.

A computer is a collection of electronic circuits that operate on input (data) under the control of a program (software) to produce the desired output (data). For our example the input is our fictional movie *Visage* and the software is what is first locating and tracking the objects in the frame and secondly identifying what those objects might be. The desired output in this example is locating, tracking, and identifying Object A = Bill Character = Frank Actor, in a single frame of *Visage*. Figure 2.6 illustrates how our frame from Visage moves through the system and identifies Object A.

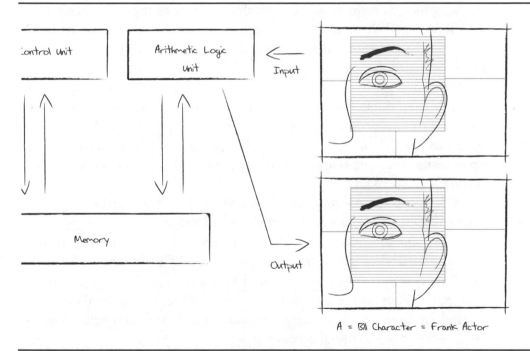

Figure 2.6   Functional Overview of Computer Architecture

To begin this analysis we need to go through some basic steps. We start with a processing unit that can execute a our image identification and tracking program. It will also need to be able to accept input data from our video frame, and generate output data such as the identification A = Bill Character = Frank Actor. This core of inputs, processing, and outputs is known as a central processing unit (CPU). It is composed of control circuits to guide the data and operation, and arithmetic circuits to operate on the data.

To identify A = Bill Character = Frank Actor in the single frame we will also need a way to provide the video frame to the CPU. This is a system bus, which links the CPU to the other components. Next we need a means to input the frame data to the CPU. This can be data stored in a memory or a direct connection to a live data source like our movie. Once we have the frame data sent to the CPU, we need to store intermediate data results that might be required for the CPU to execute the program. This is typically specialized memory such as registers and buffers that are part of the CPU architecture. Finally we need a means to output our identification data generated by the CPU per the program. Like the input data, the output can be stored onto a memory device or directly connected to a live data source.

From a high level, that's how the CPU works and how we can go through that single frame to identify A = Bill Character = Frank Actor. As you can imagine, it is a bit more complicated than this. Our broader computer system that we will use to identify and track the frame is made up of some core components. For the sake of our later discussion, I've listed and defined them here:

CPU: central processing unit, also known as microprocessor. This is the primary computing element that we described above.

DSP: digital signal processing. The specialized computing used to analyze "signals" or inputs from the real world. DSP also stands for digital signal processor, a processor specialized for digital signal processing, and an unfortunate reuse of the same acronym used for the more general definition. In modern computers, both the microprocessor and the digital signal processor are capable of digital signal processing.

Platform: the major hardware and software components that comprise a useful description of the computing capability.

System memory: the available memory for software and data storage. RAM is typically used for fast access to smaller amounts of memory, but is not preserved without power. The hard disk drive is an example of large amounts of memory that can be stored without power (nonvolatile), but run much slower than RAM.

Software: the description of the processing required for an application. Software is usually written in a human friendly way (such as in a high level programming language such as C++ or C), then compiled into a processor-friendly format (such as executable binary code).

Algorithm: a description of the output(s) generated by a series of processing steps taken on input data. This term is thrown around in the field of computer vision without a precise sense of what is happening, and algorithms can usually be decomposed into a sequence of smaller algorithmic tasks. For example, an algorithm to detect an actor is composed of blob detection, blob tracking, classification, and spatial-temporal boundary matching; each of these can be further broken down.

Computer vision: enabling a machine, typically through a computer program (yet another algorithm) to act upon captured video data. In science fiction, this means ill-intentioned computers reading the lips of astronauts, whereas today's reality is closer to having a reasonably accurate count of the number of people who pass through a door as long as they don't use canes, wheelchairs, stand up straight, don't block the camera, don't walk closely together, don't run too fast—you get the idea.

Data flow: how an algorithm processes data.

Control flow: the decisions based on the algorithmic steps and subsequent branches available based on the decisions.

Video analytics: the creation of a semantic description that a step in the data flow can provide. Often many steps in the data flow are required before a meaningful semantic can be formed.

Analytics frame resolution: the height and width of the input image presented at the start of the video analytics data flow. In general, the higher the analytics frame resolution, the greater the ability to distill information within a frame.

Analytics frame rate (AFR): the rate at which new input images are processed. If the analytics frame rate is too slow, critical events are missed. Too fast can mean spending energy without much improvement. For example, an AFR of 10/s is considered okay for typical human activity, whereas an anti-missile guidance system may need 1000/s.

Image operations: these are the "primitives" used by the video analytics algorithm developers. Examples are convolution, correlation, histogram, absolute subtraction, matrix row-column multiplication, matrix element-by-element multiply, dilation, and erosion. Sometimes these are referred to as the image processing library functions, but even this can be a bit misleading when the library includes functions like "face detection," which is actually composed of the simpler image operations.

Let's apply this back to our fictional film *Visage* example. Before we looked at a single frame of *Visage,* let's now look at an entire scene. What does it take to identify and track the objects in the scene? We are going to use the four steps of Figure 2.7 as a guide.

The crux of the problem is that what is easy and natural for humans to describe and relatively simple for us to do (watch the movie) is actually very difficult to describe to a computer in a way that feels natural, is easy to understand, and is flexible and adaptable in the way we would like. It's true that a good portion of the problem is that we don't have a good description and specifications of what we want and need, but it's also true that we don't have a way to get computers to understand all the factors that make this problem simple for humans.

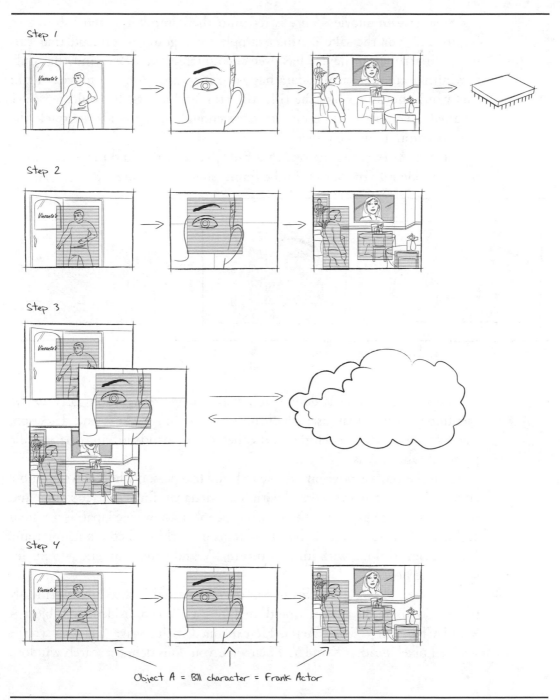

Figure 2.7   *Visage* data flow

Step 1: Our movie *Visage* is fed into the computer system, shown in Figure 2.7. For the sake of this example we're going to pretend that this is the first time our device has ever encountered the movie and that only a minimal amount of metadata has been included with the movie. Again this would be things like the title, director, and actors. It would not have detailed scene-by-scene information or enough information to track the objects throughout the movie.

Step 2: As the computer watches Bill Character run into the restaurant it begins to identify the objects in the frame, shown in Figure 2.8.

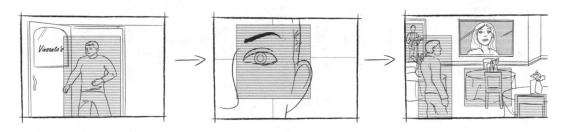

Figure 2.8   *Visage* data flow Step 2 - detail

This identification is done through the image recognition software we mentioned before that uses algorithms to do things like scene detection, tracking, boundary matching, and other means of identifying the specific pixels of Object A as a person.

Now before we move on I'd like to bring in a person who knows far more about this than me. I've worked with Suri Medapati for years. He's quiet and soft-spoken and also one of the smartest people I know. Medapati is a system architect for Intel where he builds systems on a chip, silicon, and software. I have been working with him on future TV and entertainment systems for some time now.

We were talking about this step in the process and I asked him specifically to describe how the system would analyze the scene and identify Object A = Bill Character = Frank Actor. He explained it this way: "Let's say you've selected pixel location X and Y. Then what you do is define a search window.

Let's say you pick 200 pixels in either direction. Then you begin to search all the pixels and you learn that at location 150 and 151, there is a change in pixels. We have found the edge of an object, the edge of Frank Actor." (See Figure 2.9.)

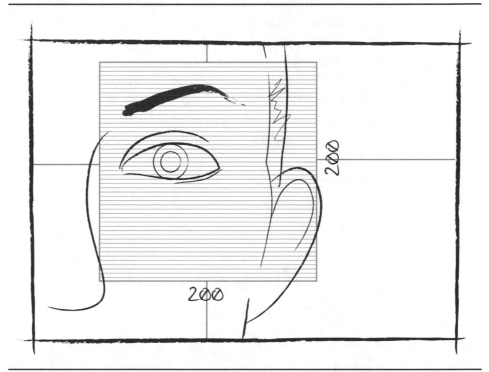

Figure 2.9 In a 200x200 search field the edge of the object is discovered

"Now that you have found a change in the pixels you try to create an outline in that neighboring region of a particular object. The algorithm looks for gradients, and shades of pixels that are changing. It also tries to use the next frame to determine if there is motion in the object. It looks for where the last movement was in the previous frame and it can determine the size and shape of our object."

But how does the computer and the algorithm "see" the differences and outlines? How can it tell if an object, like Frank Actor's head in Figure 2.9, is moving from frame to frame?

Medapati pointed at the Figure 2.9 and replied, "Frank Actor's head and all the objects in the frame are sitting against a background. In this case the front door to the store. We're lucky it's easy to see in this frame. The algorithm is looking for the difference in either grayscale or color or some gradient between the two. If it can find those gradient differences then it can create an outline of that object. Frank Actor's head. Just like this example"

"But I should point out," Medapati continued. "We don't know it's Frank Actor's head yet. We just know it's an object. The algorithm says 'hey, this is what the object looks like at this boundary of pixels' but we still haven't determined what that object is, the algorithm has only determined that 'this is an object at these pixels are surrounded by these other pixels.'"

The hard part is identifying the object and that's our next step, shown in Figure 2.10.

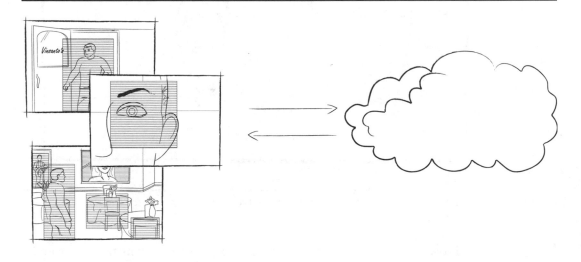

Figure 2.10   *Visage* data flow Step 3 - detail

Step 3: Everyone will tell you that this is the most complicated part of the entire process. It isn't compute intensive, meaning it doesn't take a lot of computing power like analyzing the video in Steps 1 and 2. The identification is hard because of all of the variables and possibilities.

Medapati explained it like this: "The next step is trying to determine what that object is. If you have detailed metadata about the movie and that metadata is linked to images of the actors then you could use the metadata to match to our image of Frank Actor. But today this doesn't exist. So what you need to do is take the object along with some really high-level information about the movie; like the title and genre. Then you try to do your best level matching you can to determine what the object is.

Let's say we know it's the fictitious movie *Visage* and that it is starring (1) Frank Actor, (2) Karl Hero, and (3) Sam Villain. So we can begin to narrow our search by searching if Object A is either 1, 2, or 3. Based on this criteria you would quickly learn that Object A is 1, Frank Actor.

But unless we have this information this is probably one of the tougher problems, because we have no parameters to take Object A and match it with other examples of Frank Actor outside of his image in *Visage*. This is where we could use some clues from the stream data or the movie to narrow our search window instead of trying to identify all the objects in that particular frame. What we would like to have is data that gives us hints and clues about what each object could possibly be. The fewer the set of things that we need to go look for to see if this is Frank Actor or somebody else in the movie, the better.

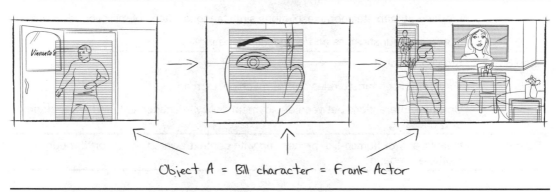

Object A = Bill character = Frank Actor

Figure 2.11   *Visage* data flow Step 4 - detail

Step 4: Once we have located and tracked the object and crossed the hurdle of identifying Object A = Bill Character = Frank Actor, as shown in Figure 2.11, then this information is combined and fed back to us. The simplicity or the complexity of the information delivered in Step 4 depends upon the algorithms, programs, and services that are on or connected to our devices.

Now that we have identified the objects using the algorithmic analysis of the video frames we have turned them into data. Now this data can move through space and time inside the frames, throughout the duration of the movie and even as data separated from the movie itself. We can also attach hooks to the objects and make connections to other movies, information, and better yet services. Such services could allow you to buy, share, and personalize your *Visage* experience.

At each step in this process it takes work to identify, compute, and deliver this information varies, as shown in Table 2.1.

Table 2.1   The work that needs to be done by the system to watch *Visage*

Step	Processing Work Load
Step 1	Very large amounts of input data
	Lots of relatively simply, but memory intensive arithmetic operations
	Spatial and temporal filters
	Segmentation, tracking, classification
Step 2	Small-to-medium data rates
	Simple spatial and temporal filters
	Working at many temporal resolutions simultaneously (tens of milliseconds to days)
	Complex, heuristic rules and/or machine learning
Step 3	Small data rates
	Very complex heuristic rules and/or machine learning
	Complex interactions between deployment policy, management, and lower stages of processing
Step 4	Human and/or human-like processing with context awareness to sort through multiple scenarios

Out of the Home and into the Cloud

Remember back at the beginning of our *Visage* example I mentioned that we were assuming that this was the first time our device had seen *Visage?* We did this to simplify the example. But as you would expect, in the real world things are a bit more complex.

In the future there could be instances where a good portion of the data about *Visage* could be generated by the producers, studio, or a service provider. This means that a lot of the work could be done "in the cloud." Figure 2.12 gives an illustration of this. Massive server farms could have analyzed the movie before you even watched it.

There's another scenario that says a lot of the information needed to enable the experiences we have been discussing in this chapter could be collected by the camera at the time of production. It's not too much of a stretch to think of sports and news programming generating this increased data at the moment the footage is captured by the camera. This would make it easier for the news editors to do their work and easier for consumers and news junkies to get to the information they want faster.

But with that said, it is impractical to know all the information that people are going to be interested in all the time. Examining and processing every pixel in every frame really isn't an efficient use of bandwidth and processing power. How we determine this can be approached in a number of ways:

1. **Profit**: Those who are going to profit from the information include it in the file. If we use the information about Vinsanto's Italian Restaurant in our *Visage* example scene to buy a gift certificate to the restaurant that means that Vinsanto's, it's media agency, or the producers who get the product placement dollars would make sure that the information is included. The more information they have embedded in the stream the more revenue opportunities there are for them. That's a pretty good incentive.

2. **80/20 Rule:** The 80/20 rule is used all the time to reduce the amount of information added for the mainstream consumption. The idea here is that 80 percent of the people only really care about 20 percent of the information in any given piece of video. Go big and don't sweat the small stuff.

3. **Experts, Geeks, and Enthusiasts:** Let those who have a passion for the idea do the work. Just like the Internet was expanded by enthusiasts before larger companies came in to make money, we could use an army of people who are passionate about their content to develop their own additional information.

4. **Regulation:** Like many instances in the history of television the national government or regulatory body could step in to set a standard that needs to be followed by all content producers, broadcasters, and service providers. This would be akin to the HD standards.

Figure 2.12 Broader system of multiple servers and client partitioning

Deep Thinking and a Lot More Possibilities

Trends in computing and entertainment are moving us to a future where TV is transformed from video images and frames to objects and data sets. What I find exciting about this future are the possibilities. Right now we can't really know the broad range of exciting and captivating experiences that producers and directors will dream up when TV becomes data.

Medapati and I talked about this. "Right now, we're working on the computer science and the science of making this possible," he said. "We know it's possible from a compute standpoint, we just need to do some engineering and get it built. But the next step is to get people to actually begin to dream up and build these new experiences.

"It's fairly hard for us to fathom all the usages and things people will want to do at this point in time. You know it does require a lot of deep thinking, but it does open up a lot more possibilities."

In the following chapters of this book we'll explore some of these possibilities. In the end, this idea of transforming entertainment into data is quite simple really, and because it's simple, it's beautiful. I don't mean that it's simple in its execution, the variations of algorithms, business complexities, and computer science are actually quite complicated. To make this happen will be complicated but the basic idea is simple. It's beautiful because of what we might be able to accomplish and because it's going to be a heck of a lot of fun.

Chapter 3

From *Star Trek* to *Paranormal Activity*

A CONVERSATION WITH AMY REINHARD

A little over 30 miles southwest of San Francisco, California, sits the Ritz Carlton at Half Moon Bay. The sprawling hotel is perched high on cliffs that overlook the Pacific Ocean. The day I was there for a conference the wind was coming off the ocean with such intensity that you could see the glass in the windows tremble. Paramount Pictures' Amy Reinhard was on the agenda just before lunch. Reinhard gave a fascinating and concise review of the motion picture industry's business flow and the challenges, and the opportunities they face in the coming years.

Amy Reinhard is the Senior of Strategic Planning and Business Development for Paramount Pictures. Reinhard has a unique role within Paramount. She coordinates the green light process. This is the process by which a studio goes about putting a film project into production, assigning a budget and a production team. Reinhard facilitates the communication between the creative side and the business side as Paramount gets ready to *green-light* a film and make a production investment in that film.

Reinhard also manages the long-range strategic and financial plan for Paramount. This plan looks ahead, analyzing the various segments of the business and exploring areas of growth and opportunity within the industry. She also analyzes mergers and acquisitions with Viacom, Paramount's parent company.

To set up our conversation, Reinhard started off by giving me a quick rundown of the economics of the movie business.

AMY REINHARD: I like to say we are in the gardening business. We plant a lot of seeds, develop a lot of different ideas, and see which ones grow into viable movie options. If you look at the time from when a movie is green-lit until it hits the screen, the time frame is typically 12 to 18 months for most live-action major studio releases. We have a marketing group that's getting very involved with the filmmakers from the start to understand the heart of the story. They also work to understand who the target audiences are, how they're going to be able to reach these audiences, and what is going to be driving people into the movie theater. A marketing campaign starts up to six months out from releasing the movie. With a new property or new franchise, the thrust of our marketing campaign and spend is concentrated on the six weeks leading up to a film's release. We have six weeks to reach our audience and drive them into the theater the opening weekend. If it's a sequel to a franchise, that's a very different beast to market, because there's already a known entity involved and big expectations.

Opening weekend is so important, because opening weekend is most always the biggest box office weekend for major studio releases. If we do not finish in the top three on that opening weekend, there's much less chance of making a big push at the box office in the weeks that follow. Our box office revenue will generally decline from that opening weekend. Sometimes positive word of mouth gets out into the public and changes that trend but it's a very rare occurrence when a movie does better in its second or third weekend than it does in its first. "Platform" releases are the exception. A platform release is when a studio does a very limited theatrical release the first weekend and then expands the theater count in the weeks that follow, hoping that positive reviews and good word of mouth will build an audience. But platform releases are certainly not the norm in terms of distributing a major studio release.

Major studios like Paramount usually go wide, generally over 1,500 screens, and they go hard and if it doesn't work the first weekend then you reel back your marketing because the following weeks are a derivative of the first weekend box office.

Our windows refer to the release pattern that is employed, meaning the availability on various platforms for a film throughout its life. The theatrical window is the first and for the major theater chains, this first window is generally about six weeks. A film can be in the discount run theaters anywhere from two to three months after initial release depending on how the film performs in its first several weeks. More successful films have longer theatrical lives. Rental and sell-through DVD and digital windows can vary quite a bit depending on the studio and that space is changing a lot. Rental and sell-through used to be "day and date," meaning they premiere in both retail and rental outlets on the same date. Now some studios are launching this DVD window with either rental or sell-through exclusively depending on the title. Some studios are doing a 30-day rental window. We did this on some of our fall 2009 titles, like *Dance Flick*. Some studios are doing a 28-day exclusive sell-through window. Then there's the VOD window. Some studios are releasing VOD day-and-date with sell-through while others premiere the VOD window anywhere from 7 days to 30 days after the sell-through date. Then after the VOD window, about a month to forty-five days after it, the film is made available on a pay TV window for anywhere from twelve to eighteen months. This pay TV window includes premium services like HBO, Showtime, and our new service Epix. After that window the title enters its "free TV" window and is licensed by basic cable or network channels depending on the film.

***

BDJ: A lot of the vision for the future of entertainment that we talk about happens in the home or specifically with consumer electronics devices. A good portion of Paramount's business takes place in the movie theater. When you think about the future of entertainment outside the movie theater and in people's daily lives, what do you see?

AMY REINHARD: I think there are two opportunities and two ways that we think about the future. One is from a marketing perspective.

When we are launching a new movie, particularly a tent pole or potential franchise film, we invest a lot of marketing money to craft the marketing message and get the word out. We want people to be familiar with the characters and to some extent, the plot line. We're always thinking about how to reach a very large audience that's becoming increasingly fragmented.

When we are trying to reach people through marketing avenues, TV is still important. It's the biggest way to capture eyeballs and attention right now. Even with the advent of the DVR and TiVo[†], it's still the best place to capitalize on those big events like the Super Bowl or those heavily watched shows like *American Idol*. It's a way to capture our core 'four-quadrant' audiences and get the message out about our movies.

But there are some cases where we concentrate on platforms other than TV. Different age groups are flocking to different devices for entertainment so we need to be aware of those trends. It's a little different when we're looking to market a smaller budget movie that's meant for a very specific audience. Then we search for different avenues of reaching a much more defined audience. We have a pretty good idea of who makes up that audience. With a smaller movie, we may target our message to a specific medium, device, or platform we know that niche audience is using. Specifically, we've had success with going online. But there are many avenues to find an audience, whether it be outdoor campaigns or targeted print campaigns. In the end for us it's about engaging that audience and getting them interested in the film.

So that's one area outside the theater where TV, connected devices, and other platforms are of interest to us. We want to use them for marketing our films and in these times we need to think about all of these different devices and screens.

In recent years we've also been thinking about these other screens from a development and creative perspective. Do different age groups think differently about their entertainment consumption and the mediums they use to watch this content? Is there a way to use these different devices and platforms as a means of expanding the realm of the film or exploring ancillary storylines or characters? This is really true when it comes to those franchise films I mentioned. *Star Trek* is a good example for us. Under the vision of our management, we've rebooted and reinvented the Paramount franchise *Star Trek*. It's the perfect genre to use all those screens to reach our audience and immerse a very dedicated and particularly tech-savvy fan base in a world they love.

Star Trek was a particularly interesting relaunch because the property has a lot of history. On one hand, we wanted to use that history to tap into the built-in audience but on the other hand, we wanted to expand the audience to a new generation of *Star Trek* fans. One of the approaches we used initially was to create content, in this case a teaser trailer, that we debuted online. This content focused on the shipyard where the new *Enterprise* was being built. The piece was iconic and set the tone that this was the dawn of a new era and a new *Star Trek*.

We created a variety of content that was rolled out on the Web. This included a Web site for the film that allowed users to delve into the world of Star Trek…both new and old. They could view content created by the studio and users were encouraged to generate their own content, like creating their own version of the *Enterprise*.

While we wait for the sequel, we are working to keep the audience engaged outside the theater. One way to do this is with video games. In today's world, most franchise movies have a game developed for consoles like PlayStation[†], Xbox 360[†], and Wii[†]. The most successful video games are the ones that don't necessarily replicate the movie experience but explore ancillary storylines or back stories with a mix of new and existing characters. Atari is launching an online *Star Trek* game and marketing it by using innovative social marketing tools. For example, they use a campaign that takes user "tweets" and converts them into the Klingon language. It's these types of features that really engage the audience and core fan base.

Another experience in today's world is casual gaming, which is a different experience from the console games and reaches a different audience segment. It may be a less immersive experience for the end user but it still ultimately engages the user with the brand.

On most major films, we also have a merchandising campaign that allows consumers to identify their affinity for specific movies. This can include sales of ring tones, screen savers and wallpapers for the cell phones…and now apps. Traditional merchandising is often a step removed from this multi-screen idea but it's another way we interact with consumers outside the movie theater.

Then once the movie is out of the theater we work hard to come up with appealing content to include on the Special Edition DVD. This could include a director commentary or a vignette on the production and set design for the movie. There's so much content that is collected during the filming of a movie and we make it our job to try and figure out what type of content would appeal to a DVD buyer. What special features can we include to make consumers want to purchase the film?

Now after saying all of this, this is the way it is today but the future is evolving quickly. Just recently, we're seeing the iPad[†] and smart phones opening up a whole new way of consuming content. Looking ahead, it will continue to be about tailoring the world of our movies to the devices or screens that are used by the audience we want to target. The opportunities are endless for a platform like Blu-ray[†], which can connect via the Internet and allows a consumer to download new content and extras. The video game industry has experienced a lot of success with downloadable content that enhances game play for consumers or adds new levels. Will we discover something similar in the film world?

BDJ: As you start to develop this new material that is not a traditional movie, is it difficult for a traditional theatrical movie company like Paramount to make that shift? Is there a culture or creative shift when you develop for other screens?

AMY REINHARD: I would argue that one of our core competencies is creative development and that is incredibly complex and tricky. So certainly developing content for the big screen is where our focus lies right now because that is where the financial upside lives. But that creative process involves many different people and resides in other parts of the business. The people who work on those other screens—the marketing group, our home video team, and our digital groups—work closely with the creative group. We also have people in our digital group who are solely focused on acquiring and developing content for smaller screens, be it online or on various devices which are used to access the Internet.

Another core competency is marketing and it's an important differentiator. Because if you can't open a movie, as we discussed, then that movie is dead in the water…twelve to eighteen months of incredibly hard work down the drain. We usually get one chance at really making a big push with the movie or it's done. So I think that is why marketing is such a huge focus and a definite core competency for movie studios.

***

BDJ: So consumers don't see a difference between the movie and the content for the other screens. For them it's all content. For Paramount it might be your two core competencies but for the consumer it's all content. That would seem to be a golden opportunity for Paramount. What needs to happen to take advantage of this?

AMY REINHARD: There needs to be a business model that's developed around taking this content to other screens so we can make money from it. Right now our focus is driving people to the theaters or the retail stores to pick up the DVD, because we know that's how we are going to monetize our marketing campaign and monetize our content. Right now it's very difficult with film content to monetize some of these other screens in a meaningful way. We know that there are a lot of different devices and platforms out there, which makes it a bit harder to drive volume on any one device or platform.

To make that other screen content significant we need to figure out how to create content in a cost-effective manner. Otherwise there's no tipping point for investment in these other ways of viewing content. We have faith that ultimately all these different ways of reaching people with our marketing campaigns is going to drive them into the theater or into the store to buy a DVD.

The function of marketing is to drive people to a business model that works. So it's driving people to the movie theater, which then also ties into our windowing strategy that I told you about before. The marketing drives people to consume content in the manner that works for them, be it in the theater, on DVD, or on VOD. That business model works. It's worked for a long time. It's always changing certainly, but it's proven.

So to really take advantage of these new devices and technologies we need to see them generate their own significant amount of revenue. There are obviously a lot of changes going on in the media space so we need to keep our hand on the pulse of these changes.

***

BDJ: How else do you see your business changing with technology?

AMY REINHARD: I think there will always be a theatrical movie-going experience. There are groups of people who enjoy the social nature of going to a movie theater and seeing a film on the big screen with an audience. But I think the in-home access and experience will continue to evolve. Whether this will be through your cable or through some kind of over-the-top or Internet-delivered method remains to be seen. But I think ten years down the line these are the two windows left standing. What's going to be interesting is how it migrates over the next ten years. Physical media like DVDs are still a major part of every studio's revenue at the moment. The interesting thing is going to be how the studios navigate from now until the time when distribution is focused on access into the home. Will that be day and date with a theatrical release, meaning people will have access to the movie on the day it's released into the theaters, or will it be a couple of weeks after the theatrical release? That would be a big shift. That's going to be very interesting.

When we think about going direct into people's home we're faced with a lot of questions. It's a big marketing hurdle to reach a consumer in the home. It's a different approach than what we do now. What is the messaging to let them know that when they turn on the TV they can choose to watch *Transformers*? If a consumer has satellite and he or she has hundreds of channels, how do they know that the new Paramount movie is out and it's ready for them to purchase or rent in a couple of clicks? How do we market to those folks in the home? In an industry comprised of six different studios with different release strategies, is it confusing for the consumer to keep track of when a Paramount title is available versus when a Sony picture is available, versus when a Fox picture is available? I think that can be very confusing to the consumer.

While Paramount is a known brand to consumers, it isn't a brand that necessarily influences purchasing behavior. Our movies are individual brands that influence purchasing behavior. There are certain studios that are brands.

With some studios, a consumer knows what he or she is getting. That would be Disney and Pixar. You know what type of content these studios put out. When you buy a DreamWorks Animation movie you know you are getting a family-friendly animated film. But a Paramount film could be a drama, it could be a comedy, it could be a big action movie.

In a growing digital world we want to try and replicate the impulse buy we often get on the retail side. We know we need to explore new ways of marketing and reaching our consumer base and we need to invest in research. In a retail store, people pick up a film as they pass by the bin of titles and a piece of key art or a famous actor catches their eye. The same thing happens in rental. You used to go to the rental store, thinking I'll just pick up one title and then something else would catch your eye and there would be an impulse rent. We want to encourage this type of consumer behavior in the digital world and replicate the impulse buy in the home. We need to establish a direct relationship with the consumer but that often gets back to branding. How do we do influence consumer behavior with such a wide range of films that can vary from year to year? Ultimately we have to connect with consumers in a way that we can market to them directly.

I'll give you an example of what we did on one of our really recent titles that was a big surprise for us this year. It was a psychological horror movie called *Paranormal Activity*. It was a film that we had acquired for a very small price and we decided on a platform approach because we saw how the film played with audiences. We started with an on-demand campaign. To raise awareness we marketed on different Web sites and drove traffic to a very sparse *Paranormal* Web site with a general message of "sign up if you want this movie in a theater in a town near you." We were targeting college students because we wanted to make it an event and play the film at midnight showings to play into the psychology of the film. We started out by releasing in the top ten markets where the demand was online. All these showings sold out. We had people forming lines around the block at the movie theaters. It was a huge success from a marketing perspective, driven somewhat by a scarcity strategy. Then we expanded the next weekend to the top 30 markets, again with the on-demand model. At the same time we saw fans using Facebook[†] and Twitter[†] to talk about the movie. To a large extent, we let the core audiences market the film for us. Each weekend we expanded to more theaters. Because it was a horror movie right around Halloween we could take advantage of the seasonality too. It went on to do over 100 million dollars [USD] at the box office. It was a huge financial success for us.

We carried out a similar approach to the DVD marketing campaign as well. All through the theatrical marketing campaign we had people sign up and register their names. Then when the DVD was released, if you had signed up on the Web site, your name would be in the credits of the DVD release. We had over one hundred thousand people sign up. That's the type of marketing campaign that can forge a direct relationship with the consumer. Part of the reason why it was such a financial success was because we didn't overspend on the movie. The acquisition cost was low and the marketing cost was also low. We didn't engage in any mass TV campaigns. There was no theatrical trailer. There was an online trailer that we released, but we weren't spending a huge amount of money on a media campaign. We really let the viral marketing speak for itself.

Now it should be said that *Paranormal Activity* was like lightning striking. It was a movie that our creative and marketing heads had a lot of faith in and really got behind it. They saw how it played with an audience. That made them really support it from a creative perspective. They remembered similar success with *The Blair Witch Project* back in 1999. Both movies were a real crowd favorite.

So when I think about *Paranormal Activity* I think it's a great example of a perfect melding between our creative instincts and our marketing team, our two core competencies. Together they came up with this very clever way of marketing the movie. It was really quite novel and new. Having those two in sync, the creative and the marketing, were the key factors. The movie really took off.

I'm not saying that we can replicate that again on every movie going forward. But it shows that when those two core competencies, creative and marketing come together, we achieve true success. Each one needs to feed off of the other to create that success.

If you have a great movie, but not a great marketing campaign, the film likely won't achieve its full potential at the box office. At the same time if you have a bad movie and a great marketing campaign, you can only get so far before word of mouth gets out there and arguably limits your box office figures. Then really it's up to the audience and if the movie isn't good —the movie isn't good and it won't do well. But having those two pieces together is what it's all about.

In the future, we're always looking for other ways to really synergize those two competencies together. I don't think it's a genre phenomenon. Some people think we can only get this type of buzz with a small-budget horror film. But I think it's just about connecting the right creative instincts with a really good marketing team that can ultimately tap into the right audience.

***

BDJ: What things, for your industry, are you excited about and looking forward to?

AMY REINHARD: I am excited to see how the windowing structure plays out and how this impacts the industry. Some people anticipate some sort of consolidation in the industry. I think there is a lot of opportunity. Arguably, the industry tends to be like a pendulum. If one was to look back five or six years ago, there was an influx of financing in the industry, and there was a big increase in the volume of independent films. Now we're in a place where that's all contracted. The money has gone away and a lot of the studios are focusing more on big budget, franchise films with built-in audiences. But hopefully it's just a matter of time before it swings out the other way. We as an industry need to figure out how to tap into the social nature of this digital world to access those smaller audiences. There is a demand for all different type films, whether it be drama, or action, or horror, or comedy. There is always an audience out there for something. We need to figure out how our business model can adapt in a successful way.

I am excited for 3D. I would love to see how that evolves as more theaters have the capacity to show films in 3D. It will be interesting to see if there are more live action 3D movies like James Cameron's *Avatar* in addition to the animated 3D movies. It's a little further out in terms of mass adoption but I'm excited for 3D in the home. We are just at the infancy of it but it will be interesting to see how it evolves.

It is going to be fascinating to see a generation of kids who have grown up accessing content on their computer and multiple devices relying more on these platforms than their TV. I want to see if that behavior continues as they get into adulthood or if there is a shift as they become wage earners. It's all going to be very, very exciting.

Chapter 4

Ubiquitous TV

U biquity is a funny word. *Merriam-Webster's Collegiate Dictionary* defines it as "presence everywhere or in many places especially simultaneously." *Random House Dictionary* describes it as "the state or capacity of being everywhere, especially at the same time." Simple enough right? Well, hang on—there's more to it.

Ubiquity really isn't a term that is in most people's everyday vocabulary. Computer scientists and social scientists have been using the term to describe a vision for how we will interact with computers in the future. Imagine what our world will look like when all of our devices—our laptops, phones, TVs, cars, and any other device that has a computer in it—are all connected together. Don't worry about the details just yet; we'll get into that later. But imagine a world where data flows freely between your devices and they are always connected to each other, to the Internet and to any other service or network you need.

When put that way, ubiquitous TV makes a lot of sense. We can easily imagine a world where we can watch TV shows wherever we are, enjoy movies whenever we want, play games, and chat with friends. This vision really isn't that hard to conjure up in your imagination because, well, it's already happening. Many aspects of this ubiquitous future are already here. So, taking the next logical step and imagining that all our devices are connected to each other isn't too much of a leap. This ubiquitous vision has even seeped into our popular culture.

Like in the previous chapter on informative TV, let's use an example from science fiction to illustrate what we're talking about. These science fiction visions will allow us to be specific as we explore our ubiquitous TV future. In the case of our next example, the future isn't that far off.

Ubiquity Takes Over the World!

It's 2009. Rachel Holloman walks out of a bar after having drinks with some friends. Her cell phone rings (Figure 4.1).

Figure 4.1   Rachel's cell phone rings.

A pleasant female voice tells her to look into the window of the McDonald's across the street (Figure 4.2).

Figure 4.2   TVs in the windows of the McDonald's across the street.

In the window the flat panel TVs switch suddenly from a cheeseburger advertisement to surveillance video of Rachel's son, Sam, on a train (Figure 4.3).

Figure 4.3   The image on the TVs changes to video surveillance of Rachel's son.

Figure 4.4   Rachel's son on surveillance video

One of the screens shows Sam safely sitting in his seat chatting with a friend while the other gives an aerial view of the boy's train headed from Chicago to Washington DC. The pleasant voice on the phone informs Rachel that she's been *activated* (Figure 4.5).

Figure 4.5   Rachel is informed that she has been *activated*.

The voice tells Rachel the she must do exactly as she is told or the mysterious voice will derail her son's train. In a panic, Rachel hangs up and tries to call 911 for help but her cell phone is blocked. The mysterious voice calls Rachel back and gives her instructions....

This begins a massive and elaborate chase sequence in the 2008 futuristic thriller *Eagle Eye*. With executive producers Steven Spielberg and Edward L. McDonnell, director D.J. Caruso, producers Alex Kurtzman, Robert Orci, Patrick Crowley, and a screenplay by John Glenn, Travis Adam Wright, Hillary Seitz, and Dan McDermott (who also wrote the story), the movie follows two strangers, Jerry and Rachel, on a breakneck thrill ride to save Rachel's son, the United States government, and possibly the world. The Internet Movie Database sums up the plot this way:

Jerry and Rachel are two strangers thrown together by a mysterious phone call from a woman they have never met. Threatening their lives and family, she pushes Jerry and Rachel into a series of increasingly dangerous situations, using the technology of everyday life to track and control their every move. (IMDB)

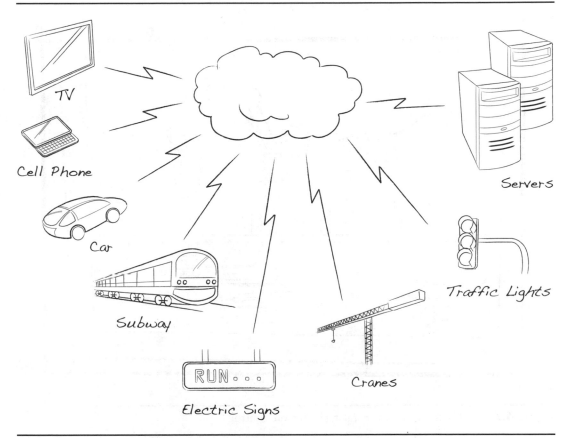

Figure 4.6   *Eagle Eye*'s interconnected devices

The chase scene that begins with the call to Rachel unfolds magnificently and bombastically through the streets of Chicago as everyday technology becomes a character in the drama (Figure 4.6), Subway trains are controlled remotely. Messages are given to Jerry and Rachel from electronic signs.

Traffic lights are flipped from red to green to aid Jerry and Rachel's escape. Car navigation systems become a tool of the mysterious voice and even control of the car itself is hijacked. The grand finale of the chase shows our heroes and the police racing through a scrap yard while wrecking cranes with gigantic claws pluck cars from the ground like a coin operated arcade game, as shown in Figure 4.7.

Figure 4.7   Wrecking cranes operating by remote control

The tension and excitement of this scene comes from the mystery of the pleasant female voice's power. How is she controlling all of these devices? As we continue to watch the film we learn the truth behind the plot, but in this early chase scene much of the adrenaline that fuels the fun comes from ubiquity. All of the devices in the world are interconnected and working together to force Rachel and Jerry into a sinister plot. Somehow they are under the control of the mysterious woman. Her ability to use these everyday devices to have the "capacity of being everywhere" and a "presence everywhere or in many places especially simultaneously" is precisely why the scene works so well. For a short period of time, ubiquity, it seems, is a tool for taking over the world.

On September 26, 2008 when *Eagle Eye* opened it was the number one movie in America. I can pretty much guarantee you that the crowds of people that flocked to the movie didn't consider themselves to be ubiquitous computing advocates. No. They just thought it was cool and the tension from the "eagle eye" just made sense. The notion that devices could be interconnected together in this ubiquitous way was plausible enough to suspend their disbelief. It *could* happen.

In 2010 ubiquity is a concept that most of the mainstream media and average people accept. Just like in *Eagle Eye* most people believe it *could* happen. Many would say it *is* happening. But what is ubiquity really? What does it mean? It started as a complex computer and social science theory and over the last two decades or so has made its way into popular culture without most people even knowing its name. That's fascinating!

To better understand the future of ubiquitous entertainment let's track the origins of the vision along with its twisting, turning. and transforming path into popular culture. Connecting these dots and understanding these subtle changes over the last two decades will be helpful as we think about the coming two decades.

Ubiquity: A Long Strange Trip

Around 1988 Mark Weiser began to use the term *ubiquity* while working as the chief technologist at Xerox Palo Alto Research Center. These computer and social scientists saw ubiquitous computing as the coming third stage of computers. This vision helped to guide them in their understanding of how computers might work together in the future and how humans would interact with them.

The first stage of computing is widely seen as the age of the mainframe computer. From the 1950s to the 1970s, these computers were typically used for large scale tasks like data processing or statistical analysis. Often these mainframe computers, like the one shown in Figure 4.8, took up an entire room, so they were owned and managed by big corporations and universities.

Figure 4.8   Mainframe computers typically took up an entire room

The second stage of computing picks up in the 1970s and 1980s with the personal computer (PC). These multipurpose machines were designed and priced for home and single user usage. This was a giant shift. No longer did you have to be a global corporation to own or work on a PC. Now that people had access to these machines an entire new industry of hardware and software companies sprung up; all competing and innovating for the attention of consumers. From desktop publishing and personal finance to word processing these machines were used for both the home and small businesses.

Typically the PC is thought of as the desktop PC (Figure 4.9) but it can also include laptops, nettops, netbooks, tablet PCs, ultra-mobile PCs, home theater systems, and Pocket PCs (Figure 4.9).

Figure 4.9   A whole range of "personal computing devices"

This brings us to Weiser's third stage; ubiquitous computing. This is some-times referred to as pervasive computing as well. The idea behind ubiquitous computing is that by the third stage there are so many connected computers that they begin to disappear in the background. No longer will we think of computers as those massive mainframes that took up a whole room or even the PC that took up an entire desktop. These new computers would be low cost and we would be able to find them everywhere. This new type of device would still work with our existing laptops and netbooks, but with this new pervasive computing, new usages would begin to reveal themselves. Weiser predicted that the number of ubiquitous computing devices would surpass all others by 2005 (as shown in Figure 4.10).

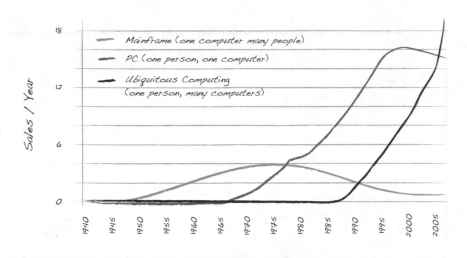

Figure 4.10 The major trends in computing (Weiser 1996)

The principles behind ubiquitous computing were that a computer was there to help its user, that the best computer was a quiet and invisible servant, that your computer should extend your unconscious, and that technology should create calm (Weiser, Chen).

To accomplish these principles ubiquitous computing requires low cost computers, sensors, device interconnectivity, and even augmented reality. It was a vision that set itself apart from the previous two stages because it saw computers as devices that would be so pervasive in our lives that it would fundamentally alter our relationship with them. We would no longer think about computers and computing as we had in the two previous stages. With ubiquitous computing devices and computational power would surround us, enriching our lives and our interactions with each other.

That was around 1988. For the next five years or so people played with this vision for the future of computing, exploring what new experiences people might want. Asking, how it could make their lives better? What steps would need to be taken? Also by examining this next stage of computing many futurists began to imagine what an interconnected world might look like.

Probably the most famous take on this future came out of the Massachusetts Institute of Technology's Media Lab. In 1995 Nicholas Negroponte, a Professor of Media Technology at MIT and the founding director of the Media Lab, collected his thinking in this area with the book *Being Digital*. Echoing Weiser's vision Negroponte wrote, "Computing is not about computers anymore. It is about living."

When it came to thinking about the future of TV, Negroponte challenged how we thought about the very nature of what a TV might be. If computers were changing everything else around us, why would they also change TV?

In his writing he explained how computers were becoming TVs. "The growth of personal computers is happening so rapidly that the future open-architecture television is the PC, period." (Negroponte, *Being Digital*, p47). Now to Negroponte's credit you have to remember that he's writing at the beginning of the 1990s. The global and commercial internet was still very new and untried. In 1990 fewer than 4 percent of people worldwide owned a computer and little more than 1 percent had a mobile phone (Euromonitor. 2010). There was no Google, YouTube, or Hulu...there really wasn't even a Napster.

With the long promised (even in 1995) coming of high definition broadcasts and the even then long looming digital switchover, Negroponte imagined a world where TV was delivered digitally to a computer that could decode and show the program. Pretty futuristic stuff for the time. This meant that not only would we have devices everywhere but we'd also have TV everywhere as well. But for Negroponte and many of the futurists at this time the vision was very much rooted in the computer. It was about the future of computing devices. They were imagining the good and bad affects that all these computers could have on people. But no one was really talking about TV. Why?

To better understand this I'd like to introduce you to a colleague of mine, Dr. Genevieve Bell. Bell is a cultural anthropologist who did a lot of her growing up in the Australian outback. She's an Intel fellow and heads the consumer experience group. She's been studying people and how they use technology for nearly twenty years. She maintains that to truly understand the future of any technology you must understand people first. For over ten years now she's been studying how people use TVs and enjoy entertainment.

Bell sees this glaring lack of TV-centric thought and language in an interesting way. She wonders if entertainment as a leading experience for these emerging ubiquitous computer networks just wasn't serious enough. "I wonder if it was initially as silly as it being a waste of the technology or as being a waste of time," she explained. "I think there was a kind of Calvinistic approach to technology development happening back then. You know, the kinds of visions we want to have are big and serious and life-saving and world changing. Computer scientists and the high tech industry wanted the future to be about bridging the digital divide and making work more efficient and creating wonderful advances in education and health.

"When you look at it like that no wonder they never talked about TV seriously. There are a lot of really smart people who don't know how to value entertainment appropriately. They see it as a frivolous use of these really re-markably sophisticated devices, but you know—frankly when I think about it—the most popular technologies of the last century, television, telephones, radio, electricity. All of these made possible storytelling, and I think that TV just wasn't seen as being sufficient or important enough.

"Think about electricity and the radio. In the past people would tell these stories about how electricity saves people's lives because you can have hospitals or that the radio is important because it can communicate to the masses during a disaster. These are the things that people say to justify why these technologies are important.

"But there's a really weird kind of thing where people can't let the capacity of those technologies to be the medium for storytelling and a means for people to gather together and communicate with each other. Electricity and radio give us nontechnical things like shared moments and shared opportunities and shared stories—and I somehow think that for a lot of engineers and scientists that wasn't serious enough.

"I think scientists sometimes burden themselves with a high-minded goal of what they think of as real science. They think real science has got to be big. Real science can't be about frivolous things. It needs to be significant and I just don't think that people give entertainment enough credit for what it really does."

Around this time there was at least one place where TV was really important: *TV Guide.* In the late 1990s, away from the scientists and futurists, advertisers and marketers where starting to take notice of the Internet and all of these connected devices.

In 1998 Brian Seth Hurst was working as the managing director of Convergent Media at the Pittard Sullivan entertainment marketing firm, known for its design of the original TiVo user experience which is still being used today. *TV Guide* came to his agency and wanted to extend their brand from the TV to the Internet and other devices like the PDA. At the time personal digital assistants (PDAs) from companies like Palm and Trio were a new class of personal devices that were just hitting the market. It was on the *TV Guide* project that Hurst first coined the term "cross-platform."

"So, *TV Guide,* when they came to Pittard Sullivan, they said look, we want to build a new brand and we want people to be able to know *TV Guide* as the source for all information that they want about television," Hurst remembered as he talked to me from the offices of his current firm, the Opportunity Management Company, where he is CEO. "So, what we designed and built was a consistent brand experience in terms of look, tone, feel and even navigation for *TV Guide* across all platforms; magazine, TV, interactive set top box, Web and handheld."

The desire to develop this cross-platform experience didn't grow out of any ubiquitous vision of interconnected devices. It was about brand experience and advertising. *TV Guide* wanted to put its brand across as many platforms, as many screens as possible and to do that successfully they needed to make sure that the experience on each device was consistent with the global *TV Guide* brand. Hurst and his colleagues at Pittard Sullivan began using brand and the consumer experience with those brands on multiple devices as the basis for their development. It wasn't about technology at all.

"What we were doing was teaching the consumer because this was behavior that had not occurred yet," Hurst explained. "At that time you didn't have interactive TV program guides. You had a certain amount of Internet behavior, but search wasn't anywhere near what it is now. So, we thought if you knew *TV Guide* the magazine then you should be able to use any of the platforms and it will still feel like *TV Guide*. That was important. We had to teach these new cross platform behaviors because the technology was new and it really wasn't happening yet."

By 2000 connectivity and computer sales had skyrocketed: 940 million people owned a PC and 1.2 million people had cell phones. The Internet had grown to over 395 million users and built many online businesses; something that would have been unheard of five years before (Euromonitor. 2010).

As Hurst and I continued to talk I asked him what he thought had changed between 1998 and 2008.

"By 2008 you have an audience that's enabled by technology. They are power users. You also have influencers and communities and blogs. Looking back at 1998, these are all very new and very important. You also have people like hardcore game testers and really a whole community of people that function without us. They function in a world away from advertisers and brands and entertainment companies. They're out there and they're creating their own content or their commenting on content and they're all participating."

Hurst makes a good point. The past ten years has seen the rise of the blogger and the citizen journalist. The Internet has given a platform for individuals and smaller groups to have a voice on a national and international level.

But that can't be all of it. Bloggers alone didn't move ubiquitous TV and entertainment into the mainstream. I asked Hurst what he thought were the other factors that moved the industry to get their shows and movies online and on multiple devices.

"First of all you had pirating of video happening again and you had the major entertainment networks and studios saying to themselves: Well, you know, this is our content and YouTube is making money from it. This type of activity isn't fringe anymore. It's going mainstream. It's no longer small guys like Limewire anymore. It's now about YouTube. It's too easy for people to post content and we, the copyright holders, are not making money off of it. So, they decided to actively find a way to make money from their properties. And, they quickly realized that they would have to cooperate with each other in order to do it. They finally took P.T. Barnham's advice: Give the people what they want otherwise they'll take it anyway."

Hurst is not alone in his view. Many see the late 2000s as a key turning point for industry attitudes toward cross-platform entertainment. The trouble with this new ubiquitous entertainment future was that it was incredibly complicated. No longer did an entertainment company like Disney or CBS just have to worry about their traditional distribution and line of revenue. Now they had to work with device manufactures, service providers, and online services. Likewise, consumer electronics giants like Sony and Samsung now would need to coordinate their products with multiple entertainment companies and advertisers as well.

"The 2007 Consumer Electronics Show marked a watershed in coming to terms with the digital future of video and other media by the broadcaster, computer, consumer electronics, and film industries," writes Dr. Alexander B. Magoun in the 2009 version of his book *Television: The life story of a Technology*. Magoun is the executive director of the David Sarnoff Library. He goes on to say that "All realized they stood to benefit by helping to connect broadcast and Internet content on the same household display" (p. 180).

With computers and TVs now the same thing in technologists' and entertainment executives' minds it made sense for Gary R. Edgerton to proclaim at the end of his book *The Columbia History of American Television*, "The key to thinking about television in the digital era is to re-envision it in terms of screens (of all shapes and sizes) rather than merely households (which no longer captures a complete and accurate picture of TV penetration)" (p. 417).

Egerton's point is very much rooted in the TV and advertising world of eyeballs and ratings. He's saying that now that we have TVs in all of our devices then we must think of each new screen as its own entity. He's making the business argument for the fact that TV has now gone ubiquitous.

Over the last two decades we have seen a subtle but major transformation of ubiquity from computers that disappear to devices that entertain us, wherever we might be with whatever shows, movies, games, or services we might be interested in.

So is ubiquitous entertainment the wave of the future? It certainly seems that people want it. It also looks like the vast array of industries affected by this new vision are lining up to at least explore their options. Ubiquitous TV as a concept captures the original intention of computing's third wave and combines it with the market and usage realities of the last two decades. But is it more than that? Can we think of entertainment as a better driver for technology? Again I talked with Dr. Bell about this:

"The thing about television and entertainment is that it's really pure." Bell explained. "That might sound like an odd choice of words, but the stories we tell ourselves about how we use our TVs has a great deal more truthful resonance than the stories we tell ourselves about a lot of other technologies in our lives. I think we delude ourselves about how important technology needs to be. Yes we feel bad [about] the amount of time we spend on the television, but I don't think we bought a television thinking it was for education or exercise or our kids or to help save the planet. We're honest that we bought [a TV] to entertain us. I think unlike a lot of other technologies, TV is one of the few that has a purer motive. We just want it to be entertainment."

Ubiquity: From an Eastbound Train to a Downtown McDonald's

So if our futures are headed toward a world were all devices are seamlessly connected together, delivering us our favorite movies, TV shows, games, and applications, then what do we really need to do to make it happen? This is a great vision but certainly it isn't happening today on any large scale. To get into the nuts and bolts of ubiquity let's go back to our *Eagle Eye* example and look at what it would take to bring about the movie's form of ubiquity.

We are back in Chicago and Rachel Holloman has just left the bar and gotten the menacing cell phone call from the mysterious female voice (Figure 4.11).

Figure 4.11   Rachel Holloman is blackmailed by the mysterious voice

How do we go about getting the live security camera feed from Sam's train that is traveling to Washington D.C. to the flat screen TVs in the window of a McDonald's in downtown Chicago? Well we know the short answer to that is ubiquitous computing! The longer, more specific answer to that question requires a network diagram, shown in Figure 4.12.

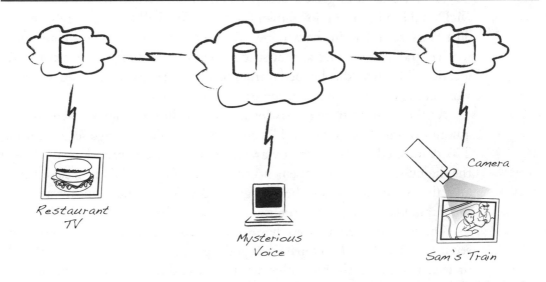

Figure 4.12   Ubiquitous computing used to patch the security camera feed from Sam's train to the McDonald's in Chicago

First we begin with Sam's train. On the train there will need to be a wireless security camera or a network of wired security cameras that feed into a central server on the train. Of course this could make sense if the railroad was monitoring all of the security cameras on the train in a centralized location. This kind of centralized security occurs in most buildings today so it's possible that it would happen in the train as well. This centralized train security server would then need to be wirelessly connected to a larger server network that is off the train. Again, this could make sense when you think that all the security cameras from the trains could be monitored from a single security or train dispatch location. Ultimately to get the live feed of Sam on his train we need a wireless connection somewhere between the specific camera that is filming Sam and the Internet.

In this illustration we are not going to worry about security. In the movie the security is hacked and overridden. In the real world there would be protocols and accounts that would help with this transfer assuming we were allowed access to all the servers and cameras, but we will get to those details later.

Next we need to get the security feed of Sam from the Internet to the McDonalds window in downtown Chicago. This will be considerably easier. The flat screen TVs in the window will need a wired or wireless connection to a central server either at that specific restaurant or off site at a corporate location. This wouldn't be too far from reality. Currently there is quite a bit of work going on in the area this industry calls *digital signage.*

As the manufacturing costs for flat screen slim TVs goes down and the amount of intelligence in the TVs goes up, the digital signage sector is using TVs connected to the Internet via wired and wireless connections to change the digital signs and advertisements that appear on the TVs. It's cost-efficient and allows for the signs to be changed and tailored much quicker and in a more targeted manner than traditional signs or advertisements.

Once the mysterious voice has made the connections between the train's security server and McDonald's digital signage server, transferring the file or feed is easy. Again remember we are pretending for a moment that the security is handled. The wireless and wired connections between devices, servers and the Internet allows for the ubiquitous transfer of Sam's image to the TV screen. The nuts and bolts of transfer are quite banal but the affect, as seen in the movie, can be both magical and frightening, especially if you are Sam's mom.

Getting back to reality, let's look at the specific real world components needed to make up this ubiquitous system.

Three Pillars of Ubiquity

If there is anyone I know who is going to help bring about a truly functioning ubiquitous world it's Jeff Foerster. Foerster is at Intel with me. Like Suri Medapati, who I introduced you to in the Informative TV chapter, Foerster and I have been working on the future of TV for several years. Foerster is a natural born skeptic, so when he says he can see how we could bring about the reality of Ubiquitous TV—I listen.

Over the years we have seen that to bring about seamless device inter-connectivity, three technology areas come into play. Each of these three technology pillars addresses a different section of the device and network infrastructure, as illustrated in Figure 4.13.

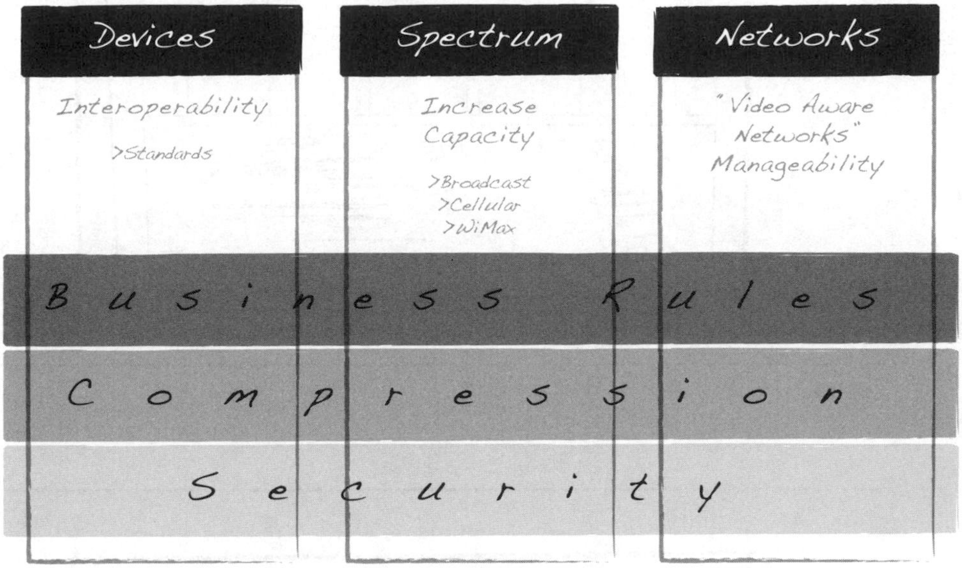

Devices	Spectrum	Networks
Interoperability >Standards	Increase Capacity >Broadcast >Cellular >WiMax	"Video Aware Networks" Manageability

B u s i n e s s   R u l e s

C o m p r e s s i o n

S e c u r i t y

Figure 4.13   The three pillars of ubiquity

The basic requirements to set up this ubiquitous vision for TV and entertainment are quite simple. You'll need a computing device capable of connecting to the Internet and possibly directly to other devices via a wired or wireless connection. This could be your laptop or any other device plugged into a modem or connected to a wireless network. The device could also be a cell phone or smart phone that is connecting to the cloud via a cellular network. We could even use a hybrid approach where an Internet-enabled set top box connected to a TV to received broadcast data and send data via an IP connection.

Figure 4.14 Wired or wireless network

Figure 4.15 Cell network

Figure 4.16 Hybrid Multichannel

"But as we look deeper into these three areas," Foerster explained, "we can see that we're also going to need support for efficient compression technology and high-speed wireless links if we're going to do any uploading. If we want to take advantage of connected video cameras, like the video camera on the train in *Eagle Eye,* then we're going to need some real-time capture capabilities along with more powerful radios and even more spectrum. Really as we start to move around more and more video between our devices it puts an increased stress on our wireless networks. We just need more capacity."

There are distinct differences and challenges between getting these devices connected inside the home on a personal network as opposed to outside the home. To get devices to work together in both of these environments we're also going to need standards. Standards are always a big topic of conversation when you start thinking about ubiquity and interoperability. Because you're trying to get a lot of different companies and developers to get along and work together standards can also be a very volatile and hotly debated topic. I asked Foerster about his take on standards.

"Standards are important because we've got all these hardware platforms that have all these different interconnected pieces. Now when I say standards, there's the standard's body standards, but there's also just standard ways of doing things. That means standard ways for your ubiquitous device to connect to the Internet. Or a standard way for your device to connect to another device, peer to peer.

"There's several different standards that come into play," Foerster continued. "At the lowest level, we're talking about wireless communications; you need radio standards, cellular standards, broadcast standards, even on the Wi-Fi side any of these could be relevant communication methods to connect devices. In the three *Eagle Eye* examples you mentioned, all three use each of these standards."

One way to begin to make sense of this wide range of standards is to start looking at what Foerster and others call end-to-end standards. These are meta-level standards for all devices. They are really high level and focus on a specific consumer experiences or capabilities. In our case we're interested in the delivery of entertainment or video to a personal device. I asked Jeff to give me some specifics around what would be needed for this type of end-to-end standards approach.

"For video specifically we need to think about end-to-end network protocols and hardware requirements. There are some interesting and evolving compression schemes that could be leveraged, but these tend to be implemented in hardware. It's important that the people developing and manufacturing the devices that we want to connect together agree on the hardware components they're going to put inside those devices. I'll give you an example. Compression technologies and radios are typically handled in hardware and have some specific requirements. So, there needs to be some agreement on what those protocols are. We also need broad industry agreement and support of these technologies, like compression, in multiple devices in the ecosystem in order to justify integrating them specifically in the hardware. If we can do that then our devices can be ubiquitous. They will be able to talk to a number of different sources."

But this need for standardization goes a lot further than just personal devices and interconnectivity. Foerster explained that the ability for wireless carriers and broadband service providers to manage the video and TV that is moving through their networks will become important as well. As the volume of video and high bandwidth data goes up these providers will need to use intelligent rate control to help manage the capacity of their networks. There could be so much video moving around that the network could literally break. Foerster and his team explore the specifics of the network and wireless implications in Appendix C of this book. They explore specifically what challenges we face and technically what is needed to overcome them.

Once these networks are optimized for traffic that is predominately video based and we have sorted out some standards so our personal devices can talk to each other then, technically, ubiquity will be possible. But when we're pushing around that much data were also going to need something else—capacity.

When we start envisioning a world where the majority of the data that we are pushing around our wireless, broadband, and home networks is video, then capacity becomes an issue. Most of the networks that we are using today were built for voice calls or Web surfing and e-mail. It wasn't that long ago that calls, Web surfing and e-mail were all that you could do with your phone or PC. Over the past few years this has changed dramatically. In the 1900s the majority of network traffic was either phone calls or text messages or Web surfing and e-mail.

The problem here is pretty easy to see. Telecommunications companies and broadband service providers built their networks to deliver a data capacity that we and our new devices are exceeding by far. For many broadband networks the solution is in the wire or in the fiber.

One solution for the wireless side of this bottleneck is to increase the available capacity of the wireless networks. On February 24, 2010, Joelle Tessler reported for the Associated Press that, "Wireless carriers have been clamoring for more spectrum as their customers increasingly check e-mail, update Facebook and watch video on the go. Broadband services are already choking in some markets, and next-generation services will tax wireless networks even more."

The solution that is being explored in the United States by the Federal Communications Commission (FCC) is to increase the available spectrum for wireless providers. This would mean opening up different wireless spectrums between the 300 and 700 megahertz bands, which is used by many television broadcasters, so that private companies and governments could use it for the delivering of the video and applications. "Although the potential of mobile broadband is limitless, its oxygen supply is not," FCC Chairman Julius Genachowski said in a speech at the New America Foundation in Washington. "Spectrum—our airwaves—really is the oxygen of mobile broadband service. Without sufficient spectrum, we will starve mobile broadband of the nourishment it needs to thrive."

Another way to approach this problem is to fundamentally rethink how data networks are architected and built. If you know that the majority of traffic on your networks is going to be video then you could optimize the overall network (see Appendix C for examples) as well as fine tune the wireless portion of the network for the delivery of video.

How could we fine tune the network and wireless delivery for video? Let's use video quality as an example. When people watch video they tend to evaluate the quality very subjectively. What I mean by this is that they don't judge it mathematically. When we judge the quality of video we watch it and decide if it looks good or not. Most people can't describe good quality video, we just know it when we see it. When we see the surveillance video of Sam on his eastbound train in *Eagle Eye* (Figure 4.17) we don't really question if it's HD or not. In this case and in many cases the specific data rate and quality of the video doesn't matter. When you are in your house watching *Eagle Eye* on your Blu-ray player then HD or the perception of HD matters quite a bit. But outside the home, on many devices quality is simply subjective.

Figure 4.17 HD? Or does it really matter?

Why is this important? Well, most networks and data delivery systems don't operate on this subjective quality grading system. In this case subjectivity isn't bad at all. It's just a fact. Now networks handle video much more mathematically. Taking this into consideration, one way to rethink video networking to overcome capacity problems is to use this knowledge that people judge the quality of video from a subjective standpoint rather than a mathematical one. You could apply networking schemes and routing schemes that are *video-aware*. That means rather than optimizing your network for delivering throughput and maximizing your throughput in the network, you would optimize your network for delivering minimum distortion of the video content.

One benefit from a video-aware network could be that you give more flexibility to the various points of that network. Imagine you have a video-aware network and the video you are pushing around has scalable compression. That means depending on the available capacity of the network the video file can be made smaller or larger. Video and data compression really spans across our three pillars (see Figure 4.13).

Now as that video is zipping around the network it moves through cellular base stations before it gets to your device. Now imagine that the base station knows that it is sending you video. It also knows the condition of its network, meaning it knows how many people are using that bay station and how congested the network is. You could give that base station the ability to make decisions about how much throughput it can give to that video. I can determine how much compression it needs to do on the video to keep it moving, but at the same time to preserve the video quality just enough so that it is acceptable for you when you watch it on your device. Making these decisions about the traffic on the network and the quality of the video files would allow the base station and the entire network to be more flexible, robust, and streamlined for the specific delivery of video.

Foerster and I went on to talk about multiple changes and adjustments that could be made to increase capacity of wireless networks. There are new signal processing techniques, like MIMO. That's multiple input, multiple output, multiple antenna type technology. There are also advanced interference mitigation techniques that could be applied at the signal processing level to enhance capacity. But at a certain point it became obvious that these little tweaks won't get us to the capacity we need. If we continue to make these small optimizations to get more spectral efficiency to the wireless networks we might be able to expect two to three times improvement every generation. Each generation of new technology comes about every five years and that won't be enough to handle the demand that our ubiquitous devices are putting on the network.

So what then? Well, after we have made the networks and video delivery as efficient as possible, we could create more room to push the data through. This opening up of capacity is what the FCC and other regulators are looking into. But another approach could be to make wireless networks smaller in size.

Today's cellular networks are primarily based on macro-cells, which tend to have ranges that are measured in kilometers. We could move to a micro-cell or even pico-cell architecture, which can have a range of 100 meters or less. The idea is that if you start shrinking the cell size, there is a shorter distance the wireless signals need to propagate, which allows a higher throughput for each user. In addition, there are fewer people using the base station and therefore sharing the same spectrum and capacity. As a result, the overall capacity increases, and the throughput per user also increases, which can allow for higher video quality sent to the end user. But the challenge with this approach is that it increases the infrastructure cost since more base stations are needed as well as wired or optical connections from the base stations to the Internet, referred to as backhaul. In addition, network management and maintenance costs increase due to the additional equipment and complexity. So, at the end of the day, it's a tradeoff between network capacity needs and cost.

Ultimately for wireless networks the solution is likely to be a mix of all of these solutions and technologies. But is there a solution that spans across the three needed pillars of ubiquity we've been talking about? Could there be a solution that draws from the TV broadcasters, cable, broadband, and wireless providers? If entertainment is going to be one of the leading experiences on all of their networks, couldn't all the players find a way to work together to deliver the best digital entertainment to our devices? The answer is of course complicated. Interestingly enough it is more a discussion of business complexities than technical or engineering hurdles.

This is where security and business rules become important to achieve ubiquitous TV. Like compression, security and business rules span across our pillars (Figure 4.13) because they are needed across all networks and involve nearly every business in the future of entertainment.

Security is important both for the consumer privacy and for the people providing the entertainment that is being enjoyed. Much has been written about digital rights management (DRM) for digital content. There are several competing standards and this isn't likely to change anytime soon. But it is important to note that for TV and entertainment to achieve the ubiquity that consumer's desire, content must be standardized. This also can be applied to the protection of consumers' security as well. This issue too is currently being hotly debated in both corporations and governments around the world. And just like content security, personal security needs to be agreed to and standardized for us to bring about any meaningful manifestation of ubiquity.

Business rules facilitate the transfer and handling of data, files, and intellectual property between networks, corporations, and devices. It's a catch-all term that recognizes that each TV show or song or movie that is passed from a TV broadcaster to a cellular network and is watched on a device has contracts, business agreements, and copyrights that go along with that asset. The business rules govern how that asset can be handled.

Business rules are nothing new but in a ubiquitous world the scope and scale of the rules will need to be greatly expanded. Understanding the ubiquitous world we have been discussing is the first step. Understanding how they impact content, business and data infrastructure is the next. If you are a consumer you probably don't really care about business rules. That's really the most important point to make about business rules, security, compression and the three pillars of ubiquity—for consumers, none of this matters. Consumers have a massive appetite for entertainment on the devices they love. It's up to the industry to catch up. Because in the end we all just want to be entertained.

We Just Want to Be Entertained

Ubiquitous TV is happening. We want it because we want to be entertained. We want to be entertained in our living rooms, our cars, and anywhere we might find ourselves with a little bit of extra time and the need to relax. The technology has been worked out to facilitate the interoperability of connected devices and servers. The combined industries that are needed to bring this ubiquitous access to entertainment have seen the signs and recognized that in the future entertainment will go more places, on different devices and in very different forms than it did just a decade ago.

Some fundamental changes need to take place in how networks handle video and how that video is delivered to multiple devices, often over wireless connections. Ubiquitous TV will come to pass is because people want it. Much of what is needed to bring it about has less to do with technical hurdles and more to do with business complexities. Finding a way for this wide range of businesses with incredibly different business models to not only work together but to build products and make money together is certainly not easy but one thing that would help would be a way to pay for these advances. In our chapter on Personal TV, we'll look at just what it takes to not only customize people's entertainment experience but also how to pay for it. Because the moment your TV is both *informative* and *ubiquitous,* people will want it to be *personal* as well.

Chapter 5

Your TV Won't Change but Everything Else Will

A CONVERSATION WITH DAVID POLTRACK

As I walked into the MGM Grand Casino I passed a slender woman in her 60s perched on a stool. I almost didn't see her in the casino's dim light but her fabulous white hair caught my eye. She smiled and handed me a ticket saying, "See TV free before everyone else."

I took the ticket. It read:

Television City
Your Opinion Counts
Preview & Rate New & Existing Programs
In the MGM Grand, At The End Of Studio Walk
Open Daily 10:00am – 9:00pm
Tickets Valid Any Day. Screening Every 30 Min.

I asked her, "How do I get to Television City?"

"Just go through the casino, take a left towards the Arena Theater and it's at the end of Studio Walk."

"Thanks," I said getting on the escalator, heading to the casino's main floor.

"Are you going to go to the focus group?" she called as I slid down the escalator toward the Lion Habitat where the show was in progress. A gigantic 550-pound, 10-foot-long male lion looked down at the crowd from a rock cliff two stories above.

"No," I smiled and called back to her. "I'm going to see the man in charge!"

She smiled again and waved.

As I made my way through the bings, bonks, and plings of the slot machines, Credence Clearwater Revival's "Bad Moon Rising" was playing on the sound system. It was a little after 2 p.m. and the casino had a pretty good crowd. At the end of Studio Walk, past the restaurant craftsteak and the CSI Experience, I found CBS's Television City.

If you love TV, Television City will beckon to you. Posters for the most popular CBS shows hang on the walls. *NCIS: Los Angeles. The Good Wife. Medium. The Mentalist.* A massive TV screen shows clips and teasers for the shows. Under a giant shinning CBS eye logo you can sign up for the television program screening. At the desk I asked to see David Poltrack.

The person who designed and runs Television City is David Poltrack. Poltrack is the chief research officer for CBS and president of CBS Vision. He oversees all research operations at CBS encompassing audience measurement, market research, program testing, advertising research, and monitoring of the national and international video marketplace. Poltrack has been the chairman of both the Media Rating Council and the Advertising Research Foundation. He's a trustee of the executive committee at the Marketing Science Institute and the president of the Market Research Council. Poltrack teaches at New York University, the Columbia University Graduate School of Business and the Cheung Kong Graduate School of Business in Beijing, China.

Poltrack was just finishing up with a screening group when I arrived, so I waited in the room next door. I could faintly hear the group in the next room. Poltrack and his researchers would talk a bit and the group would laugh. One researcher was telling the participants about some recent work they had done on CBS's hit show *Big Bang Theory* and one participant, a woman excitedly interrupted, "Oh I love that show!"

The research continued.

Poltrack and his team supply all media-related intelligence to the CBS Corporation, providing syndicated audience measurement for television, radio, outdoor, and Internet. One of the unique things about the media business is that they cannot directly count the number of people watching their product. Because of this they rely on survey research and research companies to define the size of the audience. Broadcasters use this information as the basis for how much they charge to advertise on each show; the more people watching a particular show the larger the group of people that advertisers can market to and the more CBS can charge for that time. Poltrack's team processes this information and converts it into materials and reports that can be used by rest of CBS.

The other primary function of Poltrack's team is more traditional. They develop primary research to help select TV shows, refine products, and develop overall marketing strategies for those products. This is the type of work that is done in Las Vegas at Television City.

Television City at the MGM Grand lets the public preview and rate new and existing programs. It's a rolling focus group; open daily with over 1 million participants a year. The back of the ticket that I was given tells you that CBS is interested in America's opinion of television programs and that the public's reactions and opinions go directly to the network executives and producers.

In the television industry David Poltrack is one of the most highly respected experts on consumer opinion and audience measurement. He spends his time getting to know what CBS's viewers are interested in and envisioning what this major broadcaster can do in the future to continue to retain its audience.

When the audience screening finished up Poltrack came into the room with a quick smile. We started talking about the future of entertainment and what the media and technological landscape might look like five to ten years from today.

DAVID POLTRACK: When I look five to ten years out I mainly think about the work we are doing right now, the research and the planning we're doing and how that is going to play out over the next five to eight years. It's going to take that long for a lot of what we are working on today to play itself out.

But before I talk about that, we should talk about what's not going to change in the next five to ten years. I don't see what people are watching changing all that much. By that I mean mainstream TV and TV shows. At this point in time, all of our research shows that people like TV. They like watching TV and don't want that to change.

The way I like to think about it is that the television industry in the United States is a very democratic business. It is supported by advertising. The shows that get the highest audiences, the ones that get the highest ratings make the most money. It's pretty simple and very democratic. People vote by what they watch. So to survive and prosper CBS has to remain a very efficient producer of quality mass entertainment. We make shows that people want to watch. When I see all these new technologies, I don't really feel that people are going to want radically different TV shows. Where they get those shows and how they watch them might change but people want dramas and comedies and reality shows that they get today.

I don't see a lot of change in the type of content, the type of shows. Of course we also see that user-generated content and short form video on the Internet is important. But the average person watches about two minutes a day of that and that's not going to generate a threat to traditional television. There could be change in traditional television shows but that evolution will happen much more slowly.

Where I do see a lot of change is the revenue aspect of the television and entertainment business. By that I mean specifically where traditional broadcasters make money. How we make money, that's going to change dramatically.

Right now the television industry needs to work through the concepts of subscription versus pay for view versus advertisement supported television programming. At this point in time, the consumer is still telling us, very emphatically, that they prefer advertising-supported free content. They accept advertising as a way of supporting their entertainment and they will continue to do so. That's how most people think about it. They think that TV is free because it has advertising.

But that's not completely true. Things have changed in the last five years. If you look at the 1960s and the 1970s, people were really paying nothing for television. They were getting it all over the air. Everyone just accepted the fact that advertising was necessary to subsidize the process. Actually they really didn't think about it at all. TV was free. It always had been free, so why would it any different?

Now today it's much more complex thanks to this: 80 percent of people who get television today are paying some form of a cable subscription or a satellite subscription to get access to that programming. They can still technically get the broadcast part of it over the air for free, but they're not doing that. They're purchasing it. They are subscribing to some service. Therefore, people are seeing costs of those services increasing because it's not just one subscription they're paying for. There are multiple layers today. People pay for the base service, the pay extra for premium channels, digital, sports, and any number of other types of content. For the past few years these layers have been built up and up on top of each other. Now people are getting much more sensitive to the fact that they are paying for a lot of different kinds of content. It's not nearly as simple as it was 30 to 40 years ago.

Realistically today it's a hybrid revenue model. People are still getting advertising, but they are also paying a subscription. So now I believe the industry and people are thinking differently. Why not just pay the subscription and get rid of the advertising completely? It can become an argument for a totally subscription based system.

Our studies have shown that most people have reached their limit about how much they are willing to pay for TV. It's a fairly definitive level. It seems to be constant over the last few years. It's around USD 200 a month. People expect to pay about USD 200 a month for their television, Internet, and telephone service combined. That seems to be the ceiling. It will be very hard to break through that.

Most people are under that number now, but that's going to change. If the entertainment and service provider industries all come out with new services and they are successful, then that number has got to go way over USD 200.

If that happens there is going to be a significant amount of consumer resistance to a collective bill that exceeds USD 200. So that is the challenge. That's one of the big things that's going to change in the next five to ten years. It has to evolve and it's going to be complicated because you have a lot of industry players jockeying for position in terms of the distribution part of the business.

As I said, the content part of the business seems to be pretty stable, but the distribution part of the business is going to go through some dramatic changes. It's going to take at least five years for the new distribution model to emerge.

***

Poltrack's observations get right to the heart of a growing debate over how entertainment and news is paid for over the Internet and broadcast TV. For over fifty years consumers have taken for granted that they can get broadcast TV, sports, and news over the air for free. All they needed was a TV set and an antenna. Likewise over the last decade the general public has gotten used to getting news, TV, and entertainment for free over the Internet. All they needed was a computer and an Internet connection. But change is coming. 2010 could mark a shift in how all of this is paid for.

"Good programming is expensive," Rupert Murdoch was quoted saying at a shareholder meeting in 2009. "It can no longer be supported solely by advertising revenues" (AP. Dec. 29, 2009). Murdoch's News Corp. owns the broadcast channel Fox and news outlets like the *Wall Street Journal*. It is looking to dramatically change how consumers and the industry pays for its TV programming and news both over the air and online. The company currently charges for online access to the *Wall Street Journal* and has discussed forming an exclusive agreement with a single search engine to pay for the rights to search through the company's content.

I asked Poltrack what issues he saw as CBS and the industry began to think about these new revenue models.

DAVID POLTRACK: It's important to remember that the broadcast networks provide a form of in-home entertainment that occupies the most hours of the day for most people. Of course you have cable television and other sources of entertainment but the most popular programs are still on the broadcast networks.

Now these most popular shows have been traditionally paid for from a single source and that's advertising revenue. Because of that we have been able to provide these shows free. That's pretty remarkable. It's something that is envied by all of the new services that are subscription based and charge. It's truly unique.

If we were to build the television system from scratch today it would be subscription based. To make the economics work the entrepreneurial forces of the business world would build the entire system on some form of subscription basis. I mean there's nothing else in the United States that offers the same amount of satisfaction of consumers that they don't pay for.

We can use ESPN as an example. ESPN is a very popular cable sports network. Over the years they have carved out a piece of the National Football League (NFL) franchise from broadcast TV. Next they went on to Major League Baseball. ESPN has gradually gotten more and more sports attractions away from free over-the-air television by the fact that it could outbid the broadcasters for these products. So you might ask yourself how they can do this. Certainly ESPN doesn't get more viewers than the major broadcasters. That's where the difference in the revenue models comes in.

ESPN doesn't have to rely on the people who watch the programs to cover their costs. Essentially every cable home pays the ESPN subscription fee. That capability on top of a strong advertising base makes it really prohibitive for the broadcast networks to compete. (With both advertising and fees, ESPN has seen its revenue grow to $6.3 billion this year from $1.8 billion a decade ago, according to SNL Kagan's estimates)

For broadcasters to continue to develop and create the entertainment franchises and television shows that people love, we're going to need some supplement, some second stream of revenue supplementing to our advertising revenue. The development of that secondary revenue stream is critical to the survival of broadcast television.

It looks like things like mobile TV and Internet could provide that additional revenue. We could offer subscription based Internet access to people. Also we could look at the re-transmission of TV shows. It's because of this that the Internet and all these new connected devices could be really interesting for us.

BDJ: So, at CBS you see the Internet as beneficial to your business? What effect do these new devices have? Soon people will have the ability to get more information about your TV programs; they'll be able to watch them on all of their devices and personalize that experience. It's not changing the nature of the entertainment or television, as you said, but it is changing the nature of how people watch it. What effect do you think that has on CBS and the other networks?

DAVID POLTRACK: Technically speaking getting TV programming on-demand is critical to this vision. Essentially the on-demand aspects of television are here. I think the most recent reports show that around 35 percent of the people in the U.S. now have DVRs. They have the ability to choose when they want to watch television programs. You also have more and more people with access to the Internet. They can watch our TV shows online. That has proven to be a positive in terms of the number of people who end up having the ability to watch our shows. They don't have to choose one show over another. They can watch more than one. They can catch up on shows they've missed. It's a good thing.

But this does create an issue with advertising support. The DVR allows people to skip advertising and that's the big issue. Also the economics of online TV advertising are very different than broadcast. You make less money from advertising with online users. Again here something is going to have to change.

Essentially consumers are going to be given a choice. They can watch live or on-demand TV programming for free but they can't skip over the commercials. If they want to they can record the same TV programming and skip the ads but it won't be live. It's a pretty simple choice regardless of where people get access to the programming. This could be broadcast or this could be the Internet. They can watch it live with commercials or they can wait and watch it later; skipping the ads. It's really a matter of what they want more.

Our belief is if you offer the programming instantly, if you give people access to the programming whenever they want to watch it, if you give them access immediately when they want to watch it with the ads in it, without the ability to fast forward, they will gravitate towards that option.

Our research has shown that ubiquitous access immediately on-demand, without any preliminary planned behavior, is something people prefer. Many people don't want to go through the bother to plan in advance. They would rather just get it whenever they want it, wherever they are. It could be online or on their TV. There are of course a certain percentage of the people who are more averse to watching commercials. They could opt for a subscription alternative that does not include commercials. Ubiquity could really become a reason for commercials. Advertising supported programming could be available live on any device a consumer has handy. Just by having the advertising in the programming and people not skip it would open up a whole new world of possibilities for how and where they watch TV.

BDJ: You've said that this cross-device viewing behavior is good for the TV business. Why is that?

DAVID POLTRACK: It has to do with the concept that the television business from the network's perspective is to develop and build program franchises. If you look at what happened in terms of the streaming of television programs on the Internet in the last several years, you can see that the ability to have streaming helped build these franchises.

To explain let's use the example of *How I Met Your Mother.* It works for any show like *NCIS* or *Big Bang Theory* as they were becoming popular. Having it online or even available on devices other than the TV gave people the ability to watch the shows and to get involved with them. It grows the opportunities for people to watch them.

Let's use a show like *How I Met Your Mother. How I Met Your Mother* is a show that is one of the most streamed shows on the Internet. It is also one of the top comedies on network television. The show airs on Monday nights on CBS. It's very conceptual, very good, and people like it. The median age of that primetime TV watching audience is 46 years of age. The same show is one of the most streamed shows on the Internet. The median age of the streaming audience is 28. Since that show has been available for streaming on the Internet, more and more young people are now watching it on network television as well. They discovered it on the Internet and they're watching it on network television. The Internet provides new opportunities for people to sample TV shows.

***

2000 to 2010 has been seen by many as the coming of age of cable TV. With ground-breaking shows like the *Sopranos* and *The Wire* cable programming is a significant cultural and financial force. But things were very different thirty years ago.

Back in the early 1980s Poltrack wrote a book called *Television Marketing: Network/Local/Cable.* It's a remarkable book because it was written at the beginning of the cable age. Reading the book, the reader gets a glimpse into a world where the three major broadcasters are about to enter a much more complicated media landscape that will be dramatically altered by cable television.

Even as early as 1982, when HBO had 8.5 million subscribers and Showtime had just 3 million, Poltrack comprehended the power of this change. In Chapter 7, "Cable TV: Past, Present and Future," Poltrack even goes so far as to successfully predict the emergence of niche cable channels like Home and Garden and the Style Channel.

Poltrack's book is insightful as the entertainment, advertising, and technology industries stand at the beginning of yet another massive change. Poltrack's observations of cable TV's effect on advertising are particularly visionary when applied to the changes happening today. In the book excerpt below, simply substituting Internet for cable illustrates Poltrack's deep understanding of change in the TV, Internet, and advertising industries.

> The coming cable [Internet] age will represent both challenge and opportunity for the advertiser. The challenge will come in the transition from an over-the-air network-dominated TV advertising universe to a complex multichannel system.... The opportunity afforded advertisers by the new cable [Internet] television medium includes both national and localized outlets for advertising. The national advertiser can choose from broad-based general-interest and various special-interest program services. The broad-based service offers larger viewing bases, but less specific audience profiles.... The special-interest services provide a much narrower audience base, but one whose profile is very specific. The advertiser whose target market is similar in composition to the viewer base of a special-interest service should be willing to pay a premium to reach that specific segment, as long as the higher CPM translates to lower unit costs. Another advantage of the special-interest service centers on the editorial content of the service's programming. To the extent that editorial content is related to the product, service, or marketplace of the advertiser, a possible synergy can be established between the programming and the commercial (*Television Marketing*. David F. Poltrack. 1983. McGraw Hill).

POLTRACK: The question we have to ask is at what point does streaming on the Internet become directly competitive to the live television distribution. This could start to happen with Internet-connected TVs and set top boxes. People could then start watching these television programs through the Internet and watch them on television and not the computer. This would give them the same experience that you would get watching them live on television. When this happens you will start to see that some of the streaming will be in replacement of, as opposed to complementing, the live broadcast experience. But if we can generate as much advertising revenue from the online version of these shows as we do from the live broadcast version, then we shouldn't be concerned.

The amount of advertising that people will watch online is a matter of debate these days. Right now we don't see the same amount of advertising on the Internet as we do in broadcast TV. I believe this is an artificial limitation that was set by an Internet model and not a TV model. The Internet video model was developed with the idea of people watching short form video, short clips and user-generated content. It was what people were watching on their computers. You can't put a lot of advertising on user-generated content. If a person is only going to watch two minutes of video, you can't put two minutes worth of advertising with the video. That' just doesn't work. But as more and more full TV show viewing takes place on the Internet, the more people will become comfortable with higher commercial loads. If the people are actually going to be viewing TV shows on a television set, then there's no reason that we can't put the same amount of commercials in this program as we do our broadcast programming. It would be the same experience for them.

I believe the Internet distribution of TV programs and the ability to stream them introduces an advertising opportunity. It's an opportunity because the nature of the experience is the best of both worlds. Consumers get to watch their favorite shows delivered via the Internet for free with advertising but there is a potential for interactivity. If they want people can interact with the advertising and that's something that advertisers would be very interested in. People can respond directly to the ad. I think that will eventually evolve into just a natural extension of those franchise programs to a broader and broader audience.

***

BDJ: What do you think is the significance of interactivity on Internet connected TVs or even other connected devices? Do you see what's happening now as just normal TV broadcaster's evolution or do you see something different play?

DAVID POLTRACK: Well, essentially if you look back in the early days of television, people had about five choices when they turned on the television. Today they have 160 choices and if you went down those 160 choices and you said to a consumer: Okay here are the 160 channels of the television. Here's what's on television. What's missing? They'd be hard pressed to tell you what's missing. They'd say they don't need any *more* television. They have enough television programming available to them.

So, the question is now not whether there's more content because I think they pretty much know the content is there. The question now is how does that content change? Interactivity introduces change. So, instead of being totally a passive medium now you're going to have the potential for interactivity while viewing. That's something that people have been talking about for years and years but it seems to be here now. The sets are out and being sold. The IP TV sets are out with widgets and all the things that will allow for an interactive experience. That not only can add to the TV watching experience but it also changes the advertising market. It allows for people to react to advertising and take actions on advertising that they weren't able to do before.

The question is whether we can integrate interactivity into television. That is a potential game changer because it makes the medium much more dynamic from the advertiser's perspective. It also introduces new opportunities for the consumer and new ways for the consumer to enjoy the medium.

Our research has shown that interactive television is something that viewers will like some of the time but not all of the time. They would love to decide when they have it and when they don't. Interactive television is fine as long as it stays out of the way when you want it to stay out of the way and is only there when you choose it.

The social viewing dynamic of multiple people watching television at the same time is also somewhat challenging. One person may want to interact with what's being watched and another person may want to passively sit back. That creates some issues as to how to execute interactivity on the screen. These things all have to be worked out, but certainly they can be worked out. There is a lot of potential for that interactivity once the Internet is integrated into the television sets.

I can see interactivity more as an extension of the total program experience. That's opposed to something that's highly intensive while the show's going on.

Now, of course from the advertising perspective, with interactivity there is a great opportunity. One of the limitations of television has always been that it can only stimulate interest in products. It doesn't allow the consumer to buy anything directly. It doesn't take it all the way. And, the direct marketers of the world who know how to do that on television, will talk about how effective that is on TV, but most marketers can't do that.

Obviously, with interactivity, the advertising opportunities become richer in terms of being able to drive somebody to a Web site. Thirty percent of the people on the Internet during prime time are also watching television. That means you're not that 30 percent out of the room to turn on their computer. A lot of them already have it on. And now with the IPTV, it'll be built into the television set. So, I think you will see, from an advertising and a marketing perspective, that does offer other opportunities.

BDJ: What about the social nature of these connected devices. At CBS do you see any potential around people being social with their TVs around your TV shows?

DAVID POLTRACK: Definitely. If you look at the social networking sites like Facebook[†] and Twitter[†] they are basically sites that people have come to for interpersonal communication. When we talk to people about why they are using Facebook they tell us it's to communicate with friends and family. That is by far the number one reason that people maintain pages on Facebook. It's the number one activity that people do on Facebook.

Now, for those social networking sites to become successful business enterprises and generate advertising revenue, they've got to figure out a way to keep people engaged on their site in something other than a direct personal conversation with someone else.

You can't interrupt people's direct personal conversations with advertising. But you can take advantage of the fact that the people are on your site and draw them to other activities. That's the key to the Facebooks of the world becoming viable commercial enterprises. It's really the only way they are going to become commercially viable and not just attract a lot of people. Social networking sites have to go beyond the use of personal communication and introduce new content that keeps people engaged.

Of course you can use TV shows to draw people into the social networking site. You can also use social networking to draw people into our TV programs. We could expand one of our shows by introducing social networking into aspects of the experience.

CSI airs for 60 minutes a week. I can increase that through interactivity and compelling ancillary experiences. I can draw those people who are watching that 60-minute telecast into a *CSI* site where there are interactive games and things to play, then I have the ability to further commercialize that program.

At CBS our approach is to make our TV shows related to Internet sites and to add social networking aspects to those sites. This then extends the amount of time people spend on those sites and the advertising and marketing opportunities as well. It's natural for CBS to work with any of the social networking sites to bring our content onto their sites and help them with their goals of trying to extend the amount of time people go onto their sites.

BDJ: What are you looking forward to?

DAVID POLTRACK: I'm excited about expanding the potential of the medium to go beyond its current creative boundaries. That could be interactivity or 3D or further creative enhancements. I'm interested in the ability of the integration of social networking with content to increase the amount of engagement with that content. I think that we no longer have to look at each TV program as something that's going to occupy 30 minutes and 60 minutes of consumer's time. You can see those programs going beyond that. As we talk about these advancements it's not just for TV entertainment. It also applies to things like sports and news. If you look at the core product that we have, I'm excited about the extension of that product into all these different areas. They are all enhancements of our basic creative product and can expand the boundaries within which we work today.

Chapter 6

Personal TV

The Intel Corporation has facilities and fabrication plants all over the world. I had made the trip down to our Chandler, Arizona site to see some new work that had been done with low level sensors and cameras. It was summer and it was hot; crazy hot. If you haven't been to Arizona in the summer it's a strange experience. It looks and feels a little like you are on the moon except it's not the lack of oxygen and gravity that makes it so foreign; it's the ever-present dry heat. It bakes the land until it looks like a lunar landscape. When I pulled into the Chandler parking lot I was still sweating from the short walk from the rental car shuttle to my car. As I opened the door it felt like I was opening a 400-degree oven. The heat waves pushed into the car, brushing aside any of the cool that the overworked air conditioner had managed to create. I grabbed my laptop and headed for the entrance.

When you enter most Intel faculties you are instantly reminded of all the other buildings you've been in before. All the buildings look vaguely alike. Intel is an engineering company, you have to remember. If a building layout works then they'll use it again, improving it just a little from the previous version. The added benefit to this copy-repeat process is that usually when you get to a new building you generally know where to go. I was headed for the TV lab.

The TV lab in Chandler was a maze of packed workbenches and squat server racks. At the back of the room were two TVs hooked up to menagerie of computers, set-top boxes and deconstructed computer platforms.

"Just step in front of the TV," Randy, the engineer smiled.

There were three boxes on the TV. One showed a trailer for a recent action film; cars flipped, beautiful people dodged bullets, and things blew up. In the second window I could see the low-resolution output from a small camera fixed to the top of the TV. The third box revealed the image processing from the camera.

"Ok, we're good," Randy said while I was still examining the boxes. "You can step away from the TV."

I took a step back and waited. "Now what?" I asked.

"Just step in front of the TV," he replied. "The program entered you as a user while you were standing there the first time. If you step…"

I stepped back in front of the TV. I could see the low-res camera seeing me but this time up in the image processing box it said "BDJ".

"See there," Randy pointed at the box. "See the BDJ? It recognizes you."

I moved away from the TV and came back again. The camera saw me and said "BDJ". I bent my knees and popped back up into the camera. "BDJ".

"We've refined it down so that it can do the detection with a low-res camera in a few seconds. It can also do multiple people." He stood next to me and the box ready "Randy" and "BDJ". "We've got more work to do but you can see how it works. We need to make sure that the low-res video feed is secure on the platform."

I moved in front of the TV, watching it recognize me as I reentered the sensor. "You mean if I had this on my TV at home then every time I came into the room I would essentially be logging into my TV?"

"Yes."

"And if you were with me then we would both be logged into the TV? The system would know we were there? Just by physically being in the room we're logged into the TV or the set-top box. No typing. No remote control. Nothing. Just by being in the room physically we're logged in."

"Yep," Randy smiled.

***

The idea of making the TV experience personalized and tailored to a specific individual (also known as you) and to the tastes and needs of an entire household (also known as your family) is both intuitively simple and realistically complex. The notion of Personal TV is really a mix of the traditional TV experience combined with the personalization of a computer; the entertainment of TV mixed with the personal choice of the Internet. As we gain the ability to enjoy TV, movies, games, and applications on all the devices we love, the nature of these devices become more computational. Meaning there are more of what we think of as a traditional computer than a traditional TV. However, as we talked about in the Ubiquitous TV chapter, these devices don't have to be anything like a traditional computer. Sure they could be a laptop but they can also be a phone, a car, or any other device that has some computational power and a connection to the Internet. Now once you have this type of device then, if you want, it's possible for that device to know who you are. This may sound a little scary but it really isn't. It's already happening today. Your iPhone[†] knows who you are. You have an account and preferences and settings. Every time you or anyone else picks up your iPhone it just assumes that they are you. Your laptop has the ability to handle multiple users with a simple log in. Some laptops even allow you to log in to your account using a fingerprint scanner. Taking all of this into consideration along with the advances I described from our Chandler site, you can see how all of your devices could know who you are simply by you using them. Physically using your device is a kind of secure log in.

Let's think about this practically. Once you're logged into your devices then you could start to utilize all of that additional information that's going to be coming along with your favorite TV, movies, games, and applications. The increased data that we talked about in the Informative TV chapter could allow you to simply find something to watch in the 500 billion hours of content that will be out there in 2015. Because your devices know you and what you like, it will make searching easier because you device can filter out the things you're not interested in. Up until recently, the way you "personalized" your traditional TV experience was by choice. You chose what you wanted to watch and the entertainment business has done a fantastic job over the decades bringing you more and more choices. But at some point, in this ever increasing world of choice we're going to need to use the computational power and intelligence in our devices to tailor our entertainment in new ways.

This type of personalization brings up a whole host of questions and opportunities. Just as Personal TV is a combination of traditional TV and computational devices so too is it an intersection of new business models, partnerships, and rivalries. We'll explore all of these in this chapter. But before we do that I have two little histories about how different people have conceptualized what it means to personalize a device. What's particularly important with each story is not just how the device was "personalized" but also what were the follow on implications of this personalization as the idea eventually made its way to mainstream adoption.

The 'N Sync Tracking Device

Over the years Dr. Genevieve Bell, my colleague here at Intel, has done some fascinating field research. Being an anthropologist in a technology company her methods and results are quite refreshing. She studies people first and technology second. She'll follow people throughout their days to better understand how they shop, work, and live with technologies. She has an amazing understanding of technology as a personal device in the lives of people. Now when I say personal device, I don't mean customizable or even in the context of personal TV. For her, devices are knit into the fabric of people's lives and social interaction. Your iPhone isn't a smart phone that gives you access to telephony and Internet applications. No, for people it's *your iPhone*. People decorate it. They give it a name. People don't think in terms of telephony. Their phone connects them with the people they love and the people they have fun with. The Internet capability keeps them from getting lost and gives them something to do when they are bored. It is their device.

Back in 1999, Dr. Bell was doing some early research on personal devices and technologies. She was working with Eric Dishman, another researcher here at Intel. They were doing field research. Their work, along with that of a handful of other anthropologists, fundamentally changed how Intel understood consumers and planned its products.

But to really appreciate this story you need to think back to 1999. The world was very different place in a number of ways. From a technology standpoint 1999 was before the rise of Google, before the social networking explosion. Amazon.com had only been online for four years, Bill Clinton was the American president and only 14.4 percent of people in the world owned a cell phone (Euromonitor. 2010).

In the suburbs of Washington DC, Bell and Dishman were at the Carter family home. Mark and Bonnie Carter were your average American family, with a three bedroom home and two kids; Raquel and Michelle. After interviewing the family for a while the researchers asked the family to design their perfect technology device. These kinds of exercises are called participatory design sessions and they are incredibly helpful when you want people to talk about new experience and technologies. The most remarkable device of the four was Michelle's 'N Sync Tracking Device.

You may not remember the boy band 'N Sync, but in 1999 they were huge. Their debut album *NSYNC* sold over 10 million copies (RIAA). and the group appeared on the television series *Sabrina, the Teenage Witch* on February 5, 1999 at the height of their popularity, performing "Tearin' Up My Heart" (Wikipedia).

In 1999 the members of the boy band (Justin Timberlake, JC Chasez, Lance Bass, Joey Fatone and Chris Kirkpatrick) owned the world and the rest of us just lived in it. And Michelle, like millions of teens before, was rabid for any and all information about her favorite band. Because of all this her perfect and expertly personalized technology device would be *The 'N Sync Tracking Device,* shown in Figure 6.1.

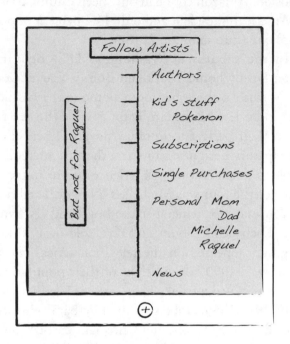

Figure 6.1   The 'N Sync Tracking Device

This ingenious little device would give Michelle up-to-the minute updates about 'N Sync: where they were, what they were doing, what songs they were working on—basically anything and everything having to do with Justin, JC, Lance, Joey, and Chris.

Now depending on your opinion of 'N Sync, you might think this device is either frivolous or inspired, but the one thing you should recognize is that Michelle's personalized device gave her the exact information and entertainment she wanted about the most important band in her life. Dr. Bell's sees Michelle's device as an example of people's clear understanding of what they want from their devices. She argues that people know exactly how they want their technology personalized and how they would like to use it in their everyday lives. She said, "Consumers….people know exactly what they want, exactly how they want their technology personalized for them. We just need to learn how to listen."

On October 28, 2003, Mark Zuckerberg answered Michelle's wish when he created the social networking site Facebook in his dorm room. On its Web site Facebook describes itself this way: "Facebook helps you connect and share with the people in your life." Facebook users can find friends and people online, "friending" them and adding them to their Facebook page. On their personal page people can update their profiles and notify their friends about what they are doing. In turn their friends can post messages and updates to each other's page,

In 2009 Facebook was voted the most used social networking site in the world with 300 million active users. As the service has grown people can not only follow their own personal friends but they can also follow their favorite bands, like former 'N Sync member and now pop powerhouse Justin Timberlake. In 2010 there were 20 Justin Timberlake fan pages on Facebook.

A few years after Facebook emerged from Zuckerberg's dorm room another social networking service became wildly popular. It asked people the question: What are you doing now? Almost as if answering Michelle's wish for an up to the minute 'N Sync tracking device, Jack Dorsey created Twitter in 2006. On its Web site Twitter describes itself this way: "Share and discover what's happening right now, anywhere in the world."

Twitter is a micro-blogging service that lets people post and read short messages and updates called *tweets*. Users of Twitter post their tweets throughout their day keeping their friends and followers up to date with what's happening at that moment in their lives. Users not only post but they also "follow" or subscribe to other people's tweets, always knowing what's happening right now.

Twitter would allow Michelle to follow 'N Sync, giving her instant updates from Justin, JC, Lance, Joey, and Chris. Not only that but it would also let her stay connected to other 'N Sync fans and even allow her to tell them what she's doing at any time. In 2010 former 'N Sync member Justin Timberlake was a registered user on Twitter with over 1.3 million followers.

The success of both Facebook and Twitter prove quite clearly that it wasn't only a boy band mad teenager in suburban Washington D.C. that wanted the capabilities of an 'N Sync Tracking device.

An Intelligent Agent for Every TV

Dr. Michio Kaku is an American theoretical physicist and futurist who has written several bestselling books like *Hyperspace* and *Physics of the Impossible*. In 1997 he wrote a book called *Visions* about how science would revolutionize the twenty-first century. The book explores three overarching revolutions: the computer revolution, the bimolecular revolution and the quantum revolution. *Visions* is a fascinating read and it is interesting to see where we are in Kaku's visions of our future.

Even three years before the end of the twentieth century Kaku was talking about the merger of TV and the Internet as well as the explosion and proliferation of what he called "wall screens" or the flat screen TVs that have transformed the landscape and look of homes, pubs, and businesses across the world.

There is one section of the book called "From the Present to 2020: Intelligent Agents" in Chapter 3, The Intelligent Planet. In this section Kaku explains that "an intelligent agent should be able to act as a filter on the Internet for the user, distinguishing between junk and valuable material" (Kaku, 59).

He goes on to introduce us to the work of Pattie Maes who at the time was at the Massachusetts Institute of Technology Media Lab and is one of the pioneers of the concept of digital agents. These digital software agents would have enough intelligence that they could act as our own private and personal secretary, planner, and even companion. Maes' vision back in the late 1990s was that "such agents will be invaluable for people who want continual updates on sports events, news items, hobbies or human-interest stories. Even as we sleep, our computers will be able to silently collect information we might need" (Kaku, 60).

In 1995 Maes further explained her concept of the intelligent agent in an article for *Scientific American*. "Some of these proxies will make the digital world less overwhelming by hiding technical details and tasks, guiding users through complex online spaces or even teaching them about certain subjects. Yet other agents may have the authority to perform transactions (such as online shopping) or to represent people in their absence…this change in functionality will most likely go hand in hand with change in the physical ways people interact with computers. Rather than manipulating a keyboard and mouse, people will speak to agents or gesture at things that need doing. In response, agents will appear as "living" entities on the screen, conveying their current state and behavior with animated facial expressions or body language rather then windows with text, graphs and figures." (Pattie Maes. *Scientific American.* 1995)

As with most projections and visions for the future Kaku and Maes got it somewhat right—we interact with intelligent agents these days without even knowing it. They filter the spam from our e-mail and assign us gates when our planes land at the airport, but we've not quite seen the popularization of the personal agent—the one that will filter out all the junk and give you only what you're personally interested in. But it is happening. Gradually over the last few years significant advances have been made. Probably one of the more publicized and watched advances came with the NetFlix Prize.

The NetFlix Prize was a competition announced in October 2006 by the online DVD subscription rental service NetFlix. The company offered 1 million USD to anyone who developed a recommending algorithm that would score 10 percent better than the company's current movie recommendation system. This recommending algorithm would be a basic version of Kaku and Maes idea of an intelligent agent.

NetFlix's web site described it this way: "The NetFlix Prize sought to substantially improve the accuracy of predictions about how much someone is going to enjoy a movie based on their movie preferences." (from Netflix site). The whole idea was to develop an agent that could give you suggestions for movies you haven't seen based on the movies you have seen and rated on the site. The agent could then go through all of NetFlix available rental library and only give you recommendations to the movies you'd be interested in. Simple enough an idea but rather tricky to pull off.

The prize was awarded on September 21, 2009 to a seven member international team called "BellKor's Pragmatic Chaos". To get to a 10 percent improvement the team had to take some unconventional approaches. Their algorithm took into consideration how people rated movies just after they watch them as opposed to a few days later. It turns out some movies drop in ratings while others get better the more people think about them. Each movie has its own curve of how different people might rate it over time. The team also looked at people's mood as they rated multiple movies. For instance when people didn't like a movie they tended to rate it and other movies lower than if they rated the single movie by itself.

All of this data and behavioral observation led to a single simple goal: better movie recommendations. For NetFlix better movie recommendations means happier customers. These customers will remain loyal and continue to rent movies from NetFlix's service. Part of the intelligence behind those recommendations was the vision that Kaku and Maes discussed back in 1990s. Now you can see it simply by going online, renting a movie and rating it.

The Business of Personal TV

The 'N Sync tracking device and the concept of intelligent agents for TV give us two distinct visions of personalization. Facebook and NetFlix are examples of the realization of these visions in the real world. To make a TV or any other device personal there has to be a company developing the software and hardware to do it. Ultimately for personalization to go mainstream there needs to be a way to pay for it.

Back in July of 2004 *The Economist* did a profile of what the digital home of the future might look like. They discussed both the reality and hype of TVs and computers coming together. Back then people were talking about the PC taking over the living room. Near the end of the short article Art Peck, who at the time was an analyst at Boston Consulting (Peck currently is President of Outlet Division and Executive Vice President of Strategy & Operations, Gap Inc.), is cited as saying that "the real money in the digital home will be made by those providing a service or selling advertising." (*The Future of Technology*. Ed. Tom Standage. 2005)

Peck's point is a good one to remember as we think about how to personalize TV and technology. Facebook, a realization of the 'N Sync tracing device, supports itself by selling advertising space to companies who want to reach its users. In 2009 the company reported that it had turned a profit for the first time, a huge hurdle for most social networking sites. The NetFlix Prize to provide better movie recommendations is an example of how a service can use abstract ideas like Kaku and Maes' intelligent agents to keep people paying their monthly or yearly movie rental subscriptions. In the real world personalization must be paid for.

Okay, so it's no secret that the TV and the entertainment business are just that: a business. We can look at the history of TV and the business of entertainment in the living room as a history of choice and personalization. Over time the industry and its technology has constantly evolved to provide the consumer more choices and better personalization. The switch from black and white to color drove the adoption of new TV sets. The desire for more channels and access to more shows brought about new service providers and devices. All the time consumers have responded with their eyeballs and wallets, watching more TV, buying new sets and subscribing to new services.

TV began in the 1920s as an expensive technological marvel, far out of reach of the average consumer. Twenty years after its introduction, fewer than one percent of Americans had TVs in their homes. People travelled to department stores and bars to see TV. Then, in four years, the media landscape changed. In 1946, Americans bought 6,000 TVs, in 1950, they purchased 7.3 million sets (CEA). The number of local television stations exploded and the range of content delivered through the television fundamentally shifted from a live-only solution to tape, expanding people's choices.

Throughout the history of television, there are lags between the development of a new technology and its broad adoption by consumers. It took more than 20 years for TV to move from the sports bar to the living room, and 18 years for color TV sales to surpass black and white. It took 14 years for the VCR to arrive in half of American homes, but only 7 for the DVD player to reach the same level. How long will personal TV take to become the norm for television viewers?

The TV and entertainment industry is not now nor has it ever been static. From the very beginning the history of television has been a history of constant change. Although the television is sometimes represented as a monolithic, stationary media object in history, the fact is, from the beginning, it has been a hungry technology, absorbing and adapting new developments in technology, culture, and consumer tastes.

In the last 80 years, the scope and nature of the content has changed dramatically and repeatedly. This also includes the technology used to deliver it. But even though TV today may look quite different than it did in 1930, two fundamental rules remain. TV is moving pictures. TV is a business.

To Watch or Not to Watch—That Was the Question

Tawny Schlieski spends most of her time thinking about TV. As one of our leading researchers in Intel's Digital Home Group, she spends her days following global TV trends and tracking consumers' evolving relationship with TV.

"TV really wasn't that personal in the beginning," Schlieski told me when we sat down to chart TV's history of personalization and technological change. "The choice was simple really; people either watched it or they didn't. I guess you could say there was a type of personalization in that. There was also the decision you could make to buy one of those early TV sets or not. If you bought one then it was your TV set so it was personal. So I guess you could look at the first personal TV choice was whether to watch or not to watch—or to buy or not to buy and most people didn't buy."

Television was first introduced in the US in 1922 with little market impact. The early mechanical sets were expensive, and global events like the Great Depression and World War II limited commercial investment in broadening the technology. In the late 1920s little content was produced. Very few people were watching these shows so consequently advertisers kept their distance. Radio, movies, and print remained the primary media for entertainment and information. However, the technology continued to evolve.

Even though today we draw a direct connection between the TV and the living room, when TV began, it was not in the home. It emerged in the 1930s as a remote experience, delivered to bars and department stores. In 1939, the National Broadcasting Company (NBC) broadcast the first baseball game to an estimated 3,000 viewers, a pretty small number when you consider that there were 33,000 in the stands (NPR. "1939: First Major League Baseball Game Airs On TV" .August 26, 2009) Around this time a new television set cost about USD 300. This was about one quarter the cost of a new car. The price tag placed these 8-inch monochrome screens well out of reach of most Americans. But even at this point, the core idea of TV was forming.

TV is video—moving pictures delivered remotely to a screen. That screen could be in a sports bar, or on a train, or in a living room, or in Portland, Maine, but the content that is displayed on that screen comes from someplace else.

The content on these televisions was largely constrained to news and sports, but consumers still flocked to these communal screens to see the revolutionary technology that transmitted images across vast distances. The government saw social value in the sharing of information through TV. Civil defense signals were relayed by television, and the government eventually started nonprofit television stations, but TV, from its earliest inception, has been a commercial medium. People produce and distribute content in order to get paid.

The people that made the content in this early ecosystem were the media giants of their day: radio studios. NBC and the Columbia Broadcasting System (CBS) created content in their existing studios and delivered it over the infrastructure they already owned. In fact, in 1947, virtually all the TV cameras produced were sold to NBC. But these powerful players at the time still didn't completely know what to do with the new medium of TV, as pointed out by Larry Gelbart, a television writer from the 1940s.

> Television, of course, is an invention. It does not suggest what you do with it, and we didn't have a clue. We borrowed, we mixed and mismatched, and we did radio material. It was just there to take the picture of performers doing stuff from other media.

I Love Lucy and the Birth of Content as We Know it Today

By the early 1950s the world had changed significantly. The average cost of a television set had dropped under USD 200 and 22 percent of the US population had one in their home. TV was moving out of the fringe and becoming a mass medium. Driven by the nature of broadcast (one signal repeated exactly across many towers), and the desire for advertisers to reach large audiences, programming and structure evolved around mainstream tastes. People had three channels to choose from, and the networks' job was to entice viewers to spend the evening on one channel. The advertisers would then pay the networks for the ability to put their products and services in front of those families.

This was that first small step towards personalization and choice. People watched the TV shows they liked. By watching these TV shows it raised the ratings for these shows. Ratings were and are the basis for how networks collect advertising revenue from the advertisers. The more people watched a particular program the more money the broadcaster could make. In response to this the networks would tailor their TV shows to the most popular tastes of the time. People had a choice of what shows they wanted to watch and when they did watch the networks made sure to produce more shows tailored for them.

In the early 1950s CBS was lagging in the ratings. The network needed a new show to attract people to their Monday night spot. CBS approached Lucille Ball who at the time was a mildly successful film actress who was also the star of CBS radio's hit show *My Favorite Husband*. Ball agreed to do the show but she had some demands.

First she wanted her husband, Cuban band leader Desi Arnaz, to play the part of her husband Ricky Ricardo. Next the couple wanted to stay in Hollywood and produce the TV show from there. This was highly unusual. Most shows of the time were shot in New York City and then broadcast out across the country. Ball and Arnaz also wanted the show to be filmed. This too was highly unusual.

In the early 1950s most TV shows were performed live and broadcast to the public. These shows were then recorded for later broadcast using a Kinescope camera. The camera filmed the performance off the TV screen as it was being broadcast live. Although it did capture the performance the quality was relatively low. The grainy, monochrome images of the early days of TV that we have today were captured using this method.

Filming the performance as it was being given by the actors in front of a live audience was new for CBS. At the time some westerns and large extravaganzas were filmed but these were rare. Part of the reason for this goes back to how the networks like CBS and NBC thought of themselves. During this time many network executives thought of TV broadcasts as live events only. Filming a show, editing it together and then broadcasting it out went against the very idea of what many thought TV was supposed to be. There was another problem with filming Ball and Arnaz's show; filming was expensive.

To close the deal, Ball and Arnaz agreed to cover some of the financial risk of the production with their newly formed production company Desilu. On October 15, 1951, *I Love Lucy* premiered on Monday night at 9 p.m. The show became the decade's biggest hit. Lucy and Ricky Ricardo along with Fred and Ethel Mertz became a classic in American television history.

To capture the comedy between the cast members in front of the live audience, Desi Arnaz used a camera production technique that was pioneered by producer Jerry Fairbanks three years earlier (James L. Baughman. *Same Time, Same Channel*. 2007. Johns Hopkins Press. p .130). It was called the three camera technique and it allowed each camera to capture a different angle so that it could be edited together in a single performance later, as shown in Figure 6.2). It was cost-effective, allowed the actors freedom to capture the scene, and has since become an industry standard for shooting a TV show.

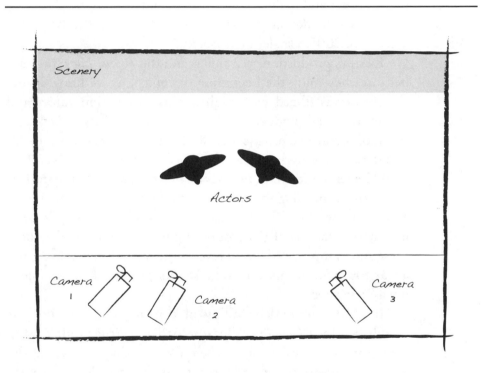

Figure 6.2   Overhead view of the three camera technique

In 1993 television writer Larry Brody for his book *Turning Points in Television* talked with Arnaz about what led him to use the camera technique.

"People say Lucy and I were big innovators. We had to innovate. This was the beginning of TV. There was nothing else," Desi said. "We had a great life in California and we weren't about to trade it in so we gave up a little money here, a little money there, to be able to shoot on the Coast.

"The only way to do things was to film the show in advance so it could be shipped to New York in time to be aired. But CBS wanted us to do it in front of an audience so we had to come up with a way so the camera could see us and we could see each other and the audience could see and laugh….

"We did the only practical thing. We set up three cameras so we could play to them and to the folks watching, and now all these years later kids like you (Brody) make out like it's a big deal" (Larry Brody. *Turning Points in Television*. 2005. Citadel Press Books).

Desilu's production techniques and the *I Love Lucy* show are significant because they mark the beginning of content as we know it today. Because the show was filmed with high quality production values and edited together, the final product became the episodes of the *I Love Lucy* show, not the individual live broadcasts. With the shows captured in this way they could be not only broadcast out to the nation from New York but they could be rebroadcast. *I Love Lucy* is often credited as being the first show to go into reruns, meaning that the show could be replayed again and again. This allowed networks to fill their daily lineups with high quality shows that cost less than a fraction of the cost of original live content. For the producers of these shows it provided a new revenue stream called residuals. Residuals were a way for them to continue to make money from their original content after it was first aired.

In 2010 our understanding of content is based upon the approach established by *I Love Lucy*. Because Ball and Arnaz didn't want to move to New York and chose to shoot their TV show in Hollywood, the economics and programming of entertainment was changed forever. TV stations could program shows across their time schedules, advertisers would still pay for access to the audience, and the creative asset could live on to be rebroadcast, shown on the Internet and sold in DVD sets.

What does this have to do with personal TV? When TV shows were no longer thought of as live broadcasts and could be re-shown and monetized again it increased the choices available to consumers. TV shows and entertainment became discrete entities separate from the TV broadcast itself. As discrete entities entertainment could be moved around and rebroadcast, giving the consumer more access to entertainment and increasing their choices. This increased choice allowed TV stations to attract more viewers at different times in the day. If the early days of personal TV were about a simple question: to watch or not to watch. Then the golden age of TV expanded that to what TV show to watch and when to watch it.

This greatly expanded people's entertainment choices in the middle of the twentieth century. But this was nothing compared to the massive amount of choice that was coming: cable.

People Will Never Pay For TV: Cable

The idea of choice and personalization that we know today really started with cable TV. Three channels really limited consumer choices and the network programmers' ability to offer a wide range of entertainment that could span the interests of all consumers. Cable changed that.

Cable television evolved alongside broadcast TV. Introduced in 1948 as a means of delivering signal to areas with poor reception, early cable systems were little more than community antennas, erected in prime locations, and distributing signal to homes connected to the antenna. By 1952, there were 70 of these cable operators, who were beginning to take advantage of their ability to pick up distant signals, and offering differentiated content to their customers.

In 1970 only four percent of Americans had Cable TV. In 1972, HBO launched the first pay TV network. What had been a 100-percent advertising supported model was beginning to change, and early subscribers were underwriting the cost of infrastructure and paying cable companies for more programming that they could get from the networks alone. This shift in revenue was gradual.

As cable programming gained popularity, the audience reach of any individual show began to decline. With more choice, fewer consumers chose the same things. Although the audience for television continued to grow, the audience for individual shows began to decline. That being said, even today, the networks still garner larger audiences than the most successful cable programming.

This raises an interesting question since most viewers continued to watch more network than cable programming, why were they willing to pay for what had been a free service? One answer could be that the promise of content is worth more than the content itself. Cable promised a dramatic expansion of the opportunity for television viewing. So even though viewers continued to consume the "free" content in greater volume, on an average of 10 channels, the promise of more content continued to be cable's selling point.

The success of the cable companies brought with it a change to the fundamental wire infrastructure in the United States. With the Cable Television Report and Order of 1972, high speed data connections to the house became the standard in new housing developments, and laying cable to existing homes began in earnest as subscriber bases grew.

By 1987, pay TV was no longer an early adopter frill, and more than half of US homes paid for a television signal. The networks continued to broadcast their signal over the air, and even in homes with cable, a second or third television receiving signal through an antenna remained common.

Further splitting the U.S. TV market, satellite to the consumer launched in the 1980s and U.S. subscriber numbers inched upward for a decade, reaching 10 percent of the U.S. population in 1998. Outside the United States, satellite functioned to expand the reach of television across the globe. Locations in the developing and developed world where the cable infrastructure was weak or missing could suddenly receive the full spectrum of television programming, for the right price. In expansion areas, where cable penetration was low, satellite companies picked up subscribers at a good rate.

With the mainstream rollout of cable and satellite systems, personal TV took another giant leap forward. Not only could consumers pick what programs they wanted to watch but they could now select entire networks that were tailored to their taste. Niche networks cropped up that catered to specific interests like cooking (Food Network), sports (ESPN, SportsCenter), science fiction (SyFy, FearNet) and fashion (Style Channel, E!). With all of these channels and a business model that now included subscription as well as advertising supported programming, consumers were offered more entertainment than they could possible enjoy. With so much entertainment now available the consumer could almost begin to act as their own entertainment programmer but to do this they needed a little more technology.

March of the Acronyms: VCR, DVD, DVR

Prior to 1970, television had undergone numerous changes. Many of these technological advancements took place inside the TV set. Other innovations included how entertainment was produced and paid for. Consumers now had access to a wide range of entertainment. They could control *what* they watched but not *when* they watched it. The VCR changed all of that.

Although available in the 1960s, the videocassette recorder (VCR) entered the mainstream consumer electronics market in the 1970s. The VCR allowed consumers to record live TV to video tape and watch it later. The VCR enabled time-shifting, allowing consumers to watch their favorite TV shows whenever they wanted independent from when it was originally broadcast. This brought a whole new world of content into the living room and even shifted the very idea of entertainment ownership.

With the VCR the broadcast and rebroadcast of content was not the exclusive purview of the networks. Even though recording of live TV remained an exception, it altered the relationship between the content and the viewer. What was high value had previously been a determination made solely based on the evaluation of the networks and advertisers. Now people and families made their own determination about what content was good enough to capture and time-shift or play again.

Something else happened with the introduction of the VCR. Collections of tapes began to appear on shelves across the nation as viewers kept their favorite content. The VCR introduced a new idea of ownership to the consumer. Prior to the VCR, video content, although recorded and reissued by the broadcasters, was necessarily transient for consumers. The VCR enabled users to record and keep programming on the TV, and as prices declined, to buy and maintain libraries of video content.

The final and most significant change brought about by the VCR was that it expanded the range of content available in the living room. Hollywood arrived on the couch, uncensored, and not on the basis of a network or cable schedule. Now people went to a whole new place to get their favorite entertainment: the rental store. The very definition of TV had changed again. Friday night TV no longer just referred to scheduled programming, controlled and monetized by the networks. The TV had become a screen managed by the consumer, gaining them access to a wider variety of entertainment that they could own and watch on their own schedule. For the first time the answer to the question "what are we watching tonight?" was not constrained by a published broadcast schedule.

Early in the first decade of the twenty-first century VCRs began to drop in popularity, replaced by the Digital Video Disc (DVD). The difference between a VHS tape and a DVD was not that revolutionary. It was still a physical copy of media that could be shared in the same way. A DVD had a higher quality picture than the VHS, it could hold more information on a single disk, it was more durable, but important, it was less expensive to produce.

When the DVD was introduced, consumers were not unhappy with the VCRs and demanding change, but the DVD had the fastest ramp of any consumer electronics technology. Why? DVD player prices quickly dropped to match VCR prices. Because DVDs are significantly cheaper to produce (on the scale of one tenth the cost), content owners leapt onto the format. In addition, the DVD was itself an evolution of a known technology: the CD. From a consumer point of view, improving on a known activity is almost always easier to sell than trying something completely new.

Even though the idea behind the DVD was not unique, it changed the content landscape. Cheaper copy prices lead to the rapid proliferation of titles. DVDs extended the reach of content producers to create revenue from their products.

At this point, the vast majority of the professional entertainment content was available and scheduled by the networks. The vast majority of this content was seen on this same schedule. The VCR did allow people to take a more active role in their content delivery, but relatively few people could program it to record and opted to watch movies instead. DVDs entered the market and provided high quality less expensive digital entertainment but there was still a need for digital time-shifting.

TiVo introduced the digital video recorder (DVR) in 1998, and the satellite company DirecTV had propagated the technology into 3 million homes by 2004. How is a DVR different from a VCR or DVD? Two differences, both evolutionary, but together produce what had the potential to be a revolutionary change.

Evolutionary change #1: volume. The hard disk stored more content than a tape. This opened up the door for "routine" content to be recorded. You could record all of your shows, not just special content. Before with the VCR you could record up to six hours of TV before you had to physically intervene with the machine and put in a new tape. Now, the average DVR could store up to 40 hours of TV. This increased capacity meant that people could be less selective and recording became a routine event. Also consumers could record shows even if they had a marginal interest in them to see if they liked them.

Evolutionary change #2: simplicity. 40 hours of storage is easier to manage than a 6-hour tape. With a DVR when you finish a program, you delete it. When you record a new program, it never records over the program you haven't finished. Simplicity extends throughout the DVR experience. It allowed consumers to manage their personal entertainment easily on a single device with a program guide for easier recording.

The VCR, DVD, and DVR brought control over TV into the living room, changing consumers' entire concept of entertainment. Mainstream consumption habits shifted to a broader range of programming and entertainment while the amount of time people spent in front of the TV continued to increase. Getting more choices over what and when to watch entertainment increased people's expectations and appetites for content. It was this expectation that content could be available when and where you wanted it that brought about the next seismic shift in personal TV: the Internet.

The Internet and TV: A Digital Frankenstein

In 2004, digital video invaded the Internet.

Initially, delivering video over the Internet was an expensive proposition and the experience of watching large files was generally unsatisfactory. Storage and transmission costs for the large files meant that relatively few files existed, and those that did were generally removed quickly. Less than one third of US households at the time had high speed broadband and that meant most viewers were waiting for long periods of time for video to download. Like other technological innovations, the possibility of meaningful streaming content on the Internet was not immediately matched by the reality. Still, adoption rates climbed. Broadband connections grew, and professional producers began to deliver their content over the Internet as well.

In 2005, YouTube was launched. In 2009 estimates placed the number of viewers who watch YouTube at roughly the equivalent of a Super Bowl audience, every day of the year. Interesting yes, but YouTube is dominated by noncommercial user-generated content, so although marketers dream of electric ads to reach that audience, from a professional TV perspective, YouTube is part of a parallel universe. YouTube introduced consumers to the idea of video on the Internet but Hulu delivered TV.

In 2010, two-thirds of Americans under the age of 24 regularly watched their TV shows on the computer, and 70 percent of Americans with a broadband connection have watched video on the Internet (CEA/Nielsen). In August of 2009, the Hulu audience surpassed Time Warner audience (the second largest cable company in the United States).

When 70 percent of the US Internet users watch online video, and Hulu garners 38 million viewers a month, the idea of watching video delivered by the Internet is no longer a novelty, or a target for early adopters. Overwhelmingly, the preferred screen for viewing professional content remains the television. The migration to PC viewing is driven by opportunities that are not available on the preferred TV screen: missed episodes, trying out new shows recommended by your friends, or watching content you can't get on your TV (CEA and Nielsen).

This isn't to say users won't continue to use the PC and other devices to watch entertainment. There are times and places where the PC is a better solution, notably, say, the lunch hour, as evidenced by the fact that 65 percent of users who stream video online stream video between the hours of 8 and 5 on weekdays (Nielsen).

"Consumer uptake of Internet on TV has also passed the fulcrum," Tawny Schlieski said as we wrapped up our chat. "The simple functionality of a deep video-on-demand library that enables consumers to find and watch the TV they are interested in is a Pandora's box that cannot be closed. The lure of the big TV is strong. Today, even though getting Internet content to the TV is often complex and clunky, nearly a quarter of streaming video users have done it. Consumers have seen the future, and they are hungry for it."

The content of TV is no longer constrained to the TV screen in the home. Viewing of that entertainment content across multiple screens has changed consumers' expectations for how television content should be delivered. Consumers now feel that they should be able to watch their content when and where they want. They assume that content recorded on the DVR in the living room should not be trapped there. Video streams from Internet content sites like Hulu or ABC.com should not be chained to the small screen attached to a keyboard. Consumer's now have the expectation that it's their content and it should go with them wherever they go.

The idea that your TV experience could be tailored to your specific interests is becoming a fairly common assumption in the minds of consumers. Like the N'Sync tracking device people can now imagine a device that gives them exactly what they want on whatever device is available to them. Software, like Pattie Maes' intelligent agents, has already begun to make it's way into the intelligence of video services like NetFlix and Amazon. For consumers personal TV is a reality that they are just seeing the beginnings of and, as Schlieski told us, they like what they see.

The problem remains how do we pay for personal TV? Looking back at history we can see that advertising and subscription have been the leading means for making money in the entertainment industries. But the trouble is that there are some massive adjustments that need to happen to make personal TV and the future of entertainment continue to thrive.

Paying for Personal TV: The Cast of Characters

"I don't know if the average TV viewer realizes the strain that is being put on the entertainment industry today by the Internet," Marcelino Ford-Livene told me once when we were discussing the dynamics of personal TV and its broader implications on the entertainment industry. Ford-Levine lives in Los Angeles. He's an attorney who's worked at the Federal Communications Commission, *TV Guide* and entertainment companies both on the east and west coasts. He's currently the Secretary of the Academy of Television Arts and Sciences and I'm lucky enough to have been working with him for the past few years at Intel on the future of TV. Marcelino has incredible insights into the legal and business sides of how this puzzle fits together.

For us to understand the drama of how we can personalize the TV experience, we first have to get to know the cast of characters (Figure 6.3). Ford-Livene separated this way.

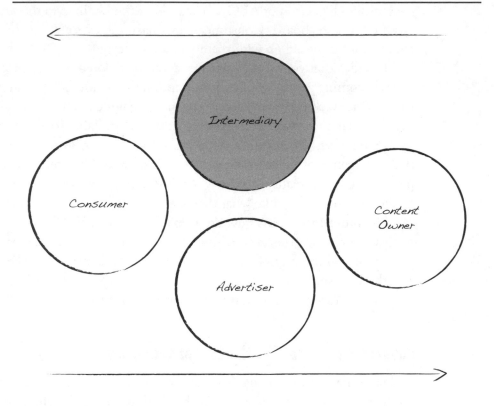

Figure 6.3   The four actors in our drama

The Consumer

The first key player in the drama is the consumer. The future of entertainment all starts with them. When you think about what this cast of characters really looks like from a monetization standpoint, the buck starts and stops with the consumer. The other three characters want to reach the consumer because ultimately it's the consumer who pays for everything.

So what needs to happen? Today consumers have a set of services, devices, and experiences that they are currently paying for. The ultimate challenge for the rest of our cast of characters is to find a way to provide something new that ultimately impresses the consumer so much that they have to have it. They will pay for it and they will seek it out.

There are plenty of examples of this: the introduction of TV over radio, the switch from black and white to color, and the introduction of new service providers like cable and satellite. Once people see this new device or service and freely engage with it in large numbers then it becomes economically viable. People have to want it en masse. It's all about large numbers.

As we start looking for what these new experiences might be, we can see that over the last 10 years there have been some interesting technical innovations. These were good ideas that had promise with some early technology adopter markets. But these ideas usually end up falling by the wayside because there's no way to effectively develop the scale and reach that's really needed for it to be widely adopted. You have to have the wide adoption to pay for itself with advertising or subscriptions. Personal TV is going to get paid for in one or three ways. It's either going to be supported by an advertiser, paid for or subscribed to by the consumers, or a kind of hybrid sponsorship model that has more functional integration and other attributes.

Advertiser/Sponsor

The next player in our cast of characters it the advertiser. The advertiser's ultimate goal is to get their product and pitch in front of the consumer to raise the consumer's interest in that product and possibly buy it. The best way to do this is to get directly in front of the consumer.

The traditional way that consumers get programming is from a paid TV operator, like a cable provider or broadcaster. If you're an advertiser, the traditional way that consumers get their branded message on television is via a value chain of advertising agencies, media buyer and stand practices that allows the advertiser to get their message in front of the consumer packaged with other ads and entertainment. This is the way that things have been done for decades.

You can do things differently on the Internet but it's challenging. You could set up a Web site and put up your branded messages and content with the hope that the consumer will find you on the Internet and think that your advertising and content is interesting enough that they will keep coming back. But this model really hasn't proven itself to be mainstream yet.

Content Owner

Another player is the content owner/creator. They are the people or companies who own the rights to the content. They're the ones that need to get paid for the use of their content, either by the consumer or the advertiser. Ultimately they want to get their product in front of the consumer. It would be ideal if there was a straightforward way to get their content in front of the consumer without having to go through any distributors or intermediaries (the fourth in our cast of characters).

The Internet provides this direct link to the consumer. If I'm a content creator, I can create my content, I can put it up on a Web site and if viewer can find it, if they can gain access to it, I can develop a one-to-one relationship with the viewer who is consuming my product as often as I can make it available and refreshed for them.

The challenge for nontraditional content providers in this new connected environment is that they have to prove their value to the consumer sufficiently so that the consumer will pay for the content or the consumer will want it so much that they are willing to watch advertising along with it.

Intermediary

When you talk about the world of broadcast whether it's broadcast television or cable network television as an example, a variety of players stand between the content creator and the consumer. These intermediaries include broadcasters, cable channels, and service providers. These intermediaries are struggling to innovate. The one-to-one connection between the consumer and the advertiser or content creator could greatly disrupt how these intermediaries make money.

Consumer habits and technology advancement are changing the landscape for the intermediaries. This is nothing new. This landscape has been in constant change since the broad distribution of TV and entertainment. One could argue that one thing that these intermediaries do well is adapt. You could also say that the reason these intermediaries are still around today through so much change is that they are a needed ingredient and player in this cast of characters.

A Tale of Two Models

We can generalize the way our cast of characters interacts with one another by breaking the world into two models or business flows. The first is the Intermediary Model that exists for the delivery of the majority of mainstream entertainment to the TV, as shown in Figure 6.4.

The content provider produces their content and delivers it to an intermediary. The intermediary bundles the content with advertising and delivers that bundle to the consumer. To get in front of the consumer the advertiser pays the intermediary and after taking a portion of this advertising revenue the content owner is paid by the intermediary.

The delivery of this content and advertising bundle can be through a number of mechanisms. In the early days of mainstream TV this was done via broadcast signal. In this case the bundle was assembled by the broadcaster and beamed to the consumer. Over the years the delivery mechanism for the bundle has changed. Cable and satellite TV are great examples of innovation in delivery technology but the assembly and delivery method of one bundle to many different users has remained the same.

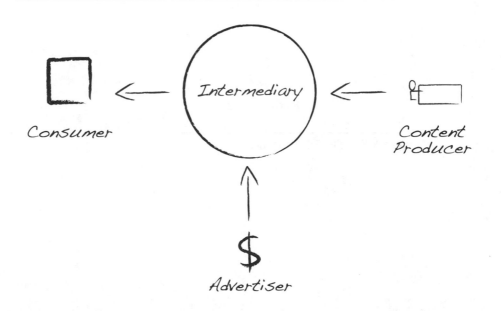

Figure 6.4 The Intermediary Model

The Direct Model, illustrated in Figure 6.5, is what can be possible when the content provider has a direct relationship with the consumer. This direct relationship is usually made possible by delivering the content to the consumer via the Internet. In the Direct Model the content provider creates their content and sends it directly to the consumer. Typically this is done by posting the TV or entertainment on a Web site that the consumer can go to. It is on this Web site or sometimes imbedded in the entertainment itself that the advertising is bundled. Here the advertiser pays the content provider directly to be included in the entertainment or on the Web site. The intermediary has been removed from the model.

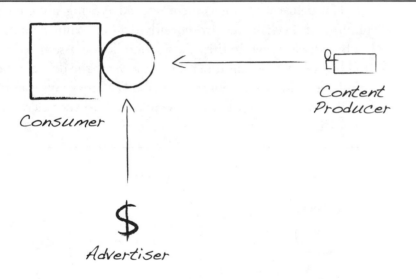

Figure 6.5   The Direct Model

Tension in the System

The differences between the two models are generating tension in the system. On one hand you have the Intermediary Model. This is the model that everyone knows and it has worked for nearly fifty years. But there is tension in the system from the Direct Model. There's pressure coming from the Internet and the promise of nearly 15 billion connected devices by 2015. As we talked about in the Ubiquitous TV chapter, these devices are not just TVs and set-top boxes. The tension is coming from the fact that TV could be available on any device that has the ability to connect to the Internet.

The Direct Model began changing things around 2005. It changed how media was distributed. Before TV and entertainment was delivered one to many. This means that a single intermediary delivered the advertising and entertainment bundle to many consumers. The Direct Model enabled a one-to-one approach, where a single content provider reaches a single viewer. It is this one-to-one connection that enables personalized TV.

The Direct Model holds the personalization and promise of the Internet. People understand that the Internet gives them personal access to the information, news and the entertainment they love. It's not a far leap to imagine that same style of personalization for all entertainment. The Direct Model is very attractive to advertisers and content providers.

But things really aren't that simple.

The Direct Model is putting pressure on the intermediaries. They are searching for ways to control their relationship with the consumer, adapting as they always have to continue to attract people to their shows. But there is a fundamental flaw in the Direct Model. It can't pay for itself. There just aren't enough people willing to pay for subscriptions directly from the content owners to make a business profitable. Also there aren't enough people watching entertainment in the Direct Model to entice the advertisers to sponsor enough programming to make a business profitable. The numbers just don't work out.

It doesn't stop there. As it turns out, creating high quality TV and entertainment is expensive. In 2007 the average cost of an hour-long TV drama was over USD 2 million and the average cost to produce a Hollywood movie was close to USD 75 million (*New York Times* and *Variety*). The Intermediary Model has a working mechanism to develop, fund, and distribute content on the scale where it is profitable. I should note that the funding approach for the Intermediary Model is constantly in flux as intermediaries and content producers innovate to bring down costs of production while at the same time raising the profit from the distribution.

There's tension going both ways. The Intermediary Model is putting tension of the Direct Model. The idealized promise of Internet distribution was that a small content producer could just grab a video camera and make their own movie or TV show. Then they could take that content and put it online, selling some advertising space. This has worked for niche content producers creating new shows but the level of money needed for long form mainstream content makes it currently unattainable and unsustainable in the Direct Model.

Ford-Livene sees the distinction between long and short form video as being important to this discussion. "Most of the short form that we've seen over the last several years has been primarily either user generated and nonprofessional. It's usually between thirty seconds and seven minutes long," he explained. "It's what makes up most of the video on YouTube. It's also what you would see on a Facebook."

The number of people watching this type of video content is not insignificant. The challenge is that nobody has really shown effectively that they can monetize this type of short form video. As we talked about earlier, Facebook has turned a profit using advertising but that is mainly based on advertising dollars from their user base, not directly from this kind of video. This is a great example of the current flaws with the Direct Model.

Advertisers want to reach as many consumers as possible. They need a large scale audience and wide reach to be affective. The advertisers also are looking for their advertising dollars to be measurable as well.

Traditionally most advertisers have gone for advertising on longer formats. These are shows and entertainment that is typically 30 minutes or longer. But this doesn't mean that they will only advertise on traditional TV. Recently advertisers have been placing ads in traditional primetime and daytime programming that is distributed via the Internet. For these advertisers the Intermediary Model has been successful for them; they use their budgets to buy gross rating points, to buy people's attention and get the ratings points they need to make their campaigns affective.

But the tension doesn't stop there. There's tension between the traditional advertising approach in the Intermediary Model and the type of audience interaction that could be provided in the Direct Model. The traditional advertising approach is designed to serve up advertising and entertainment derived from the perceived profiles of the viewer. It measures that audience, typically via a service like Nielson ratings, and then the intermediaries are able to provide whatever the advertiser wants in terms of audience size. This is also known as scale and reach.

The Direct Model allows for a advertising project creators and owners to have more of a direct relationship with a consumer. There's a feeling from advertisers that if they own their own destination and they are in charge of the content then they can communicate directly with the consumers. As an advertiser if I do this then I can start to capture more attention and save the costs that I'd traditionally have to share with others in the Intermediary Model.

So there's tension on both sides. There's the Direct Model that's struggling to try to figure out an economic model that makes sense. There's the Intermediary Model that's struggling to change the way it's currently doing business to deliver the same type of capability.

What's driving all this tension and change is the underlying technology. The changes and advancements in the underlying hardware and software are enabling changes in both models. Over the next three to five years the devices that we have in our living rooms or in our TV rooms will allow us to gain access to the Internet and to watch television at the same time. The tension between the two models is healthy. It's trying to figure out where that transformation is taking place. How is it going to happen? What is the scale and reach going to be? How is that going to be nurtured and ultimately how are you going to monetize that and then pay for the programming?

More Tension: Cracks in the Economics

The tension doesn't stop at the friction between the two models. The pressure from the shift in consumer behavior and the increasingly ability to be entertained on multiple devices is also affecting the advertising industry.

The amount of time people are spending watching video via a broadband connection is rising. In 2009 is was about 14 billion hours (Nielsen 2010). Now compared to traditional living room TV watching this is still quite small. In 2009 540 billion hours of programming was consumed on the TV (Comscore 2010). But advertisers are seeing erosion on specific shows. This means that there are some TV shows that are actually losing their audience. People are not sitting down in front of their TVs at a specific time to watch a specific show. The industry calls this appointment TV. The appointment viewing of many TV shows is being lost.

Where are these people going? How are they still watching an incredibly large amount of TV? Some are shifting their viewing times, which means they are using a DVR to record the show when it's on so they can watch it later. Also people really are beginning to watch traditional TV shows on the Internet.

This is worrisome to the advertisers and intermediaries because appointment TV, the traditional way people sit down in front of the TV at a specific time, is the foundation of the moneymaking engine of the Intermediary Model. If people are not watching during those critical hours and in that way, the underlying economics that have funded the Intermediary Model no longer work. The advertising spaces in those shows are no longer as valuable as they used to be.

We're starting to see cracks in the system just like we saw in the music industry a few years back. The foundation of the economics of how money is spent and made is no longer working. This is a problem because the advertisers need to reach their audience and if they can't reach them using the traditional approach then they will search for something new. And the fact is this has already begun.

More Tension: Deficit Financing

One of the flaws in the Direct Model is a lack of sustainable funding for projects. One of the things that the Intermediary Model has going for it is that it has been around for a while and has a functioning economic model. Production companies have a way, working with the intermediaries, to come up with the substantial dollars needed to develop and produce big budget entertainment. They do this using a practice called deficit financing.

Deficit financing is a financing strategy used by the producer of a project like a television show, movie, or any kind of big budget entertainment. To get the project off the ground the producer needs to come up with a large portion of the total budget before the project can get made. This budget is needed to pay the writer, director, and producer as well as the crew members and the marketing budget.

Coming up with this large amount of money is called the front end of the project. The producer does this with the hope that the project will make its money back on the back end of the project. The back end is after the project is made and released. The producer is then hoping to make the money back though syndication of the project or international distribution. To get the project made the producer literally must go into a deficit.

Producers and production companies don't have this large amount of money on hand so to raise the money needed they will borrow it and get a third party to finance the project. What that then means is that the producer doesn't make any money until everyone else is paid back. Because it is such a large amount of money paying back takes a really long time.

This type of deficit financing has had a dramatic affect on how entertainment is produced. As an example for a typical TV show it could take up to 80 aired episodes or more to make back enough money to repay the original loan needed to get the show produced. TV shows can cost anywhere from USD 3 to 7 million per episode. Part of the reason for this is that the production values, the look of the show has to compete with big budget Hollywood movies.

To help with these growing costs more studios and networks are coming in to underwrite the cost of these productions. This is a substantial shift. After the 2007–2008 writer's strike there have been fewer and fewer scripts that graduate out of the development cycle to get made into TV pilots. What that means is that producers and studios can't afford to test out a broad range of ideas like they used to. In 1990 about 100 television pilots for new shows were made for the three major broadcasters (ABC, CBS, and NBC). By 2009 that number had fallen to just 65 pilots (*Entertainment Weekly*).

Deficit financing puts an incredible amount of stress on the system. Clever production companies and studios have made it work but with this looming debt and already low success rate in mind you can see why many are resistant to the Direct Model. Without a clear path to profit and revenue many in the entertainment industry can't afford to gamble on the one-to-one direct to consumer model. There is barely enough funding as it is with the current model so for many the Direct Model is a threat to the entire way they do business.

The pressure from deficit financing makes it difficult for content owners to innovate. With production costs running so high and the need to turn a profit so immediate any diversion from the Intermediary Model is incredibly risky.

The Goal: Addressability

Where does all of this lead us? Well, we know that people love the idea of personal TV. Over the last few decades content and the entertainment, computing and advertising industries have been evolving to meet the consumers expectations of more choice and control. But we also know the market realities that somehow, somewhere TV needs to be paid for and that is done either through a straight subscription or through advertising. Cable and satellite TV delivery showed us that many consumers will pay for increased choice and access to specific premium content. This is an important part of the solution, but as subscription models are well established we won't delve into them here. Broadcast TV and the Internet have also shown us that advertising will play a significant role and one that is far more complicated.

When the Internet and computing capabilities are built into advanced set-top boxes and TVs, both the Intermediary and the Direct Models advertisers are interested in increasing the reach, effectiveness, and interactivity of their advertising messages. To accomplish this they look to addressability.

Addressability is the capability to send an appropriate advertisement to a specific TV or CE device based on information the advertiser might have about that household. This could be as simple as a zip code for local advertisers or as complicated as a robust user profile. Advertisers are attracted to this feature because they will be able to deliver the right advertising to the right group of people giving them a significant incremental yield through refining their targeting.

Once the advertiser has reached the appropriate audience they can then use the capabilities of an interactive platform to deepen their engagement with the consumer. This could be as simple as allowing the consumer to request more information about a product; sometimes called request for information, or RFI. Or it could be more complex like a feature called *telescoping*. Telescoping allows consumers to request and access more information on the product that's being advertised during the commercial. This is a big deal to the advertisers because this would allow them to turn an advertisement into a direct sale.

With advanced set-top boxes and TVs advertisers will be able to innovate and go beyond the typical 15- and 30-second advertising format. New advertising formats will depend greatly on the efficacy and ease of use of the user interface. Advances in how consumers interact with their TV and entertainment will be critical. Current user interfaces for entertainment are limited and really do limit the amount of time a consumer is willing to spend using them.

To make addressability a reality we'll need three key components. First we need a means for creating a consumer profile. This profile could be for each consumer or each TV viewer in the house but ultimately we really should get to a point where we have blended profiles for family groupings as well. Traditionally the data that's been used just for regular advertising in a non-addressable world were things like age, gender, income level, number of partners or kids in the household, and general location.

The goal of the profile is to build a credible, consistent, and predictable profile of who's watching the television at any given point in time. This is the most important information that an advertiser or intermediary is looking for. It's also extremely important that these profiles a locked away and are not accessible by unauthorized parties.

The second component for addressability is the ability to measure the audience. What good is targeting and addressability if the advertiser can't measure how many people have actually consumed the advertisement? Advertisers are interested in not only brand recall and brand impressions, but also in what is called *lift*. Lift measures if the advertisement is actually working. Is the viewer turning into a customer, going into the store and buying the product or asking for the service? Any credible advanced advertising solution needs to have a component that measures the audience and the resulting lift.

The third and final component for addressability is the delivery of the addressable or interactive advertisement. The delivery of the advertisement is going to be absolutely critical in an environment where there's tremendous fragmentation of content providers and intermediaries.

These three components are the main areas where the entertainment, computing, and advertising industries are concentrating to deliver a new kind of advertising. This personalized and addressable advertising provides a way to pay for personalized TV. Consumers get access to the wide range of entertainment they are interested in on all of their devices while the content owners, advertisers, and intermediaries can get paid for that content and continue to provide the funding to produce and distribute that entertainment.

The Architecture of Personalized TV

The business complexities behind Personal TV are certainly quite large. To deliver on the promise addressable advertising, whether we use the Intermediary Model or the Direct Model, will have significant hardware, software, and networking implications. To explore these implications let's lay out a possible network architecture for Personal TV that employs our actors; Consumer, Advertiser/Sponsor, Content Owner, and Intermediary. The technologies we discussed in the Informative TV and Ubiquitous TV chapters allow us to greatly simplify our network architecture, as illustrated in Figure 6.6. The key components of our architecture are a consumer device with the ability to identify the person using the device. Next we will need that consumer device to be connected to the Internet via a wired or wireless connection. For example, in Figure 6.6 we will work under the assumption that all connections are wireless. After we have established a connection to the Internet we will also need both a content server (Content Owner) and an advertising server (Advertiser/Sponsor. The content server could be run directly by the content producer or it could be managed and run by an intermediary like a broadcaster or studio (Intermediary).

Figure 6.6 Consumer, Content Owner, Advertiser/Sponsor, Intermediary: Our cast of characters are in place

Now the first step in our process is for the device to identify the consumer, as shown in Figure 6.7. The most simplistic would be for the device to assume that the person using the device is the owner. This is how most TVs operate today. The TV doesn't make any distinction between people in the household it simply lumps everyone together into a single user set. This is how companies like Nielson measure the rating points by which the success or failure of TV programming is judged. This is also the means by which the audience size is used for the selling of advertising.

Another way for the device to identify the user would be like a PC or cell phone, which assumes a single user or, if the device had multiple users, then each user would have a password to log on to the device. This is a bit more specific as it would identify who the exact user might be.

Other sensor technologies could help out here. Currently we have fingerprint analyzers on laptops and the industry is even working on accelerometers in remote controls or low fidelity camera, like I was shown at our Chandler site, that could identify the user or users of a device through a minimal amount of sensor data.

Of course, this identity information must be kept safe and protected. This can be accomplished through secure connections between the servers or even *anonymizing* the information that is sent out form the device. This type of data encryption is used for financial and medical records as well.

Figure 6.7 Consumer is identified and anonymously shared

Once the consumer is identified (marked with (I) in Figure 6.7) this protected identity is shared with a service server. This server can be managed and run by a third party or by an intermediary.

With the proper identification the content provider server can now send the person's personal TV shows, movies, games, and applications to the device, identified as (c) in Figure 6.8. With the ubiquitous connection between devices the consumer now has access to all of his or her entertainment whenever or wherever they might be. This is the same TV anywhere concept that Polltrack talked about our earlier conversation.

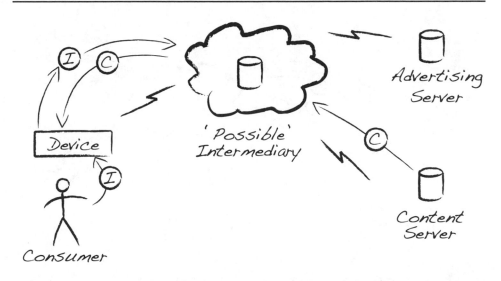

Figure 6.8 Content is sent to the consumer

The content can be pulled from multiple locations or content provider servers that are managed by a wide variety of content producers and intermediaries.

At some point in the consumer enjoyment of the content advertising will need to be inserted into the entertainment. In this case an advertising server is used to insert an advertisement into the content stream, indicated by (a) in Figure 6.9.

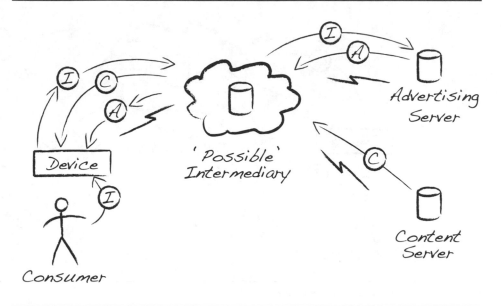

Figure 6.9   Appropriate advertising is sent to the consumer

The sale of this advertising space within the content would be done in bulk with an agreement between the advertiser and the content owner or intermediary. This could also be done on the fly with a consumer-specific advertisement sent directly to the consumer's device.

Once the consumer has watched the advertisement they can continue watching their entertainment. Behind the scenes an anonymous report, indicated with (r) in Figure 6.10, is sent back to the advertising and content server, informing them that the advertisement was delivered and watched by the consumer. This simple action is of great interest to the business of entertainment. Currently there is no means to verify that a specific advertisement was watched by a specific consumer. The return of this information makes the advertising addressable advertising.

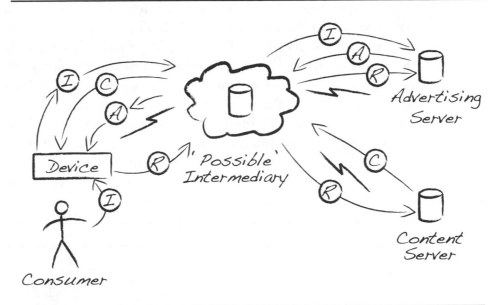

Figure 6.10 Both Content and Advertising servers are notified that content and advertising was delivered

The Magic Red Button

The infrastructure and economics needed to realistically bring about personal TV are certainly complex but no more complicated than the innovations that brought consumers cable, satellite, or even Internet TV. Television, entertainment, and advertising have a long history of technical evolution and adaptation. It is these industries' ability to adapt that has allowed them to continually capture the consumer's imagination and provide more entertainment, choice, and freedom. Personal TV is the next step in this evolution.

People will always try to personalize their devices and gadgets. Consumers have an unending curiosity and appetite for stories, entertainment, and interaction. It is industry's challenge to listen to listen to that curiosity and feed that appetite. However, as the story below shows us, there may be a few instances when not even the most brilliant innovation can bring about every consumer's perfect personalized device.

Dr. Genevieve Bell and Eric Dishman did another piece of field research on the same trip I told you about at the beginning of this chapter. This time they were in the suburbs of Baltimore, Maryland. They were talking with the Swanson family. The Swansons were in the middle of remodeling their modest two-bedroom home. Just before the interview the kitchen portion of the remodel was completed. The upstairs was still a mess and not yet done.

When they had Bill Swanson construct his perfect personalized device he put together a crude cardboard box with a red button on it (Figure 6.11).

"What does it do?" Dr. Bell asked about the personalized device.

"When I press this button," Bill replied, "my wife makes a decision about what carpet she wants upstairs and we can get our house back in order."

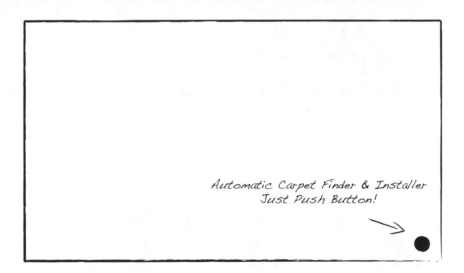

Figure 6.11 The magic red button

Chapter 7

The Implications of our Digital Future

A CONVERSATION WITH SENATOR STEPHEN CONROY

The year 2007 saw a shift in the government of Australia. The more conservative Liberal and National parties led by John Howard were defeated by the Australian Labor Party, electing Kevin Rudd to be Prime Minister of Australia. As a part of this shift Stephen Conroy, a Senator for Victoria in the Labor party, was appointed Minister for Broadband, Communications, and the Digital Economy.

Conroy's post is unique. There are very few government officials whose responsibilities touch both television and the Internet. From this vantage point Conroy is uniquely positioned as a direct contributor and steward for his county's entertainment and computing future.

On the top of Conroy's agenda is the National Broadband Network (NBN). This is the largest nation-building infrastructure project in Australia's history with an estimated cost of 43 billion Australian dollars (AUD). It is a unique infrastructure project with a joint public-private partnership designed to build out a broadband grid for the entire nation. Its goal is to build the technical infrastructure to enable Australia's digital economy—bringing reforms to education, healthcare, industry, innovation, and entertainment.

This will mean connecting up all Australian homes, schools, and workplaces to high-speed Internet by 2017.

In addition to his oversight of the NBN, Senator Conroy is also overseeing Australia's digital television switchover, which commenced in 2010, as well as changes in media law, security, and community broadcasting and its affects on Australian's national broadcasters the Australian Broadcasting Corporation (ABC) and the Special Broadcasting Service (SBS).

Conroy has a long history of public service and knows that he finds himself at a significant moment. The two worlds of television and the Internet are rapidly coming together, overlapping and radically changing each other. The decisions that he and his government make will shape an entire country's media, entertainment, and social landscape. Even with this daunting task in front of him, Conroy is energetic, generous, and has a lightening fast sense of humor. We sat down to talk and get his perspective on where the future of entertainment is going and what needs to be done to get us there.

STEPHEN CONROY: Well, I think we all know that we're going to have HD TVs with Internet enabled technology. I see this as a really good thing for a couple of reasons. One might be unexpected for you. Here's why—over the years I think families have ventured away from the lounge room where most TVs are. That's the living room for you Americans.

I think with these better TVs and more technology we could see families going back to the lounge room. When we say home entertainment center, that's just what it's going to be. It really will have everything. You'll be able to watch whatever you want and as the technology advances you'll have even more access to information and new services. You'll be able to watch it on your TV screens rather than on your computer. I see it as a kind of reconsolidation.

That's not to say there's not going to be people watching the TV screens. Everyone has got a TV screen now. In Australia it's something like 3.4 TVs per home. There's one in the family room, there's one in the parent's bedroom, there's usually one or two in kids' bedrooms as well nowadays. I think all of that will become enabled. They'll take a little bit longer for those outer TVs to convert, though they're going to need a set top box, and the new levels of set top boxes will be coming in, certainly in Australia we'll have Internet capacity.

In fact, they're already starting to have it now. So, all of those screens will become able to be computer screens as well.

Once we have all these screens connected to the Internet I think it will be much more of an on-demand world. You'll be able to download your movie from Warner Brother's direct from Los Angeles. You'll also be able to get shows from any pay TV provider in Australia as well. Now this will be great for people, for consumers but it opens up some complicated challenges for the Australian pay TV model.

Let's look at Hong Kong IP TV as an example of how things could progress. In Hong Kong you can slice and dice anything you want to. You can buy one show for one hour, you can buy a genre, you can buy anything you like. This is very different than what we have today in our pay TV model. It's not so mix and match. That much choice will put pressure on the subscription pay TV models that exist in Australia, and the rest of the world.

Ultimately, at some point I think you will need someone to aggregate your TV shows for you. When you've got a million things you can choose from, you need someone to aggregate for you. This could be an interesting model, a kind of aggregation model. If you want to watch the news you could have the Channel 9 six o'clock news—and the news director at Channel 9 pick the 10 most interesting news stories or you could pick some brand name or broadcaster that will give you the sort of stuff you're interested in. You could pick your aggregator depending what you are interested in.

This kind of thing has already started a little. It's evolving the channels we have now. You can imagine that SBS is going to bring to you a particular kind of slice of television and the ABC is going to bring you another but the choice is much broader. In Australia all of these changes are coming from multi-channeling. The analog broadcasters finally worked out that they indeed have a future in TV and that future is multi-channeling digital.

It's been a long, painful process in Australia, but I actually think in the near future you will see some interesting developments. There are three main reasons for this.

The first is, the advancing technology has now reached a stage where no one can actually stop it. Some companies and broadcasters had tried to stop it or slow it down but they can't anymore. Second, we've now got a new government that actually wants to go forward faster than we've been going forward. And third, the Free to Air Broadcasters have managed to successfully impair their balance sheets to a stage where they're incredibly structurally at the weakest point they've been in a long time. So I've been lucky that there's been a convergence of things that have all happened at once. I think we're going to see a lot of change and be able to get a lot of things done.

***

In 2007 when the Rudd-lead Labor Party was campaigning they proposed the idea of the National Broadband Network (NBN). This notion of a nation-wide infrastructure is fundamental to the other changes that the Labor party envisioned, including a "Digital Education Revolution" with a laptop on the desk of school children from their sophomore years in high school through to graduation, as well as the introduction of a national curriculum and an education-oriented Web-portal for parents, students, teachers, and communities. Following Rudd's victory, the government set about beginning the Fibre to the Home (FTTH) network to be built in Australia. The aim of the program is to provide an Open Access Network with download speeds of 100 megabits per second to 90 percent of homes and businesses in Australia. The remaining 10 percent will be connected to the Internet via wireless and satellite connections. This will be a significant change as currently only about 70 percent of households are connected to high-speed Internet.

Connecting 100 percent of Australia with broadband Internet means Conroy is faced with an interesting conflict. On one hand he is pushing to provide Internet access to an entire country but on the other hand this connection will place increasing pressure on the entertainment rights and media law that these connections will bring about.

STEPHEN CONROY: In Australia, we have something called anti-siphoning. In 1992 Australia passed the Broadcasting Services Act. It acts as a prohibition on Subscription television licensees from acquiring rights to certain 'listed' sporting events, until a Free to Air Broadcaster has the right to televise those events. This includes sports like AFL, rugby, and cricket.

Currently, it also stops those same listed events from being shown exclusively on digital multi-channels and requires the broadcaster to simulcast the event on main channels. It's probably the strongest form of anti-siphoning of sporting events, and protects the Free To Air broadcast model better than anywhere else in the world.

In the UK if you want to watch sports, you go get Sky. Sky is the UK's largest pay-TV satellite provider. If you want anything else then you can go with the Free View box. Free View is a digital TV platform that gives you free TV. But if you want premium sports you have to pay Sky TV. That's not the case here in Australia.

In fact, the UK provides a really good example of why our regime is so important. As you may know, cricket is a sport which both Australians and the English are mad about, and there's no bigger game than when these two countries play. However, in the UK, in 2006 the England and Wales Cricket Board sold cricket coverage exclusively to Sky Sports. Now two interesting things occurred as a result: average live viewers fell by about 10 times, from something around 2 million people to just over 200 thousand, and yes, the cricket board got a higher contract for their rights, but not much higher. So what you saw was a massive privatization of a previously national event. And the interesting thing is, Sky Sports have a much higher coverage than 200 thousand viewers, but of course, the cricket games were sold on a premium package, which further reduced the pool of people who could watch the game.

In contrast, the majority of sports that Australians watch are available on Free to Air Broadcast TV. That's not by accident. This is a public policy designed for the anti-siphoning list. Meaning you can't take popular and sometime very lucrative sports programming and move it from broadcast TV across to Pay TV. A result of the Broadcasting Services Act is that it protects the Free to Air business model. It's really not designed to do that. The policy is designed to protect Australians so they didn't have to pay to watch a sporting event.

Right now, this is specific to sport in Australia. I think I can say that Australians are sports mad. It's true. I haven't seen any siphoning list of any cultural events. It's just sports because they are so popular and because of that so profitable. For example, I've received a recent study which has shown that the value of sports rights in Australia has been growing significantly under the anti-siphoning regime, and are very high, in terms of dollar per population, by international standards. If you take Australia's indigenous sport—Australian Football—the rights values have grown far beyond most rights in the world, and in fact, the head of the AFL has publically stated that he is pursuing a [AUD] 1 billion contract for the next five year rights deal, which would be a rise of over 25 percent from the last contract. Now this is partly because the regime does not exclude Subscription TV completely, but says that Free TV must have first access to rights. In the end, the last rights deal ended up as a combined bid from two Free to Air Broadcasters and Foxtel.

Well, I've got to make a couple decisions around anti-siphoning in the very near future. I've got to make a decision about the Internet and while I can in the short-term protect Free to Air broadcast of Australian sporting events like women's international netball. But if a broadcaster decides that they don't want to protect Australian sports on broadcast TV then they can go to a subscription model on the Internet. Right now they could do that because the Internet is different than pay TV or Free to Air broadcast TV. In other words they could take it off the air and just offer it for 20 bucks [AUD 20] on the Internet. So being able to deliver entertainment and sporting events via the Internet to those new TVs we were just talking about has a massive affect on how traditional TV models work.

So with international sporting content that's on the list currently, if the sports rights holder wants to circumvent the anti-siphoning list, they can't show it on Foxtel as that would be a breach of their license condition, but they could broadcast it exclusively on the Internet.

For example, an overseas organization, say for a sporting event like the Olympics[†], could just start streaming the Olympics on IP TV or their own Olympic channel. If they did this it's possible then that they could make it a subscription service. Now the question is can I force it then to be on a Free to Air broadcast channel? The answer is no, I actually can't. But, at the moment you can rely on the fact that, at this moment, free to air broadcast TV is typically the most lucrative avenue for distributing you content, and in addition, to a greater or lesser extent, all sporting rights holders do have some interest in maximizing their viewing audience. In the case of the Olympics they explicitly require free to air coverage in all countries.

However, with the ability to deliver sports and TV content via the Web or IP TV, I and the Australian government need to completely rethink how we approach sports on TV in our country, especially as access to, and cost of, high speed broadband grows.

Anti-siphoning is the most interesting of the policy aspects that I'm working on at the moment. I'm about to make a decision about the Internet rights and whether they should be part of the anti-siphoning list. If I want to prevent exclusive Internet broadcasting of listed events, I can probably do it for all Australian produced sporting content, but I don't think I can do it for international content and sporting events.

It's the most interesting challenge, because when you think about it, this all affects the Australian conversion and evolution into the future of entertainment. It's also interesting for me because it's a uniquely Australian issue but will have a tremendous effect.

***

In 2010 Conroy is overseeing Australia's switch from analog TV to digital Television. Television has a long and complicated history in Australia— there were early experiments in the 1920s and 1930s but "real" television started in 1956, just in time for the Summer Olympics in Melbourne —the opening ceremonies were broadcast live. Sport has always been popular on Australian television!

From its earliest days, however, there were conversations about what the right content should be for Australian audiences. Production costs and technology barriers initially meant that much television content was imported from the United States and the United Kingdom. Local content was live, but anything that required post-production etc, came from elsewhere. According to some estimates as much as eighty percent of Australian television content in the 1960s came from the United States. Government inquiries suggested the need for support of local content production but it wasn't until the 1970s and 1980s that Australian-made content really flourished on Australian television. This paralleled moves in Australian popular culture more generally with Australian music, movies and fiction really finding distinctive vernacular voices. Yet, even with the appearance of some classic and long run Australian dramas, sitcoms and talent and variety shows, debates about what appears in

Australian television rage on. In recent years, worries about the Americanization of Australian language and culture have dominated the media. Ironically, this is happening as new Australian television shows, like *Underbelly*—a gritty drama about urban criminal activity in Sydney and Melbourne, chalk up record audiences.

The digital switchover is taking place against the backdrop of this larger conversation about Australian culture, Australian content, and Australian media ownership.

STEPHEN CONROY: The digital switchover is a key initiative for us. We've got our first region to be switched over in the middle of 2010, in Mildura, in north-western Victoria. We're switching the analog signal off in Mildura. It's a nice confined market and until recently it's only ever had two free-to-air networks.

What happened was a third commercial channel decided to start broadcasting in digital only. So, everyone in Mildura went and bought a digital set top box. They got over 70 percent penetration, which, for Australia, is very high. It's high because it was the only way to get the third channel. People went out and bought it because they finally wanted the chance to get the third channel. So that's why we decided to start the digital switch over in Mildura. It was already the highest penetration and it has a nice confined simple market.

Now this brings up an interesting and tricky topic. Ultimately all these digital set top boxes needed for the digital switchover will be Internet-enabled. The implications for media law will be quite large. In Australia, we currently have something called the 75 percent reach rule. It was also a part of that Broadcasting Services Act that was passed in 1992. It says that one owner can only reach 75 percent of the Australian viewing public. In other words, a broadcaster can only own their capital cities. This is why a channel like Channel 9 here in Australia only operates in Sydney, Melbourne, and Brisbane. We call it the 75 percent rule, that's not the official name but we call it that. Now, imagine if broadcasters start streaming entertainment live online. That means technically that they could potentially reach 100 percent of Australia.

So we've got a media law that restricts the reach of a broadcaster and yet with the flick of a switch, that broadcaster can reach the entire country.

Pretend for a moment that the National Broadband Network (NBN) is here in five years' time. When we flick that switch a broadcaster will be able to reach 100 percent of Australians via broadband. That's a reality. So there's a massive reconfiguring of Australia's media laws that has to happen.

I've said publicly that this world of Internet-delivered TV is coming. Right now not everyone has the equipment and not everyone has a connection here but in five years' time, it is going to be a serious question. So we have to start thinking about the changes to the media law right now. We've got all these archaic media laws that were based on broadcast license areas. Back then they were, importantly, trying to foster media diversity by not having one owner have access to 100 percent of Australia. But with the National Broadband Network and advances in TV technology that world is going to be dead. The whole concept of media diversity as it exists in Australia today, trying to maximize media ownership so we don't have a concentration of ownership, is completely and utterly under siege at the moment.

So another big question I've been asking myself is; how do we maintain media diversity in Australia in the future. I've been asking myself who's going to become the aggregators, because a million choices is no choice because you don't know where to walk. How would you know? So you're going to have to trust someone to aggregate for you.

At the moment, 87 percent of Australians go to the same four Web sites to access their news. So it's the ABC, it's Murdoch's News Limited - MSN News, and it's Fairfax. Australians basically go to those four Web sites, over-whelmingly. That tells us that even in a world in near infinite choice brands can survive.

That's why I say, providing the Free to Air broadcasters get their act together, they can actually survive in this world. They can still be the aggregators, and that's all they are now. They aggregate content now. They can still be the aggregators but they've got to understand the changes coming. So I think these broadcasters need to find a way to change or technology is going to run over the top of them in about five years.

Just imagine when we start getting 100-Mb connections to people's homes. Imagine the products and services that will be available. Two years ago, this didn't exist—I'm holding up an iPhone†. Now there's something like 70,000 apps. And that's just today. We don't have any idea how many apps there are going to be.

So, it's very exciting, but it's also quite terrifying. If I was going to try to take the spirit of the existing laws on the Internet—it would not be possible. Therefore massive change is coming to Australia's media laws and the media sector, massive change.

So thinking about Australian content on Australian broadcast networks; the next issue is the cost. An high quality Australian production like *Under Belly* [an intense three season drama, documenting the Australian underworld in Sydney and Melbourne] --or *McLeod's Daughters* [a long running drama centered on two sisters and their family farm] – were expensive to make: an estimate [AUD] 800,000 per episode of Underbelly, for instance an episode. But broadcasters can buy an episode of *Friends* for [AUD]50,000 and pretty much be assured that they are going to be able to attract enough viewers to sell their advertising and make money.

The question I have to ask myself is: How are we going to be able to protect Australian voices and continue to deliver Australian stories in the future? Well, ultimately you're going to have to have a strong national broadcaster.

I can see a time in the near future where the only place people are going to be able to find Australian voices and Australian stories is on the ABC and the SBS. Because of this we have already put a considerable investment into those two broadcasters. There will come a point where we've got to make a really fundamental decision about our national broadcasters.

Now an interesting point is that these broadcasters already have a strong online presence. They're following the model of the BBC (British Broadcasting Corporation). I think it's fabulous that it's cutting edge in many different ways. It's creating Internet communities and local programs. We've got money for creating virtual town halls so local content is being produced by local people.

But even having done all of that, there's a quantum jump somewhere down the track that we're going to have make. We're going to have to say, if we actually want Australian voices, Australian stories, Australian content, we have to massively invest in it because it will become harder and harder for commercial models to generate that type of content.

Now, having said that, the most successful shows this year have been Australian shows—*Underbelly 2* and *MasterChef Australia*. So, if it's good, Australians will still watch it.

Right now I haven't got the answers, but we know what the issues are going to be, which I think at the moment is the right way to approach the future of entertainment. We know where the points of contention and discussion are going to be in the next five to seven years. From where I'm sitting, those are the ones that I certainly think about.

Chapter 8

Social TV

The experience of watching television began as a social activity. People got together in bars to watch baseball games and boxing matches. Baseball's 1947 World Series between the New York Yankees and the Brooklyn Dodgers was televised from New York to Washington DC. The sixth game of the series was watched by around three million people, mostly in bars. The Ford Motor Company and Gillette shared the sponsorship for USD 65,000 (Magoun, *Television*. 2009, p. 96). But watching TV wasn't just limited to adults. Around the same time a bar owner in Hoboken, New Jersey got in trouble with the police because he would kick out the drinking regulars from 5:00 P.M. to 6:00 P.M. on weeknights so that the kids could come in and watch *Howdy Doody* (Frank, *On the Air*, p. 19).

When TV made its way into houses and apartments around the world it found a comfortable home in the most social room of all; the living room. Families gathered together to watch variety shows, dramas, and comedies. It became a cultural ritual. Watching television has always been social.

This social interaction around the TV and entertainment easily extends past traditional broadcast or cable TV. The original games consoles like the ones designed by Ralf Baer where intended to be multiplayer. All of the marketing from this time shows a family or a group of friends gathered around the TV, happily playing together. VHS and DVDs are no different. Family movie night is a tradition that stretches back as far as the devices were commercially available.

The cornerstone of the major TV broadcasters in America is prime time. Offically this is the time just after dinner lasting until the eleven o'clock news. It's the time of day when the entire family, no matter how big or small, gathers around the TV to relax. The very foundation of how TV networks and advertisers measure the success or failure of their programming is by measuring the *household* usage. The ratings for each show are based on the number of households that we watching a particular show. That's a very telling way of imagining who is watching the TV when it's on. At the moment the ratings system assumes when a TV set is watched, it's watched by everyone living in the home.

Now we know that this image is somewhat flawed. The reality of who is watching what TV when is far more complicated that this, but it is telling. The act of watching TV has for most of its existence been thought of as a social act. We get together in the same room and watch TV.

The proliferation of TV sets throughout the home is a relatively new phenomenon. TVs have moved into the bedroom, the kitchen, the den, the kid's room, and the basement or workout room. But even when we watch alone people still love to talk about TV.

The early clique was the water cooler where we got together to chat and discuss last night's episode. These days we've traded in the water cooler for the Internet, blogs, and social networking applications. On April 13, 2010, when the fan favorite TV show *Glee* returned to air, more than 16 percent of all blog postings in the United States contained the word *glee* (Trend Search). Even in this digital age there are 14 traditional print magazines specifically about TV. That just shows us that not only do we like to watch TV and talk about TV with our friends. Family and coworkers but we also like to read about what experts and complete strangers have to say about entertainment as well.

My point is a simple one—TV is social. Entertainment is social. The nature of the social activities are as vast and complicated as the people around the world who are watching it, but make no mistake, TV is social.

Why is this important? Well, in our previous chapters we have seen how the experience of watching TV and entertainment is going to change. When entertainment is delivered to a computing device (think Informative TV) that's connected to the Internet (think Ubiquitous TV) then that device is not only a means for personal entrainment and commerce (think Personal TV) but it's also a way that people can communicate with each other.

People like to talk to each other. We need it. Our families and social networks keep us company; they give us strength and purpose. It should be no surprise that if you give a person a device that can technically reach another person then we're going to figure out a way to use that device to talk to our friends and family.

Now when this whole thing gets interesting is when we combine this technology to connect people with an experience that is at its very core social: entertainment. It seems both natural and inevitable.

TV is social.

Entertainment is social.

People like to talk.

Add those very simple, very basic components together and the sum is fascinating and full of possibilities.

How will people talk to each other through their TVs?

Science fiction has given us some early visions to start with. Videophones like the ones imagined in films like *Minority Report* are fairly commonplace today with applications like Skype. Steven Spielberg and his team of designers and futurists even went so far as to put the video phone in a car for the movie, but the experience is one of the most common place, functional and boring in a movie that is brimming with technology imaginings.

The reality of social TV may be far more complicated and interesting than science fiction. We don't need an anthropologist like Dr. Bell to tell us that the intricacies of people's social interactions around the world are vast and varied. People communicate and interact with other people, their society, their government in so many different ways that they could never be captured in this book.

We don't know all the ways that people will use these technologies and entertainment innovations to connect with each other. We just know that they will and while some will be as expected as *Minority Report*'s mundane videophone many others will be surprising and wonderful.

In this final section of the book we're going to look at social interaction in broad strokes, exploring the technical and architectural implications of social TV interactions. But before we dive into that I wanted to introduce someone with a truly unique perspective on TV as a social device—Gary Wheelhouse.

Social TV from the Retail Floor

Gary Wheelhouse is the Manager for Social Media for Harvey Norman. Harvey Norman is the largest electronics and computer retailer in Australia and they are growing their presence globally in places like Slovenia, Ireland, Malaysia, New Zealand, and Singapore.

Wheelhouse has a unique position within Harvey Norman. He began his career down on the retail floor, running a store in Moore Park Australia. Anyone who is familiar with electronics and computer retailing will tell you that it is a rough and tumble business with thin margins and incredible competition. To compete you not only have to have low prices but you also have to know your customer. That means not only knowing what they want to buy and when they want to buy it, but it also means knowing how to keep them happy and how to keep them coming back time after time.

Wheelhouse is a master of this. In 2005 he was given the unique task of combining the TV and computer departments in a store called Domayne. In most big retail stores the TV and computer sections are kept far apart because for decades now people have thought of them as very different categories. But this is changing. Domayne is Harvey Norman's high-end concept store in downtown Sydney where shoppers can get everything they need for their home; from a new flat screen TV to a kitchen sink. But Domayne is far more than a typical one-stop-shopping store. It sells experiences. Wheelhouse was able to successfully combine TVs and computers into a single experience that made sense to shoppers and inspired new purchases.

Wheelhouse is also a trend watcher. I've walked around the massive exhibition floor at the Consumer Electronics Show (CES) with him and his perspective is a keen one. As he explained to me once; he not only has to figure out if a new technology is cool or not. But he also has to figure out how he could sell it to his real world customers. These are the same people he's been selling to for years. He knows them really well. He knows what they like. He knows what they will have to have, what they will put up with but even more than these I'd say he knows what they won't be interested in. What they will pass by. What will be too complicated or what technologies just aren't really ready for mass appeal yet.

This notion of social TV is one that Gary and I are equally interested in. Over the last few years he and I have batted around the meaning that it has in the real world. Not only about how we can actually build it (me) but also how we can actually sell it (him).

I asked him what he thought about the social nature of technologies and TV. What did he see was the future of the social experience through our connected devices? How does it intermingle with TV and entertainment?

GARY WHEELHOUSE: I love the idea of people tweeting and updating Facebook and being connected while they watch TV. Now they could be connected with fans of the different shows while they watch them live or after the show. In Facebook there are some really unique things people could do around TV shows and entertainment like creating Facebook events around shows and encouraging their friends and fans to RSVP and attend. There a big fan communities. I also like to think that they could socialize on the TV or on any device. It works either way.

Imagine I have a whole bunch of people following me on Twitter. They might not necessarily be the people I am connected to when I watch TV. In other words, I don't really want my friends at work to know that I have a secret habit that involves reality TV or *The Real Housewives Of New Jersey*! But I am happy to connect with fans of that genre for the duration the show is on—we have a common interest. So these are followers that are only relevant for set periods and content. This applies to all content—sport is another great example.

When you think about it it's great for TV networks, right? Imagine I'm tweeting I am watching TV live. That means I'm not time-shifting with a DVR like TiVo. Well if I'm watching live then I'm watching the commercials more than likely. When people time-shift they skip commercials and that's a problem for the networks and the advertisers. If I'm interacting with my TV and my friends while watching live TV then I'm also watching the commercials. It's the Holy Grail for networks and advertisers. It could go even further than that. Advertisers could get smart and start to appeal to social network users in those commercials.

BDJ: For you, what is a social TV?

GARY WHEELHOUSE: When I think about social TV I think about what people really do around TVs. I think about how your mates tell you what they like so you give it a look. It's the same thing with restaurants, hotels, or movies we like and recommend. People are already doing it now on different sites here and there. Maybe social TV could be something like Expedia reviews but instead of hotels it is TV shows and they are written by real people or even better your friends.

Also when I think about social TV you have to think about Twitter and Facebook these days. Social networking services like Twitter and Facebook on my TV could easily connect me to like-minded TV fans and make me part of a connected fan-base.

Here's a great opportunity: Have you seen the amount of fan fiction out there online? *Fan fiction* is where people write stories and scripts using characters from their favorite TV shows, movies, or books. Fan fiction is mostly posted on sites such as Livejournal and FanFiction.net. There is a real market for fans to link together and social media is the glue for that. Connect all the TV fans together for the duration of the show or the game. There's a great opportunity for social TV there. When you think about it there are tons of fans out there banging away writing fiction and participating in the larger fictional worlds of these TV shows, movies, and games. This isn't new, it's been around for a long time. But what is new and what is a great opportunity is to get them involved directly with the TV and the TV experience. There are some sites that are doing this now but you could do so much more with it if it was really social TV.

Social TV also makes me wonder about a time when the devices we carry around with us will start updating our social networks automatically. So if I create a season pass for a certain show then my TiVo updates Twitter or Facebook.

I want my TV and TV experiences to connect me to other people, whether that be family or fans. And I want my devices to be smart enough to remember what I like.

But it's not all just about connecting to people and talking. Social TV can also be a form of entertainment. I used to think of Twitter and those other social media applications as a way for me to just connect and chat with my friends and kids. Over the last year or so I've seen something very different.

I've seen how social media applications like Twitter can become a form of entertainment in and of itself.

The best example of this I've seen is Carri Bugbee and *Mad Men*. That was great!

***

In 2008 Carri Bugbee of Big Deal PR was a fan of the AMC show *Mad Men*. Bugbee's company specializes in social media. Her favorite character on the show was Peggy Olson, a secretary who fights to become a copywriter in the male dominated advertising world of the 1960s. After noticing that the show's main character, Don Draper, was tweeting, Bugbee immediately checked to see if @PeggyOlson was available on Twitter. She was amazed to find out it was. That's when the fun began.

Bugbee started posting short messages as the fictional character of Peggy Olson. She not only commented on the show itself but she began to answer people who asked her questions, all the time remaining true to her character.

She got one post that said: "Gee, Peggy, if you're tweeting from 1962, your computer must be as big as a house." Her reply in character was: "Yes, our typewriters are bigger, we're working with IBM prototypes" (Kristi Turnquist, *The Oregonian*, August 29, 2009).

Within a few months Bugbee and @PeggyOlson had nearly fifteen thousand people following her posts.

I talked with Bugbee about what she thought made good social content for TV. "It's not one size fits all," she said. "It really depends on the show and its storyline. You also have to have the right audience for it to work because it's not just about Tweeting as a TV show character; it's about interacting with people outside of the show. I answered every question people tweeted at Peggy. I put a lot of work into capturing her voice and authenticity of the era (1962). People would get really excited when they got a message from Peggy. Something about talking to a TV character in real time was thrilling. People came to think of tuning into the *Mad Men* Twitter feeds in the same way you tune into TV—with the most activity happening the morning after a new episode debuted. Some even said they liked 'watching' Mad Men on Twitter as much or more than watching it on TV.

Fictional Twitter accounts have taken off since then. Now it is common to have fictional characters with social media accounts. Some of them are operated by the creators of the shows or movies but others are taken on solely by fans.

The @PeggyOlson Twitter account shows how social media can become an extension of the fictional entertainment that people are enjoying on other devices like TVs and computers. It was the very social aspect of Bugbee's interaction with fans of *Mad Men* that made her successful. What attracted people to Bugbee's posts was that they were clever and she worked very hard to stay true to the AMC character and show. The social interaction of the fictional character outside of the show, talking about other topics expanded the fictional world of the show. Bugbee extended the show's entertainment value though social interactions. Using social networking programs was no longer just a way to connect with friends and family. It had become another medium for telling stories and entertaining people.

"I'm really surprised that in 2010, no TV show or network has done what fans did with the *Mad Men* characters in 2008," Bugbee told me. "I've seen a few clunky approaches to social TV and not too many clever uses. I don't understand why people are so far behind in bringing social to TV."

***

Gary Wheelhouse spends a lot of time talking to and thinking about his customers that come into the Harvey Norman stores. He told me that new technologies are all well and good but as a retailer he and Harvey Norman need to be able to sell them. I asked Gary what he's seen over the last year around social TV and what do people think about it?

GARY WHEELHOUSE: I don't think people right now have a clue of what is possible yet. I fear they learn a lot about their devices when they take them home. But really at the point we are at now, consumers have less knowledge than the industry. The industry is at a very early stage of thought on this. Both retail and vendors need to do a lot more at the last couple of feet of retail, to show consumers the possibilities. The execution at retail and how retailers, device makers, and networks market this will be critical.

The widget TV experience will really push this with Twitter Widgets and Facebook on screen. How long will it be until the networks really embrace this and use it? Because once people start seeing more interactivity and broader applications associated with TV then that will really help people understand it. They have to see it then they will love it.

I have gone from thinking of Twitter and social applications on TV as being something cool and funky with my existing followers, to something with way more defined connections. *But,* if networks and advertisers get smart and start thinking about engaging customers in real time via tweets, putting their @blabla and facebook/blabla in their advertising and their broadcast content, then it could really take off very quickly.

Advertisers have always looked for ways to have a closer, deeper connection with consumers. They have a great opportunity here to do just that. There is good talk from advertising agencies about moving some budget to social media, but it's another step then to link the TV advertising back to social media. And to respond real-time. But if you get it right those customers become very sticky—just look at a website like Zappos. They have a massively loyal base of customers just because they got shopping for shoes just right. People love it and keep coming back.

BDJ: What do you really think consumers want and how would you be able to frame it so that they would be interested in it?

GARY WHEELHOUSE: The way it has to be presented isn't really any particular message or pitch. What needs to happen is that the industry needs to start working together. Here I mean advertisers, broadcasters, technology providers, device makers, and retailers. Get that right and the opportunities are limitless. It will transform TV and entertainment from pure push to the consumer to push-and-pull, an interaction or conversation with the consumer very quickly. All of a sudden it is not just the endless pushing of content down the pipe; the consumer/viewer responds and has a voice! They can not only talk to each other, but they will also be talking to the advertiser! That would be an interesting conversation for the consumer and for the advertiser. Imagine what they might say to each other!

What Does It Take to Make TV Social?

"In the early years of TV broadcasting, there was a decidedly public and participatory element to watching programs" (Edgerton, *The Columbia History of American Television*, p. 96).

This is the strangest of all the chapters. Being social is something that humans do and something that technology can enable. Typically what happens is the technologies are released for a single purpose. Then people adopt the technology, adapt it, and remold it into something new. Usually this new thing is unforeseen by the creators of the technology or service. The VCR is a great example of this.

"The first video cassette recorders were promoted in the 1970s as an extension of broadcast television technology—a time-shifting device, a way to tape TV shows. Early advertising for Sony's Betamax told potential purchasers, 'You won't have to miss *Kojak* because you're watching *Columbo*.' But within a few years, the VCR had been transformed from a machine that recorded television into an extension of the movie theater into the home" (*From Betamax to Blockbuster*. Joshua M. Greenburg. 2008. MIT Press) In Greenberg's book he explores how local "mom and pop" video stores along with "videophiles" really took the VCR's technology and turned it into the movie experience we know today. He points out that is wasn't the technology manufacturers, TV or movie studios that did this but that it was average people who took the technology and used it in a completely different way than it was originally designed. Bugbee using Twitter to extend the story-telling of *Mad Men* can be seen in much the same way.

So why should we even bother discussing social TV? Isn't that trying to predict the future? Doomed to disaster, misrepresentation, and just plain misguided speculation? Well no, at least I hope not. The aim is to set up some guardrails and stake out the edges of how technology can enable people to connect with other people through their entertainment experiences.

For the sake of discussion we're going to examine three general areas of how people use technology in and around their social activities. Each touches on a different aspect of people's lives. We want to use what we know about people's current habits and mix that with what we have laid out in the previous chapters of this book. These chapters have laid down the technical and economic foundation for our exploration. To recap:

Informative TV

Greater intelligence about our entertainment is the foundation for TV's evolution. But the transformation of entertainment into data, turning entertainment into a compute task, allows us to create the social connections and intersections that we need. This data state of entertainment provides the raw materials we need to begin connecting people via their entertainment technologies.

Ubiquitous TV

Having your entertainment and devices with you all the time with unlimited access is another initial step towards social TV. Just as mobile phones, smart phones, net books, and laptops have become personal devices that we use to communicate with our social network, so too will this same type of activity grow out of the connected entertainment experience. If we create technologies that drive the ubiquitous interconnectivity of devices, then what we are in fact doing is connecting the people that own and use these devices.

Additionally when we enable technology and devices to collaborate and work together to enhance our entertainment experience, we are also enabling this same type of cooperation between people.

Personalized TV

Associating a device or a collection of devices and giving you as the user a presence on those devices also allows for you to connect and interact with your social network via those devices. Once your preferences have been identified and they can be shared across these devices then there is an incredible opportunity to personalize not only your entertainment but also the advertising that pays for that entertainment. This same human presence on multiple devices mixed with an ability to pay for the experience that uncovers new opportunities for developers to create social applications that are tied to both entertainment and our social network.

***

It's important for us to work in broad strokes so that we leave room for innovation. Earlier in the book, in my conversation with Henry Jenkins, he made the point that people must have the ability to make and remake technologies to suit their lives. As their lives change or the technology is adopted by others with different social requirements, the technological, business, and economic infrastructure we put in place must be able to account for the complexities of people's socials lives.

Jeffrey Cole is the director of the University of Southern California Annenberg School for Communication Center for the Digital Future. He has been studying people and their usage of TV and technology for over ten years. Cole has an interesting take on the ebb and flow of social media.

He sees all social networking sites and technologies as if they were nightclubs and everyone who joins a social network is just going to that nightclub.

"Now just imagine you're a teenager and you're at the nightclub," he explained. "All teenagers go to nightclubs first, it's what they do. They have the free time to do it and they are looking to get out. Now imagine you're this teenager and you're at this nightclub and you're having a good time and it's packed and more and more people keep showing up. At first it's cool. You like meeting new people, that's why you came to the club. But more and more people continue to show up and it starts to become too popular. Not cool anymore. You decide it's time to move on to the next nightclub; there are plenty of them and it doesn't cost you anything to leave. On your way out your Mom shows up at the nightclub and you know for sure it's time to leave. No one likes to party with their Mom."

People are fickle and funny. So it's only logical that the social technologies that connect them will come and go as taste and culture changes. Because of people's fickle nature, predicting the exact technological needs to enable social TV would be pointless. We do know that people are social and that people will always want to connect with other people using their technology. The rest of this chapter looks at three different ways that people are social with TV and then explores some basic technical implications to this these social interactions.

Watching TV Together

In the spring of 2008, one of my colleagues at Intel, Dr. Alex Zafiroglu, was conducting ethnographic field work in Chengdu, China. Zafiroglu is an anthropologist and she related this story to me about an interview she had with Mrs. He, a municipal employee in her mid thirties.

"I was shown a seemingly mundane little stool, sized, I thought, for a small child. But when Mrs. He told me the story behind the stool it really showed me how dramatically our relationships to television, and more broadly video content, has both changed and not changed in the past thirty years.

"Mrs. He showed me a miniscule stool (Figure 8.1) handmade by her father when she was a small child. She had kept it all these years. Mrs. He grew up in the 1970s in *danwei fang,* or housing provided by her father's work unit. In her case, these were small apartments arranged around a central courtyard. At the time, only one family in the entire complex owned a television, which they kept it in a cardboard box to protect it when they weren't using it. When it was time to watch TV they'd take it out and invite all the neighbors to watch with them, for a charge of the equivalent of 10 cents US.

"Mrs. He would take her stool with her into the courtyard to sit on while she watched TV with other kids and neighbors in the building. Her dad would attach the stool to her wrist with a string so that she would not lose it—she admits that she was a little absent-minded!

"As she got older she would take the stool with her to the movies that were shown in public spaces in her neighborhood. Now with a family of her own she still likes to watch TV in her own home perched on this little stool—not because she's nostalgic for her childhood, but because it's still her favorite seat for eating snack food while watching TV at home. In some ways, her TV habits have remained stable; yet her other favorite 'small' TV item is a hot pink MP4 player she uses to watch downloaded TV shows and movies while waiting during her daughter's piano lessons. The contrast between the stool and the MP4 player encapsulates both the stability and the dramatic changes in our TV watching habits in the last 30 years."

Figure 8.1   Mrs. He's little stool

The experience of watching TV has always been social. Before TV made its way into the living rooms, lounge rooms, and bedrooms of the world it was shared between complete strangers in bars and department stores. Even when the TV did begin its move into homes there was only one to start. In American in 1939, only a few hundred TV sets received the first presidential address on broadcast TV and when TV came to Australia and China in the late 1950s it reached only a few thousand households (CEA, Austrian Broadcasting System, and Museum of Television). But as I said, even in the beginning there was just one TV. Like in Mrs. He's story someone was always the first to get a TV. Media historian James L Baughman, in his history of TV *Same Time, Same Station*, paints a clear picture of what it was like to be "the first one on the block":

The first person in a neighborhood to get a television paid an additional price: friends and neighbors dropped by. "Families that purchased the town's initial television sets had delicate social problems," one contemporary recalled, "coping with friends and relatives, who devised ingenious ways to visit during prime time hours." Just over three-fourths of TV owners surveyed early in 1949 reported having more adult guests that before. Nearly as many, 72.1 percent, said they had more children coming to their homes. Some owners endured multigenerational invasions. When Teddy Ryan of Chester, Pennsylvania, bough a set around 1953, his five brothers—and their mostly male offspring—came to the house every Friday night to watch the fights on NBC. (*Same Time, Same Station*. Baughman. 2007. p. 1.)

In 2009 the average American home had 2.5 people and more than 2.8 TV sets (Nielsen 2009). Some argue that this has led to the breakdown in the social nature of watching TV. What started as a room full of strangers in the pub and evolved to the room full of friends in family in the living room has now become the solitary viewer watching whatever they want by themselves. That is one way to look at it. We can also begin to see a new kind of interactivity making its way into our entertainment culture; the beginning of which started with VHS and DVD.

Starting in the 1970s but growing fiercely over the decades people started sharing content, loaning moves to their social networks. Today it has grown into the online sharing of content typified by the e-mail with the Internet link that says, "You have to see this!" In 2009 more than 125 million viewers watched over 10 billion videos a month on YouTube (Comscore 2009). Building on this people have even been enabled by YouTube to publish their own content, shot, uploaded, and shared with the world.

The experience that started in the local bar has moved to the email in box, but it still has the same quality of sharing, of discussion and a shared experience. At Intel we developed an experience concept called "poker night" that shows how TV can be social regardless if you are sitting together in the same room or sharing via a digital connection.

Imagine a group of friends are playing poker together. Two of the friends are in the same living room while the other two players are located in their own homes (Figure 8.2).

Figure 8.2   Poker Night: Friends connected both physically and digitally

The friends use their smart phones and handhelds as their private screens (Figure 8.3) to display their poker hands while the TV acts as the shared screen between the four players (Figure 8.4).

Figure 8.3   Poker Night: The handheld is the private screen.

Figure 8.4   Poker Night: The TV is the shared screen

A camera in each other devices allows all the friends to see each other during the game (Figure 8.5).

Figure 8.5   Poker Night: Video camera allows all players to see each other during the game.

With experience concepts like this you can see how people would connect and have a shared experience both physically in the same room and digitally via their TV and their devices. Just like Mrs. He grew up watching TV with all the members of her apartment building, these friends can get together regardless of where they are in the world.

The challenge for emerging social TV applications will be to uncover social interactions that can naturally be extended with technology and entertainment.

Making Bravery Fashionable

From its beginning TV has been a way for average people to connect with their government, community, and the wider world. TV has given people news from down the street and across the globe. The Scottish inventor John Logie Baird made the first TV newscast from London to Glasgow in 1926 and in 1928 he made the first transatlantic transmission from London to Hartsdale, New York. On October 5, 1947 President Harry S Truman gave the first presidential speech to be televised from the White House, asking Americans to conserve food in order to help their recovering European World War II allies.

As a mass medium TV has done more to bring the world, the living, breathing, dying, and changing world into people's lives than any of other medium. This increased access has allowed people to be better informed about their government and their community. It has allowed them to be socially aware in a way that couldn't be accomplished with radio or print. TV has allowed the public to form an opinion about their world.

One of the more famous examples of the socially aware connection formed via the TV screen was with the American journalist Edward R. Murrow and his very public fight and denouncement of Senator Joseph McCarthy. In the 1950s the United States and Russia were locked in the middle of the Cold War. Anti-communist fervor gripped the American political scene. Many believed that communists had infiltrated the American government and industry and were actively working to destroy the country. At the center of this paranoia and fear was a Wisconsin Senator named Joseph McCarthy and the House Committee on un-American Activities (HUAC).

By the mid-1950s the general public and the media were beginning to question HUAC and McCarthy's methods. On March 9, 1954 Murrow denounced both HUAC and McCarthy.

> We will not be driven to fear by an age of unreason," Murrow said, commenting on the fear and paranoia being spread throughout America. "If we dig deep in our history and our doctrine, and remember that we are not descended from fearful men—not from men who feared to write, to speak, to associate and to defend causes that were, for the moment, unpopular. (Murrow. *In search of the light: the broadcasts of Edward R. Murrow* 1967)

Murrow's words shocked and galvanized an entire country. The cultural affect of his TV broadcast was massive. It didn't matter if people agreed with him or not, he had touched the social consciousness of an entire nation.

Again Baughman chronicles the affect in his book *Same Time, Same Channel*:

> "Television came of age," Crosby declared. "I can never recall any other time when a network…has told its listeners to straighten up and act like free men with the clear implication that they are not doing so now." Colleagues found the forcefulness of Murrow's critique heroic. "One of the great acts of political courage of our time," wired the syndicated Columnist Joseph Alsop. "Mr. Murrow," wrote Alistair Cooke for the *Manchester Guardian* "may yet make bravery fashionable."

While TV gave access to events, images, and opinions, the Internet, at the beginning of the twenty-first century, has allowed the same average people to interact and participate with their society. One of the more well known and debated examples of this occurred on July 23, 2007 in Charleston, South Carolina and around the world.

The first televised presidential debate between Richard Nixon and John F. Kennedy took place in Chicago in 1960. For the first time people across America were allowed to see their candidates discussing the issues of the day. Forty-seven years later the cable news channel CNN and the Internet video site YouTube teamed up to bring American a televised debate where average Americans were able to ask questions via the Internet. Eight candidates seeking the Democratic Party's nomination were asked questions selected from of 3000 Internet users who submitted video via YouTube. Many touted this as giving the average voter "a seat at the table." The event was highly publicized and highly criticized for its use of the technology, its choice of questions, and its general merit to the national debate. Regardless of your stance, the event, followed up by a Republican debate on November 28, 2007, signaled a very different sort of political and social interactivity that the American Political process had ever seen before.

The combination of the mass appeal of TV and the participatory nature of the Internet gives us an interesting proposition as we attempt to enable people to be more socially active with their governments, communities, and world. However we cannot make assumptions about the outcome or benefit of this combination. The technology is simply a tool and it is up to the community and society to remain involved, using the tool to connect with the world around them.

Henry Jenkins, who I had a conversation with earlier in the book, has an interesting take one this:

> Too often, we have fallen into the trap seeing democracy as an "inevitable" outcome of technological change rather than as something which we need to fight to achieve with every tool at our disposal. Too often, we have sought to deflect criticism of grassroots culture rather than trying to identify and resolve conflicts and contradictions which might prevent it from achieving its full potentials. Too often, we have celebrated those alternative voices which are being brought into the marketplace of ideas without considering which voices remained trapped outside…we must continue to ask ourselves the hard questions about the practices and institutions which are taking place. (*Convergence Culture*. Jenkins. 2006)

Again here the challenge for social TV programmers and developers is to search out appropriate spaces for people to interact with their government and community. This type of interaction can give people access to their political leaders in new ways but it can also provide a platform for regular people to engage with each other. However as Jenkins points out this engagement and this new platform will always be complex. Communities and individuals must continue to ask the "hard questions" never assuming that technology is a solution in and of itself.

The Shining Center of the Home

"The lecture, the lesson, the demonstration, and the class have all been taken over from educational practice into television. In many cases the possibilities of the medium have been extensively realized. Large audiences can be reached by exceptional lecturers and teachers. Visual demonstration of rare or complex material has markedly improved presentation of aspects of the physical sciences, of medicine, of geography, and of elements of drama and history. A developed educational service, such as the BBC or IBA or

American Public Television schools programs, or the British Open University, is a remarkable demonstration of some of the true possibilities of television" (*Television*. Raymond Williams. 1974 p.50).

Raymond Williams, the British cultural thinker and sociologist, wrote this critique on television in 1974, long before cable TV, on demand programming, and Internet video. Yet he captures the power of TV as an educational tool, recognizing the medium's affect even before the significant changes that were to come.

From the beginning of TV and the Internet, their use as an educational platform has been an ongoing discussion. For TV, which was primarily a business, entertainment, and advertising venture, education along with emergency broadcasting was seen as a way for TV to give back to the community. Proving that TV could do good was one way, early in the development of the industry, that it could be seen as valuable and acceptable. The Internet on the other hand originated in 1960s with the United States government and DARPA but eventually made its way to universities like Stanford. The Internet was primarily used for education, research, and communication before mid 1990 when it became a commercial platform.

Many saw TV as simply a commercial engine but some had a different view of TV's potential "Television is a miracle," NBC's Pat Weaver said in a 1954 interview and "[TV] must be used to upgrade humanity across a broad base." Sylvester "Pat" Weaver was an American radio and TV executive. In 1954 when he was president of NBC he said, "TV is a miracle and must be used to upgrade humanity across the board." Weaver believed deeply in the power of TV to educate and better the cultural lives of its audience. He believed that TV "must be the shining center of the home" (Thomas Whiteside. "The Communicator (part 1)," *The New Yorker*. October 16, 1954).

Both the Internet and TV are filled with educational sites, shows, and content. Some of these are funded by government or private donations while others are for profit, generating funding either by subscription sales or advertising. The funding of educational content has always been a hotly debated topic and rightly so as the content and educational merit of the programs and sites becomes of increasing importance when the audience for the content are minors. These issues of funding and regulation will only grow as the reach of TV is married with the interactivity of an Internet connection.

Basic Technical Implications

As we begin to think about how to enable people to connected with each other, their community, and to educators via their TV, some high level architectural implications and technological considerations pop up right away. To help us explore these implications I talked with Jack Weast. Weast is an Advanced Consumer Electronics Solutions Architect at Intel. He works directly with our customers all over the world to determine an appropriate software architecture for their product vision. These are the products that will end up on our TVs and in our living rooms.

You Need a Common Language

As we think practically about how we would build social TV applications, Weast called out that the biggest hurdle is the complexity of the various users and the state of their devices and connection speeds. First we have to assume that people will have vastly different connection speeds to the Internet. Also we can assume that the devices that people are physically holding in their hands will be made by different manufacturers. These devices could and probably will have different hardware and software requirements. The problem of getting all of these various devices, software, and connections to work together is a lot like getting a room full of people to work towards a common goal when they all speak different languages.

One way to overcome this challenge is to use an abstract application platform like Flash or a web browser as the common language between these devices. Essentially you are looking for something that is likely to be common across all of the devices and you can you this to unify the experience from a technology perspective.

Once you've been able to normalize the language between these devices then we can start to work on the shared and social experience.

How to Connect?

As we begin to build software applications so that people can connect with friends, their community, and educational institutions we have to consider how these devices will be connected together. At the highest level we have two options: centralized or local. Both approaches can work but each comes with unique benefits and problems.

A centralized server is a very simple approach that allows people to connect to each other through the Internet, as shown in Figure 8.6. A centralized server is sometimes called *cloud computing*. This means that most or all of the processing and interconnections of the poker game take place in the *cloud* or in the centralized server that is located outside of the consumers' homes.

A centralized server would suggest that a large well-funded organization is delivering the entertainment and social connections to the consumers. By having the social connection in the cloud, it means that potentially millions of people could connect across the world, which in turn could help pay for the service.

A centralized server also means that the organization or company that is running the connection between people has to maintain the server and answer any questions that consumers might have. In many instances this approach will work just fine. The CNN debate was hosted on a centralized YouTube server but there may be instances where having a large company hosting the social interaction may not be optimal.

In some cases the centralized approach may not be the best solution. There could be performance problems if you had people geographically dispersed at multiple sites. The round trip latency and lag for packets to go to travel to a single server could be a problem. It might be more efficient to route the traffic through multiple servers that are geographically better positioned. Additionally some countries have specific regulations that require servers to be located in the country where the customers are accessing the service. In this case a single centralized server wouldn't work if you wanted to have people from more than one country access it. But the biggest arguments against a completely centralized server approach are a decrease in robustness and an increase of bottlenecks. Distributing your service or site across multiple servers means if one of them goes down then you won't lose your entire operation. Multiple servers also allow for better load balancing, spreading your traffic across multiple sites and cutting down on any bottlenecks or slowdowns if the amount of people using the servers shoots up suddenly.

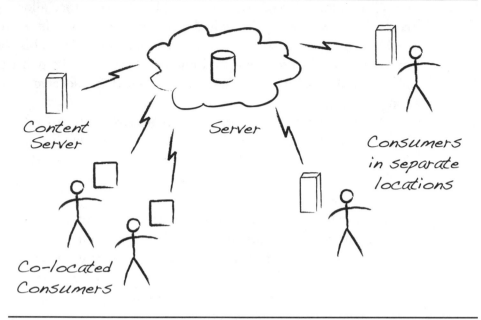

Content
Server

Server

Consumers
in separate
locations

Co-located
Consumers

Figure 8.6   Consumers using different devices connect to each other and content via a centralized server

A decentralized model to enable the social interaction could be what is commonly called the peer-to-peer (P2P) model, shown in Figure 8.7. This means that each device has the ability to connect directly to other devices involved in the social interaction. An example of this would be like how a Bluetooth[+] headset connects to a cell phone. It is a direct connection and doesn't need to connect to the Internet or rely on a server outside the consumer's home. Now in many cases consumers may still want to connect to the Internet and then they will have to use some kind of centralized server. But if your applications and content are local then you could connect P2P in your home or neighborhood with a local server.

In some ways the P2P approach is superior to the centralized approach because it distributes the bandwidth across multiple devices instead of depending upon a single centralized point of access. In effect each of the devices is load balancing and distributing the aggregate bandwidth needed to deliver the experience. It also provides a fail-safe functionality because if one of the devices goes down or breaks then the entire P2P network can auto-adjust to find another device or peer to route through and continue the connection.

This P2P model suggests a grass roots application authored by an individual or small business as opposed to the larger business that might be needed for the centralized server model. Because the devices are connecting directly to each other there is no need to "host" or pay for the offsite servers. Each device in the decentralized network is by definition capable of being a "host." The device that ultimately ends up being the "host" can change from session to session. This type of flexible approach is a trend that's come about because of more powerful computing devices. Not too long ago your laptop, handheld, or TV would not have had enough bandwidth or computing power to "host" a session. The author in the decentralized model of the application that is running the interaction would look to pay for the work by simply charging for each copy of the software that is installed or it could be funded by a much smaller government or local organization.

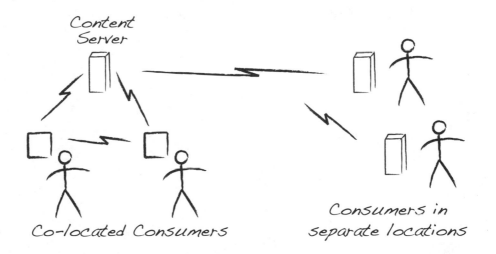

Figure 8.7   Consumers connected directly to a local content server and other users via a direct connection (P2P)

There is a third option that could deliver the social TV experience, shown in Figure 8.8. This would be a hybrid model that takes advantage of both a centralized server as well as the ability for the devices to connect directly to each other. This would mean that the application could be purchased from the developer and installed on all of the devices. The majority of the connections could be managed on a P2P basis but if additional information were needed or a device could not connect P2P then a larger Internet connection could be utilized. In some hybrid approaches you could use a centralized server that authorizes all of the P2P devices, the ones that are connecting directly to each other. An advantage of this authentication is that it enables the social TV service to make sure that all of the devices are running the correct software so that they can communicate and share with each other. If there is a device that is not up to date then the centralized server can have the device connect to the closest device that is current and get the needed software update. This approach allows the devices to update each other much faster and more efficiently than if we were using the centralized or the decentralized model. Also if the social application were commercial it could connect people directly via P2P but use the Internet as a way to deliver advertising that could help pay for the development and hosting of the service.

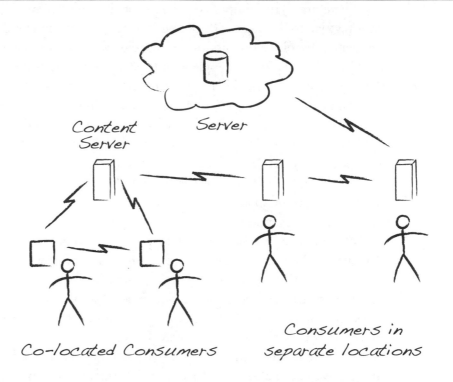

Content Server

Server

Co-located Consumers

Consumers in separate locations

Figure 8.8   Hybrid approach combines a centralized server with direct (P2P) connections for optimal flexibility and performance

Rule Sets

Facilitating conversations between people, governments, and educators can have complicated legal and cultural ramifications. In many public conversations some language may not be appropriate. Rule sets could be defined that represent allowed/disallowed speech or words for each participating member of the conversation. When consumers form a communication group, the set of rules could be applied in aggregate so that what results is a new rules set that governs the conversation so that it is compatible with all participants.

Other aspects that could be relevant to enable this social interaction would be whether the conversation is public or private. Is it verbal or text-based? We could also approach different topics in different ways depending upon their sensitivity.

There are many simplified versions of this rule set model that are used on a regular basis today with online forums around the world. Bloggers will frequently disable comments on certain controversial posts. Forum moderators may limit interaction to people who have registered with the site, presuming they are trustworthy. There are even mechanisms to shut down further comments once the discourse has degraded to an inappropriate level.

Most of the current practices described above depend on a person, the moderator or organizer, to set the rules for the conversation. When these are public or sensitive interactions these rule sets usually need people to help enforce them. Rule sets can be very useful to keep public conversations within the boundaries of appropriate communications but they are no replacement for human intervention.

We can use our previous "Poker Night" experience described in the Personal TV chapter to give us an example scenario where rule sets could be used. In this scenario let's imagine that all of the players are located in different countries, each with different legal and cultural rules. Player #1 is located in the United Kingdom where online gambling is legal and so Player #1 is playing with real money. Player #2 is logged in from the United States where online gambling is illegal, so Player #2 is playing with virtual money. We could also have Player #3 who is playing from Germany and the local government requires that all Internet content be screened for sensitive and objectionable terms. Imagine if Player #2 has a screen name that is accidentally very close to one of the terms that Player #3's government has deemed objectionable. We could also have Player #4, who is playing from an Internet cafe that has specific rules and terms of use agreements for not only what Player #4 can play but for how long. And finally we could have Player #5 who is of legal gambling age in Italy but not of legal gambling age for the United States. All of this from a simple game of international poker. As you can see these rule sets can become quite complicated but will be necessary for services that want to operate in a complex legal and cultural marketplace.

"I Would Pay Money Right Now for This!"

The ultimate test for any new technology is if real people would actually buy it and use it.

Over the past five years we have conducted several studies at Intel testing people's interest in the experiences and products discussed in this book. We use consumer testing as an integral part of our long term technology development process. These tests range from simple surveys and questionnaires to in depth ethnographic field research. Anthropologists here at Intel like Dr. Bell and Dr. Zafiroglu actually do go into people's homes and watch how they watch TV. That may sound bit odd but this rich understanding of how people use and live with technology is required as we design these types of experiences so far out into the future. Technology changes quickly; people generally don't change that much.

Another approach we take to consumer research is to explore what people think when they actually experience a product for the first time. This kind of experience testing (UX) involves early stage prototype technologies that are built out just far enough so that consumers can use and interact with them. Our social scientists and human factors engineers then sit with the people, talk to them (see Appendix A for more detail), and ask them questions as they explore the experiences. The knowledge and feedback we get from these sessions allows us to make adjustments and changes to the technology so that people will enjoy using it. Sometimes this approach just gives us an honest reality check from real people. It tells us if the technologies make sense and if real people would actually go out and buy them.

In 2008 we used a simple global survey to get a general idea of people's interest in social TV. We tested the interest in "connecting with friends and family via your TV." This usage was ranked second out of all the usages and experiences we asked people to consider (Intel Global Usage Survey. 2008).

To further explore social TV we conducted an UX study in 2009 the United States. The results were even more positive than the previous year. We showed people a concept where they could use their TVs to connect with family and friends to talk, share photos, and sometimes just watch TV together when they are located in different states. Half the participants picked this type of social interaction as a feature they would like to see in a TV or a device. People wanted to sit in front of the TV with their families and use the screen to connect with people. They not only saw it as a way to simply share photos but also as a way for their children to be able to show off their drawings from school to grandparents and extended family. The specificity of this vision is important because these families were already applying the technology directly to their personal lives.

One participant noted that "We would use it a ton, all the time…daily." While another person called out quite loudly, "I would pay money right now for this!" (Intel Experience Study. 2009).

These two studies were incredibly helpful because they showed that even at an early stage of development the concept of social TV was something that consumers intuitively understood and would purchase given the chance. We started off this chapter talking about how TV and entertainment are inherently social activities and that humans are inherently social as well. The combination of the two seems to be natural. The interesting part will be the various ways they will be combined and the different solutions developers will come up with to connected people to their communities and to each other. The potential of social TV makes me think of Carri Bugbee's quote from earlier, "It's 2010…I don't understand why people are so far behind in bringing social to TV." I think all of us want social TV to hurry up and happen.

Chapter 9

Being Bullish on TV

A CONVERSATION WITH JEFFREY COLE

Early winter mornings in Los Angeles can be strikingly beautiful. At 6 a.m. the air was still cold but the sun was coming up and the sky was cloudless. It was going to be a beautiful day.

I stood outside my hotel and waited for Jeffrey Cole to pick me up. Cole and I were going to make the over four-hour drive together from Los Angeles to Las Vegas. The 2010 Consumer Electronics Show was just about to kick off and we had a party to go to that night. We couldn't have picked a better day to make the drive, the landscape was stunning, the weather was perfect, and there was no traffic at all.

Jeffrey Cole is the director of the University of Southern California Annenberg School for Communication Center for the Digital Future. Once we had passed Barstow California on U.S. Highway 15, I asked Jeffrey to tell me about his work at the center.

JEFFREY COLE: As a television guy, I was always taught that we blew it with television. We lost this great opportunity. Television is the only mass medium we knew ahead of time was going to be a mass medium. Every other medium took time to develop. Newspapers took a hundred years before we learned the power of newspapers. Film was a scientific toy for 15 years before we saw its value as a medium. Radio got shorter, was two years. Television, we knew ahead of time was going to be a mass medium. There was no question that radio listeners were going to embrace radio with pictures.

So, what I was taught that we should have done, but didn't do, was we should have tracked people before they had television and gone back to them year after year as they acquired and used it, to see how their lives changed. We could have learned simple things; where did the time for television come from? When people were watching three hours of TV a day, and they were asked where did that time come from? They didn't know. They just grabbed it out of the air. We could have learned if the time came from talking as a family, reading books or newspapers, sleep, or from some other place. How did television change our buying behavior? Did it make us more likely to buy the goods and services we saw advertized? I think we know it did. How did it change our connection to the civic process? Did it make us more engaged in politics? Likelier to participate and vote? Or more cynical and detached? How did it affect our desire to travel? And a thousand other things.

I became convinced in the late 90s that the impact of digital technology, first the Web and now mobile, was going to be far more powerful than television. Television is mostly about leisure and entertainment and digital is about how we work, how we play, how we communicate, and probably its most important long term impact will be how we learn. So, believing that we lost this great opportunity with television, and if the impact of digital was going to be even greater than television, 10 years ago we launched this massive project. This tracking of the Internet that we thought should have been conducted of television.

We started in the U.S., we've gone back to the same people 10 years in a row and watched as nonusers went to dialup, dialup users moved to broadband, saw that almost immediately, broadband changed everything. We watch as about 2 percent drop off the Web each year, and we want to know who are these people who leave? And why? And more importantly, do they return? And if so, when? And what brings them back?

In 10 years we track the never users. So that if we want to see for example, how has the Internet affected television use or newspaper use? We actually have data on people before they were online and how much television they watched, or how much time they spent with the newspaper and watch how that changes as they go to dialup. We started in the U.S. We're now in 30 countries around the world, and what we have are pretty amazing insights into behavior.

Now, people don't always know what they want in the future, we're not good at getting that from data. We can try and interpolate some of that, but we have really powerful insights on how people have used this in their lives, and where and how that has affected the rest of their lives. The most interesting part of our work is seeing how offline behavior has changed based on being online.

One example of this is how offline behavior has changed shopping in stores. The way people shop in stores, one of the powerful things we saw that happened because of the Internet, is people now shop in stores and buy online.

In the beginning we saw that they would shop online and then buy in stores. Offline behavior, the decline of newspapers, changes in television, increased desire to travel, booking people's own travel. One of my favorite examples of one of the impacts of the Internet, well, we'll back up for a second.

I would argue that there is not a business or activity that has not been affected by digital technology. Most have been transformed, but everything has been at least affected. Sometimes, we'll ask an audience; name something that hasn't been affected by the Internet. The best answer I've gotten is, and it's not total, is getting your haircut. And you're right. You're never going to have your haircut on the Internet, but you're going to make your appointment on the Internet, you're going to buy your hair care products on the Internet, you may decide what style you want, but that's a business that's just been affected.

My favorite example of a business that has been transformed by the Internet is the funeral business. Because who would ever think the funeral business would be completely turned upside down by the Internet? And it has. It's really an interesting case study.

So, to answer your question I'm a TV guy that tracks and studies the Internet because I think it affects TV. The Internet is changing television and changing everything else. We really are at that point.

In the TV, entertainment, and high tech industries we have a lot of words that we use to explain what I'm talking about. We've expected this to happen for a long time. All of us have been waiting for computers and the Internet to begin to affect TV. In the past when it didn't happen we got frustrated and there's a backlash and everyone goes around saying it's not going to happen. But then all of a sudden it's happening without us realizing. Convergence is one of those words. And we really are at the point where it's only a semantic argument as to whether the Internet is a channel on the television set or television is a URL on the Web. It's meaningless today. We're just talking about words and the names of things. We can call it whatever we want. The fact is it's happening right now.

If you look up ahead…can you see that line of buildings up there? That's the Nevada border. See all those big casinos?

***

Crossing the California-Nevada state line we passed Whiskey Pete's and Terrible's Resort and Casino, I asked Cole what he thought was the point where the Internet and TV started to affect each other, when did the two begin to blend?

JEFFREY COLE: That's the easiest question you're ever going to ask me. The answer is simple: broadband.

People's time is finite. People only have a limited amount of free time when they are home. One of the things we look at is how people are spending that time. Not just how they are spending it but where the time for new tasks come from. It's got to come from somewhere.

Imagine this: you get the Internet in your house for the first time. Well, that's a new thing. If you get online and surf the Web then that time needs to come from somewhere and there's a lot of places it can't come from. You still need to eat and sleep and take care of the house. So the question we look at was where did this time for the Internet come from?

From 2000 to 2004 more than from any other place the time for the Internet was coming from television. But it turns out that it wasn't the Internet that was a threat to television. It wasn't the Internet that was taking time away from TV, it was dialup. With a dialup connection to the Internet people were dialing up for 20–30 minutes at a time. They would be online for about 20–30 minutes because they aggregated their tasks. They checked e-mail, went to their favorite Web sites, maybe bought some things but they viewed dialing up as a big deal. So, they went on for 20–30 minutes.

Now some people had television with them and did multitask from day one, but generally your computer was located in a different room that didn't have a TV. It was the den or the kitchen or someplace like that. There are of course a number of technical and infrastructure reasons for this. It was where your phone was located mainly and many people didn't have phones in the TV or living room. So people left the TV room and went to the computer and went online for their 20–30 minutes, got their things done and came back to the TV. That's where people want to be anyway when they are home. Television has always dominated our at home awake time. Most of us turn the TV set on the moment we enter the home, leave it on until we go to sleep, some of us go to sleep with it on. Some of us even leave it on when we're not at home so that people think we are at home. So, if you're going to carve out time at home to do anything, take a walk, take a nap, take a shower, go online, that time almost had to come from the TV. But it wasn't the Internet that was taking people out of the living room and away from the TV, it was dialup. Broadband changed all of this.

The moment people got broadband we say that they were going online not 2 or 3 times a day for 20–30 minutes, but 30, 40, 50 times a day for 2 minutes. Because you didn't have to aggregate your tasks anymore because of the always on. You could do two things, and then if you remembered something a minute later, you went right back to it. And all of a sudden broadband meant that you were going online before the show started, after it ended and even more worrisome for the broadcasters, during the commercials.

Also broadband is what's allowing the Internet to escape from the home and be watched on PCs and be watched on mobile phones. So, we saw this change and it all came from broadband because truly, the Internet was an enemy of television in the dialup era, and it is now becoming I think the best friend television has ever had.

With broadband TV has moved onto the Internet. I consider YouTube[†] and online video Web sites to be TV. So now the fear is that Internet TV is going to kill broadcasters. I think this is an important point. Internet TV isn't going to kill TV. Internet TV is going to kill television broadcast networks.

With broadband, wireless, and these Web sites, consumers don't care where they see their content. They just care about their content. The war that is going on now, and maybe one of the reasons you're seeing Internet companies and service providers getting more closely involved with TV content. These companies are terrified that they are going to become irrelevant. I don't know if you're following this "TV Everywhere" campaign, and cable companies want to say "Okay, you can watch *True Blood*, you can watch any of these series anywhere you want once you authenticate to us that you're paying for cable, but one of the things, the younger you are, people don't want to pay for cable. Part of the problem with cable is that you have to buy; you can't get a la carte pricing.

I have two cable subscriptions; I'm a subscriber in California and in New York. I pay $8 [USD 8] a month for ESPN, which I don't watch on the two coasts. So, a lot of people want away from cable, and they want to go on the Web and the cable company's answer is "Well, pay us the $60 [USD 60] a month and then we'll let you watch it on the Web." I think television has an extraordinary future, and I think it's going to explode with growth and I think we're going to watch more than twice as much television, because we're going to watch it outside the home.

Now TV broadcasters love hearing me say that, but I don't mean that the broadcasters are going to have a great future. I don't think there's enough room for four networks anymore. The Jay Leno decision on NBC came because of I think some poor decision making at NBC five years ago. But beyond all that, the way they got themselves into that dilemma, the Jay Leno programming decision is also NBC saying we can't afford to program our network anymore.

The first thing they tried to do was go to reality TV programming, which was cheaper to make. But when reality became popular, like *Survivor* or *The Apprentice,* it wasn't cheaper anymore. Reality became just as expensive when it was popular. So, then the networks started repurposing. They started saying "Well, very few people watch on Saturday nights, so we'll run shows over again, we'll borrow shows from our sister cable networks." And then Zucker at NBC about three years ago got a lot of flack when he said "We're going to give up 8:00 [p.m.]. We're going to make 8:00 reality and game shows." And he backed off of that, but essentially that's what they are now doing with 10:00.

Before the Internet, there hasn't been enough money to fund four networks at 22 hours except for Fox at 15, so while I think television has a great future, I consider YouTube television, I consider Hulu[†] television. It doesn't mean that the four networks are all going to prosper the way they did before. Because long before anybody looked at an Internet, in 1975 90 percent of television viewing in America was on three channels. They divided 90 percent of the audience, and therefore to be a successful show, you had to stay on, you had to have 30 share. A 24 share and you were canceled. There was a guy that used to drive Los Angeles in a big fancy car that said 40 share, because those were the days when a *M*A*S*H* or an *All in the Family* could have a 40 share.

Today a 17 share is a hit! You can sometimes survive if your demographics are good with a 7 share and this was before the Internet. So, television is going to thrive, it doesn't mean that the studios and the networks are all going to thrive. Clearly, one or two of them are because even though the three networks, let's not count the CW, say the four networks only account for about 30–35 percent of all viewing, they still accumulate bigger audiences than any other medium. Cable as an industry amasses about a 60 share, but that's across over 100 channels, many of those channels never have bigger than a 1 or 2 share, the exceptions would be HBO during *The Sopranos* or a really significant event. So, networks still are the place that people watch the most.

People's interest in programming and their shows will never change. What's changing is the way a network works. Back before the Internet it was brilliant the way networks scheduled their primetime TV shows. They would take two successful shows and put in that hammock between them a new show, because people knew that much of the time, people back in the 70s and 80s turned on one channel and left it on all night. That's why the 10 o'clock hour was so successful to the 11 o'clock news. That's all dying.

The Internet video, DVRs like TiVo[†] and other technologies are moving everyone to an on-demand type of schedule. The idea is that people may still sit for three hours, but it is going to be three hours programmed by them. Even today many people don't know when the shows they watch are actually broadcast. They know generally which night they're on, but not the time.

Let me give you an example. I'm a big fan of the show *Scrubs*. I have no idea what time *Scrubs* airs. When I was growing up, most of my classmates could have recited the entire schedule and you planned your life around that schedule. It's all moving to on-demand. The real difference is that before the Internet and these technologies you'd spend an evening with CBS. Today people still want to see their shows from CBS, but they're not going to spend an entire evening watching CBS. They're going watch their shows on their own schedule when they have the time. They're going to watch what they want and maybe some advertising as well.

One thing we see that bodes well for broadcast networks and studios. At the Center in our studies we're finding people are getting better at telling the difference between professional and amateur content. That's new. We haven't seen that before because really before recently we never really had much amateur content in our lives. YouTube has become a cultural phenomenon. Over the past few years we've seen the emergence of those occasional viral videos that do reach 50–100 million people. Some of them are amazing, but we find most people go to those viral videos through links. We found the people who go to YouTube directly are going to look for TV shows like *The Daily Show* and *Saturday Night Live*. People can distinguish between the two. There are different behaviors associated with professional versus amateur content. We've seen that people know the value of good writing, good directing, and good production values.

But this new world of professional and amateur content together brings up an interesting economic issue. You can have popular amateur videos on YouTube that go viral and are seen by millions of people but they are flukes from an economic standpoint. There really is no business model or way to make money from them for the people who produce them. YouTube can make money possible but what's the economic engine that's feeding amateur video? There isn't one. They do it for the love of doing it or as a way to get attention. That's very different than professional mainstream entertainment.

High quality entertainment, like the television shows and movies people love are really expensive. It takes an entire industry to develop and support the sustained interest in a show over time. You need to be able to get it out there, to market it, and finance it. You could have somebody who has a camcorder and a lot of talent, but it's very, very difficult because people have that appreciation. It's very difficult for people who aren't professionals because they don't have the economic underpinning to make the next one, or to make the next three. That's when it becomes economically viable. It will be hard for YouTube to kill the traditional TV because people love traditional TV, just like they love YouTube. They love both of them, but they spend more time with professional TV. It's that preference for high quality content that can save TV.

***

BDJ: So, when you look at the future of TV, when you start thinking 5–10 years out, what do you see?

JEFFREY COLE: I see content seamlessly shifting from platform to platform. I see people going on vacation and saying I'm going to take a lot of stuff on my mobile phone. I see people saying I'm going to be home on vacation, or I'm sick this week, I'm going to watch more of it on my big screen. It's going to move seamlessly from place to place. Television is going to become our constant companion.

Our constant companion right now is our mobile phone. If we're stuck at the airport waiting for a flight, most of us pull out our phones and start saying "Who should I call?" And it's after the person answers, they figure out what they're going to say to them.

I think we're going to pull out our phones and watch television. Television is going to move into every role and every place and every spot in our life; in the backseat of our cars, on airplanes, at airports. We're going to watch television when people are late to lunch. Television will move into all of the spots of our lives and become more important than it's ever been. But that also means that the ability of branded networks to get people to sit in front of the big screen is going to get smaller and smaller.

I also love the idea that people who put chips and technology into set top boxes say that within two minutes they can tell whether the remote control is being operated by a man or a woman and within 48 hours they can profile every member of the household. I'm intrigued that you can start delivering advertising that could see CPMs go up by 1000 percent. You don't need the huge audiences that the networks used to be able to deliver this. I like the fact that the consumer benefits from this, not only because they don't have to pay or pay as much for content, but they actually begin to receive advertising that's interesting and useful to them.

Now, of course the minute I start down this path, this really serious issue of privacy arises, an issue I work very closely on. I believe that if targeted advertising is going to succeed, and I think it needs to succeed for the consumer as the alternative is to pay. I believe it's going to succeed; but it has to be under a couple of simple rules. Advertisers have to explain exactly what they're collecting and why. There have to be privacy policies not written by lawyers for lawyers. There have to be clear, serious penalties for anyone who violates that.

And for the consumer all the technology and all the business models don't matter. That's an important thing to remember. I used to ask my class of 500, "How many of you could tell me semi-intelligently what goes on under the hood of an automobile? And if the car broke down, you could open the hood and have a reasonable chance of figuring out what was wrong?" I'd get 5 hands. So, I would turn to the other 495 and say "You don't know a thing about cars, but you know how to use them in your lives." Same thing is true with television. You don't have to know anything that's happening under the hood. You just have to know that television has an on/off switch and a volume control and a channel changer and that's all you have to know. All the technology changes are irrelevant.

I should digress for a second, there is Las Vegas right in front of us!

Conclusion

What is the Future of the Future?

I can pretty much guarantee you that by the time you read this book something in it will be out of date. We have a lot of things going against us here. The technologies that we've been talking about are in a rapid state of development. Much of this work is going on behind closed doors for the sake of business strategy. A good many smart people right now are doing great work to bring about the future we have been discussing. It's hard work and takes time, but we don't hear a lot about that. What we do hear is when the product is launched. Then the public's first introduction to the technology is a press release or a slick piece of advertising. It's here that the technology looks its best with its hair combed straight, wearing its best suit. What we don't see is the messy hard work that went on behind the scenes. We won't see the long nights of development or the brutal contract negotiations. No, we see these products as if they have sprung to life overnight, fully formed and looking great. So it's a pretty good guess that by the time you've read this book at least one or two of these products will have sprung onto the scene, making parts of the book seem outdated.

While I was writing this book it seemed like every week there was another news report or posting or event about the future of TV. Reporters and industry specialists heralded the changes coming to the entertainment industry and the media business; some were full of doom and gloom but others were quite refreshingly excited and not jaded. Pundits talked about the changes to our culture, about use of all these new devices and how the very nature of our interaction with entertainment and the world around us is changing in monumental ways. These business and cultural fluctuations seem to happen faster and faster these days. I would guess that even before I send this last chapter to my editor there will be another new development, another fascinating change that will affect what we've been talking about.

It seems we are doomed. Like the Isaac Asimov quote about writing about the future at the beginning of this book; it is a "hopeless, thankless task, with ridicule to begin with and, all too often, scorn to end with." But fear not, there is a higher goal that we can strive for. One that is far better than being outdated. What is that goal? There is a far better outcome than just finding yourself out of date. The ultimate goal when writing about the future is to become mundane.

Back in 2003 the science fiction author Bruce Sterling tried his hand at futurism with a book called *Tomorrow Now: Envisioning the Next 50 Years*. In the introduction he writes "...the victorious futurist is not a prophet. He or she does not defeat the future but predicts the present. Futurism doesn't mean predicting an awesome wonder; rather it means recognizing and describing a small apparent oddity that is destined to become a great commonplace."(Bruce Sterling. *Tomorrow Now: Envisioning the Next 50 Years*. 2003. Random House.)

In the 1980s Sterling made his name as a part of a group of science fiction writers that wrote what was called *Cyberpunk* science fiction. Along with authors like William Gibson, Sterling imagined a world of interconnected computer networks, free flowing data, and whole new interactions between humans and machines. What the Cyberpunks were describing in the 1980s is what would become the commercial Internet of the 1990s. In the 1980s these visions were both lyrical and revolutionary but by the 1990s with the popularization of the Internet, the Cyberpunk movement became a cliché. The ideas and technologies that they had dreamed about had become commonplace. Servers were those boring things locked away in the IT department. Getting online and chatting with someone halfway across the globe was easier that making a phone call. Sterling describes that he and his contemporaries' fantastic visions of the future only earned a shrug just ten years later.

Being outdated is inevitable, but becoming commonplace—now that's a goal! This is the ultimate compliment for any future vision: to earn just a shrug ten years later, to be mundane. Of course becoming mundane means that some portion of the vision has happened but it is a little more than that. To be mundane the vision needs to be so ordinary, so thoroughly woven into the lives of regular people that the very idea that it was once futuristic seems silly.

Sterling has a well grounded understanding of how the future comes to be. Later in the introduction he goes on to say: "Nothing obsolesces like 'the future'. Nothing burns out quite so quickly as a high-tech avant-garde. Technology doesn't glide into the streamlined world of tomorrow. It jolts and limps, all crutches and stilts…."

There is nothing streamlined about the future. It is just as messy and complicated as the present. The goal of this book is to start and facilitate a conversation rather than make hard and fast predictions. As we move day by day into the future of the screens that surround us, it is the conversation that will be most important.

Through the pages of this book that the future of TV is varied and exciting. The next paces that TV must take are both technological and economic. Working out the business complexities of the future of entertainment are just as important as developing the algorithms, data infrastructures, and microprocessors. The fact of the matter is that people love TV. People love entertainment and that is the reason why we having this conversation. We cannot lose sight of the reality that the future of all of our screens is dependent on the TV and entertainment that will play on those screens. The conversation we need is a collaboration between a motley collection of industries that aren't really used to talking with each other. That's why I saw, it's all about the conversation. Each industry needs the other to move forward. The good news is that consumers, real people all around the world as really excited about the future of TV. They can see it. They can imagine it and they want it.

So if you ask me what's the future of the future? Truthfully I can't tell you exactly but what I can tell you is that we'll all be watching it on TV.

***

It was lunch time and the café at Intel's Jones Farm Oregon campus was hopping with activity. Teams of engineers ate and gabbed at long tables while others popped in, grabbed some food, and then headed back to their cubes to eat. I sat in the middle of the pleasant hubbub with Justin Rattner, our Chief Technology Officer. Justin was not wearing his signature Hawaiian shirt but he was in a good mood, happy to be out of his executive conference room, near some windows and surrounded by people.

"So what do you think you'll say when you go on the Oprah Winfrey show?" Justin asked me with a smile.

I looked back, shocked, and had no idea what to say. We had been talking about *Screen Future*, this book and more specifically the conclusion that you are now reading. I had told him the overarching ideas in the book and how I was thinking about wrapping them up. That's when Justin asked me the question.

"I don't know," I finally replied. I understood that Justin wasn't really expecting that I would go on the Oprah Winfrey show and talk about the future of TV. He was making a point.

"That's really the question isn't it," he continued. "What does the future of TV mean to everyone, to people, to the people who watch the Oprah Winfrey show?"

It was an excellent question. We were both quiet for a while as the engineers rushed past with their food and a new team sat down at the table next to us and began to play dominos.

I can tell you what we know for sure about the future of TV: people will love it! Over the past few years we have an ongoing test that we do with consumers all over the world. This is a part of the UX testing we talked about in the Social TV chapter. As a part of the UX testing we ask people: "If your TV or laptop or smart phone could do anything to improve your experience with entertainment or computing what would you want it to do?" We keep it an open question to see what they fill in. It gives us a snapshot of their desires and imagination.

Consistently for the last few years the answer to this question has always been the same: people want more TV. They want access to their favorite shows that they missed. They want to be able to watch shows from last season or shows they just heard about from their friends. I guess when you think about it that way the future of TV, entertainment, and the devices we love is simple—it's just TV.

Now we know that "just TV" is actually quite complicated but it must be complicated behind the scenes. The increased functionality we gain by transforming entertainment into a compute task will happen off in the wings, behind the curtain. It's entertainment that will remain on stage. The economic and governmental complexities too must work themselves out up in the rafters among the lights and rigging. TV and entertainment are ultimately simply just about that—TV and entertainment. It's the TV shows, movies, games, and applications that will always take the main stage. They are the stars.

So to answer Justin's question: "Well Oprah, the future of TV will be better than it is today. You'll be able to watch your favorite shows when and where you want and through those shows you'll find other shows and movies and games. And through those shows and movies and games you'll connect with your friends and get to know a little bit more about what's going on in the world. There will be great new shows you haven't seen before and cool little applications that will connect it all together. The TV of the future will be a lot like the TV of today—just better, smarter, and more personal to you. You're going to love it!"

Brian David Johnson

2010

America

Appendix A

Consumer Experience Architecture: A Framework for Design

Consumer Experience Architecture (CEA) is a standardized methodology for developing products and technologies. The framework accommodates a wide range of inputs during the technology design and planning process. These inputs include computer science research and early development, theoretical computing, and social science research, along with traditional market analysis, demographic profiles, technological surveys, competitive analysis, and even science fiction visions. Additionally, the framework helps companies and designers to identify, document, and validate specific experience metrics, derived from these multiple and varied inputs. CEA's holistic approach to technology and product development lets an integrated development team not only gather and use innovative research but also validate the application of these ideas throughout the development process.

Conceptually we can divide the CEA framework into four stages, each serving as a key point of intersection between research and the industry development team. Additionally, each stage produces a set of standardized documents, practices, and workflows to inform the industry-accepted product- and service-development process.

Stage 1: Experimental and Theoretical Insights

The initial information-gathering stage provides input into the planning cycle.

The goal is to determine who your consumers or users might be along with what they value and how they understand your product or application. At Intel, a team of anthropologists, ethnographers, technologists, human-factors engineers, and design researchers work together to gather important and influential information.

The development team then uses the early research and development to develop a deep and well-rounded vision of end-user needs and reservations. At this stage, insights into human behavior and needs as well as technological advances can influence a product or system's early design.

Stage 2: Experience Definition

As the planning cycle moves forward and the product offering becomes more defined, the development team and research experts create a set of standardized documents that outline the specific consumer experience with the product or service. These documents have a particular resonance, because they're based on academic experimentation and real-world consumer insights.

This stage provides every member of the development team with a holistic understanding of the desired consumer experience. Consumer experience is the sum total of multiple inputs related to the consumer's understanding of a product. All these inputs provide a mental model to help the consumer better understand and use the product.

From the technical developers to the marketing team, this knowledge about the consumer proves invaluable during the development cycles. It informs the design process and becomes a shared understanding between all members of the development team. It gives them a shared goal to which they can return when addressing wider technical problems.

Stage 3: Early Product Definition

After the development team identifies the experience opportunities and maps the consumer's experience, they must deconstruct these opportunities into usage models and value propositions.

Usage models are an industry accepted standard format for developing technology specifications and prototypes. From the experience opportunities and usage models, the development team, research and domain experts then develop the product's value propositions.

These value propositions act as an expression of the product to the consumer, using their own language. Documenting these value propositions in consumer-specific language is an essential part of the framework. This stage also serves as a point of reflection and iteration. It lets the team make minor adjustments to the experience and product they're developing. This articulation of the product experience can serve as a way to discuss the product's attributes and value to people both inside and outside the development team.

Stage 4: Production and Validation

This is the longest stage—and it's the most complex to execute. During product development and validation, the development team applies a consumer experience (UX) validation process.

This process employs a variety of systematic methods to evaluate and understand people's perceptions of and experiences with the product. UX's targeted methods examine the user experience with concepts, prototypes, and functional product. UX isn't market research or focus-group testing; rather, it's an assessment of people's actual interactions with a prototype or product.

At each key milestone in the development process (such as the development of a prototype or release of an alpha or beta version), the development team uses UX to validate that the product addresses the original consumer experience goals. The test protocols for the UX validation are based on the core documents of the CEA. The earlier experience specification describes the test environments and how the product should present itself to the consumer. The team can even test the value propositions to see if they do indeed offer value to the consumer and if the product is meeting the promise of these propositions. Likewise, the team can develop and test possible solutions to overcoming adoption and usage barriers.

The UX validation process provides iterative feedback directly from the consumer regarding the product's successes and failures. By performing this validation process using early versions of the product multiple times throughout development and basing all stages on a consistent framework, UX lets the development team refine the product multiple times to meet the original experience opportunities outlined for the product. The results of the UX validation process are valuable to the development team. However, coupled with the experience documents from previous stages, they also help provide a clear and compelling picture of the product, even before it has shipped. The results of the UX validation can provide clarity to upper management, possible partners, and the investment community.

Technical Detail: Informative TV

WITH ANDY KUZMA

Andy Kuzma specializes in video analytics here at Intel. Over the past few years he has been working on a coprocessor approach that get's right at the heart of what we need to technically accomplish Informative TV. He would be quick to point out that some computer systems today already offer the types of capabilities described in the Informative TV chapter. Now these are not TVs, set top boxes, or DVD players. Usually these systems are rather complicated security and tracking systems made up of cameras and video analytics software. Andy will tell you that even it is possible to identify Bill Character and Frank Actor and track them throughout a scene of our fictitious movie *Visage*. This type of capability opens up a whole new range of experiences people can have with *Visage*, their TV, and entertainment.

However, qualitatively, we have reached a plateau for video analytics, and we need a substantial breakthrough to get to the level of performance required for video analytics to be generally useful, as shown in Figure B.1. In general to have the image tracking and image recognition be accurate takes a lot of computer power. At a certain level Frank Actor and Karl Hero both look very similar; both are male, Caucasian, with dark hair, and so on. Because of this, identifying Frank Actor as opposed to Karl Hero takes more processing power to get it right.

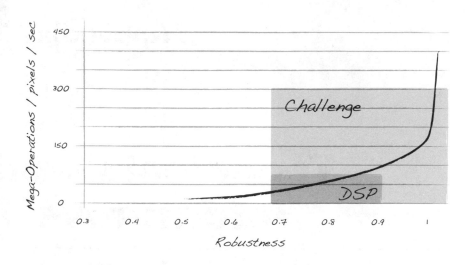

Figure B.1   Required mega-operations/pixel/second versus robustness

Many approaches can used to solve this problem, and each has advantages and disadvantages associated with it. The predominant approaches are to use a general purpose central processing unit (CPU) platform such as Intel® architecture like we described in the Informative TV chapter. You can use a general purpose digital signal processor (DSP) such as Texas Instruments DaVinci[†], Also you could use a combination of CPU and DSP, or a combination of a CPU and a media signal processor (MSP) such as StreamProcessor).

Implementations range from multi-chip solutions to single-chip solutions (SOC) that integrate the various combinations above. Just as there is no free lunch, there are implications to these choices, and this appendix hopes to bring more clarity about the technical differences and their associated implications.

The algorithms and processes needed to allow the computer to watch the scene are complex and compute-intensive when we begin to include processes like classification, tracking, segmentation, and pre-screening. This generates a new set of data, like metadata or an additional stream that is played along with the movie. These operations become more complex as the computer executes object recognition and tracking, generating more data to go along with the video. Figure B.2 gives more detail into the specific operations and low level algorithms needed to accomplish the task.

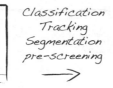 

Figure B.2   Low level operations and tasks needed to identify objects

As an overview of the computing, let's break the computing down so that we can further analyze the situation with the illustration in Figure B.2.

Step 1, the video is captured.

Step 2, we begin the processing stack. These initial steps are used to determine which pixels of the incoming video might be of interest.

At Step 3, more complex algorithms, which are built upon the earlier algorithmic steps, are performed.

An important point to note is the metadata is available at every layer of the algorithmic stack. The compute tasks needed to perform the steps in Figure B.2 vary depending on the information being processed. In Step 1, when the video is captured a large amount of data from the video stream enters the system. This information is then broken down and analyzed using video analytics. Figure B.3 shows that data rates for each task. The analysis of the video stream results in a metadata stream which contains the spatial and temporal description of the objects in the video (for example A = Object of Interest). The metadata stream is then further processed so that the information in the metadata will match the natural languages we humans use to describe scenes. (A = Bill Character = Frank Actor). Though this difference may seem simple, this transition from raw data to natural language data allows us to make use of the metadata in ways that make sense to TV viewers.

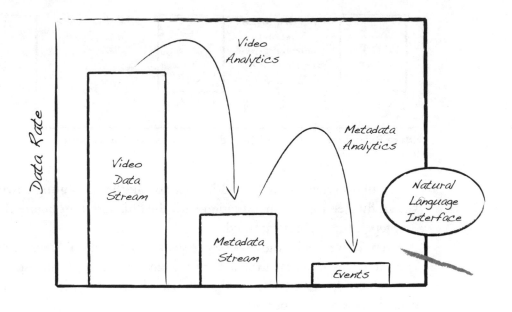

Figure B.3 Data rates for each task

Image Processing Arithmetic Operations

Analyzing the analytics data flow a bit more, we see there is a core set of arithmetic operations, as described in Figure B.4.

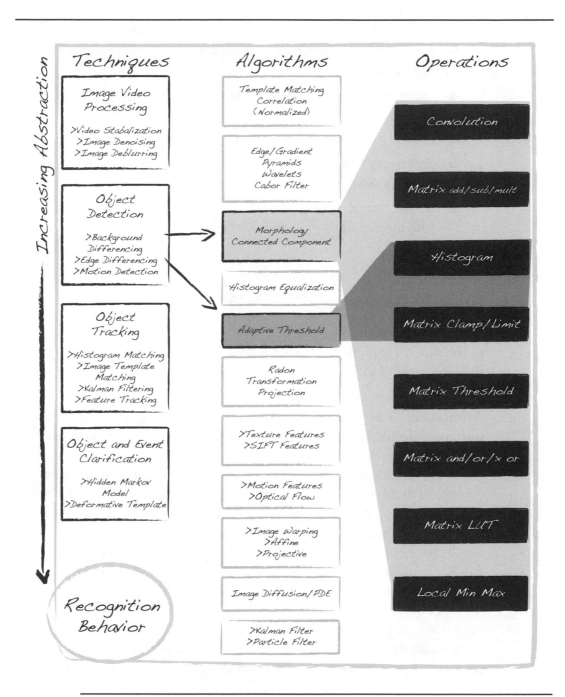

Figure B.4 Image processing arithmetic operations

A typical video sequence might be composed of the following operations:

■ Spatiotemporal filtering / convolution are 60–80 percent of total operations.

■ Geometric transformation, affine, projective are 10–20 percent of total operations.

■ Distance transformation, dilation are 10 percent of total operations.

■ Statistical, histogram, moments are approximately 10 percent of the total operations.

■ Image transformation, FFT/DCT could be a substitute for other filtering operations, but are more likely to be a used in a complementary manner.

Technology Barriers

Three primary technology barriers to computer vision and video analytics processing directly impact the algorithm by limiting the throughput of the image operations: arithmetic throughput, memory bandwidth, and memory size.

Arithmetic Throughput This throughput is the set of underlying arithmetic operations (multiplies, adds, subtracts) that comprise the image operations. Many of the interesting image operations involve operations between large, two dimensional data (the image) and smaller, two dimensional functions that combine a small neighborhood of the target pixel (the kernel), which is passed over the image. The number of arithmetic operations required climbs as the square of the image size and or the size of the kernel, and there's really not much that can be done about this effect, though approximations can be helpful. For example, a 3x3 convolution requires 9 multiplications and 8 additions (17 DSP operations) and a 7x7 convolution requires 49 multiplications and 48 additions (97 DSP operations). Over the years, engineers and scientists have developed a number of approximations in order to reduce the workload; such tradeoffs have to be considered at all times, but often the higher-level application programmers are unaware of the implications and their impact.

Memory Bandwidth This is how quickly the data can be provided to the arithmetic calculation, and just as importantly, how quickly the data can be written back to memory. Most memory interfaces are either reading or writing, and there's an overhead to switch from reading to writing. Small buffers can help reduce this problem, but there's a practical limit beyond which little is gained. A cached memory system is often used to help with the memory bandwidth problem.

Memory Size Images tend to be large amounts of data. As mentioned earlier, simultaneously reading and writing of the large image would be helpful. In modern microprocessors and digital signal processors, the available cache is smaller than the analytics frame resolution, and we typically need several images worth of memory at one time. But other pieces of code also need to be help in the cache, so large images can end up being swapped in and out of the memory cache several times. Further, because the objects of interest within the video scene are not constrained as to where they happen in the scene (people walk from a set boundary to boundary), it's very difficult to divide up the scene into smaller sections that could allow us to divide and conquer the memory size challenge.

But don't despair. Useful systems are possible within the constraints that we'll talk about later in this appendix (see framc-oriented versus pixel-oriented discussion), but these can bring out difficult issues in terms of programming and maintainability.

Several other factors must be considered in addition to the selection of the hardware components. Important factors are discussed in more detail in the following sections.

Software

In our rush to provide immediate solutions, we often overlook a reality of modern systems: software development, maintenance, and licenses become the dominant costs over the product life cycle.

We must consider software development, management and investment. An often overlooked aspect of product development and support, especially for technology products, is the cost of software: the initial development, validation testing, compatibility testing, maintenance, support, and new product development. Both the final customer and the supplier bear these efforts, affecting both the external costs of the deployment, and the internal costs of operation. (Hence the interest, from a business perspective, to add business intelligence capabilities to surveillance networks in order to generate an easily-measured output.)

Frameworks and Standards

Frameworks and standards provide the customers with several benefits: interoperability, competition, innovation, and cost effectiveness.

Open Systems

Open systems describes the condition whereby many providers and users have access to similar capabilities due to ready-availability. For example, the personal computer is considered an open system because of the wide availability of PC-based solutions. Microsoft Windows and Apple MacOS are good examples of typical application development frameworks. Within signal processing domains, Microsoft's DirectShow and the Linux gstreamer other types of frameworks.

Scalability

Scalability is the ability to add functionality in several dimensions relevant usually to industries like video surveillance:

- Algorithmic performance at each node, such as the number of objects that can be tracked.
- Number of concurrent algorithms running at each node, such as running a loitering application and people counter simultaneously, perhaps from two separate algorithm vendors.
- Number of nodes in the system, such as a system that effectively partitions the video analytics workload appropriately as the deployment grows from a small installation of four cameras to a system of ten thousand nodes.
- Ability to deploy, maintain, and manage a large system, such as the ability to configure, remotely manage the software and algorithms, restore the configuration, set the configuration to best match security scenarios.

Compatibility

Not to be overlooked is the compatibility with modern IT procedures and networks. The total cost of ownership (TCO) is a an important aspect of the deployment. Having a ready-source of IT-tested software and hardware improves the confidence of the customer to adopt and deploy systems.

Models for Implementation

Let's take a brief look at implementation options. Minimally, we need a CPU in order to host the application, and if there are other components in the system, to host them, too.

It would be ideal to have only a CPU. Why? Because then we could use a single part to run everything required. And as we mentioned the importance of software earlier, using a single CPU is a big advantage because all the code is developed, controlled, debugged, and integrated within a single software development environment. That means tracking down bugs, fixing them, and validating the fix works without breaking something else (all too common) is simpler, an especially important attribute for the large software development efforts that are common. Further, if the CPU is widely accepted, then we can take advantage of the ecosystem of applications, middleware, and development tools that are available, not to mention a pool of developers already familiar with how to develop programs.

There might be reasons why a single CPU won't work, however, such as power dissipation limits and computing power relative to the set of tasks (also known as workload). It might be that the CPU is good at most of the workload, but needs help with some of the tasks. In this very real scenario, there are options to add specialized processing devices to the CPU. These devices are Field Programmable Gate Arrays (FPGAs), Digital Signal Processors (DSPs), Application-Specific Signal Processors (ASSPs), and Media Signal Processors (MSPs). And all the variations in-between, even integrating the CPU and these devices onto a single die to create a System-on-Chip (SOC).

Table B.1 Devices and Examples

Device	Example
CPU	Intel Atom, Intel Core2Duo, Intel Xeon
DSP	Texas Instruments '642
DSP + MSP	TI '6467
MSP	Mobilygen H.264 encoder
ASSP	Techwell multichannel baseband video decoder
FGPA	Xilinx or Altera

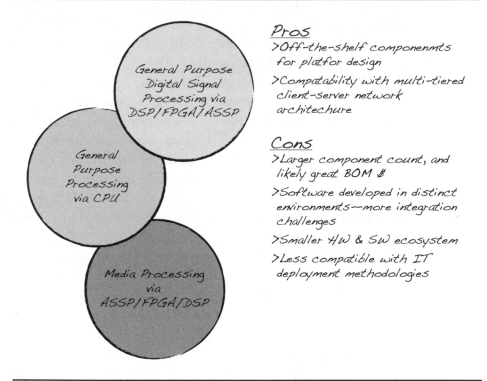

Pros
> Off-the-shelf componenmts for platfor design
> Compatability with multi-tiered client-server network architechure

Cons
> Larger component count, and likely great BOM $
> Software developed in distinct environments--more integration challenges
> Smaller HW & SW ecosystem
> Less compatible with IT deployment methodologies

General Purpose Digital Signal Processing via DSP/FPGA/ASSP

General Purpose Processing via CPU

Media Processing via ASSP/FPGA/DSP

Figure B. 5   CPU + DSP + MSP model

CPU + DSP + MSP

The model shown in Figure B.5 partitions functions across the several processing elements. In general, larger combinations are more effort on and hardware design and development because different tools and development teams are required, and integration and testing of the integration is challenging.

CPU + DSP with Integrated MSP

In the CPU + DSP with integrated MSP model shown in Figure B.6, the CPU requires that additional processing be done by a more specialized components. This model is really an extension of the prior model (CPU + DSP + MSP) except that the MSP functions are now closely coupled to the DSP. In fact, they are only accessible as part of the DSP (such as Texas Instruments DaVinci DM64XX with the VICP).

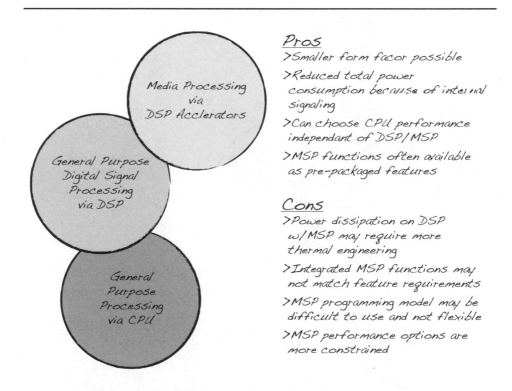

Figure B.6   CPU + DSP with Integrated MSP model

This model partitions functions across the several processing elements. In general, larger combinations are more effort on and hardware design and development because different tools and development teams are required, and integration and testing of the integration is challenging.

Integrated CPU + DSP with MSP

In the integrated CPU + DSP with MSP, or SOC model, shown in Figure B.7, is a further extension of the prior model (CPU + DSP with MSP) with further integration to include a CPU core.

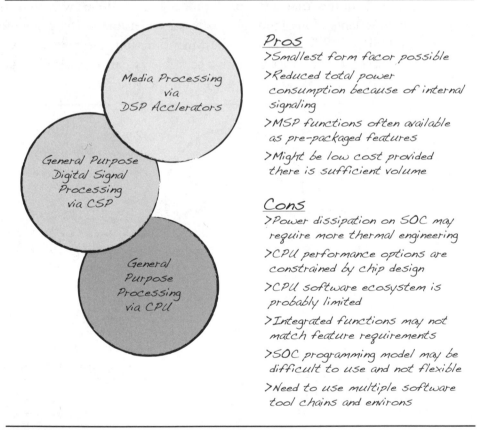

Media Processing via DSP Acclerators

General Purpose Digital Signal Processing via CSP

General Purpose Processing via CPU

Pros
> Smallest form facor possible
> Reduced total power consumption because of internal signaling
> MSP functions often available as pre-packaged features
> Might be low cost provided there is sufficient volume

Cons
> Power dissipation on SOC may require more thermal engineering
> CPU performance options are constrained by chip design
> CPU software ecosystem is probably limited
> Integrated functions may not match feature requirements
> SOC programming model may be difficult to use and not flexible
> Need to use multiple software tool chains and environs

Figure B.7   Integrated CPU + DSP with MSP (SOC) model

In general, larger combinations are more effort on and hardware design and development because different tools and development teams are required, and integration and testing of the integration is challenging. It's unlikely that the CPU in this model has as broad and deep a software and hardware ecosystem, further complicating the development.

Most people initially assume the SOC is the ultimate product goal. However, as the ability to create an SOC has evolved, the analysis has evolved from simple cost reduction to a more complex analysis of which functions it is sensible to aggregate, both for the chip supplier and the product designer. For example, the SOC requires very large quantities in order to pay back in the expensive engineering development and support, whereas if the product developer wants platform-level flexibility, the SOC might not provide the solution. Unless one-size-fits-all is appropriate, the SOC approach doesn't work.

CPU + Coprocessor

The CPU + coprocessor model, illustrated in Figure B.8, is a specialization of the CPU + DSP model with important benefits. The coprocessor can be realized as a specialized chip similar to the floating point math coprocessor. The advantages of this approach are that it is not disruptive to the software and hardware ecosystems; rather it is complementary. By focusing the operations specific to video analytics, the performance and performance per watt can be much greater than other solutions. The coprocessor can be presented to the software in a way that makes it simpler to adopt, and the software can be compatible between software-only and coprocessor-accelerated, allowing a flexible deployment strategy.

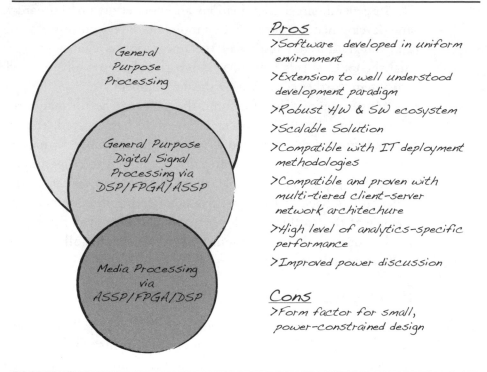

Pros
> Software developed in uniform environment
> Extension to well understood development paradigm
> Robust HW & SW ecosystem
> Scalable Solution
> Compatible with IT deployment methodologies
> Compatible and proven with multi-tiered client-server network architechure
> High level of analytics-specific performance
> Improved power discussion

Cons
> Form factor for small, power-constrained design

General Purpose Processing

General Purpose Digital Signal Processing via DSP/FPGA/ASSP

Media Processing via ASSP/FPGA/DSP

Figure B.8 CPU + Coprocessor model

Addressing Performance Bottlenecks

One of the ways to address performance bottlenecks is to use a *specialized accelerator*. Either integrated or physically separate, accelerators provide enhanced performance in terms of computation throughput and power dissipation. A good example of a specialized accelerator is a hardware-based MPEG-2 decoder.

A memory cache has proven to be extremely effective in many areas of computing because access patterns in typical computer applications have locality of reference. Cache memory is a general system resource.

The challenge of larger caches for general purpose processing elements (CPUs and DSPs) is the additional costs are borne by all applications, most of which do not need the large cache sizes required for video analytics.

Private memory is data storage and data access that is dedicated to a particular function. This memory is not a general system resource; that is, when the function(s) associated with private memory are not used, the memory is not usable by the system.

A good example of a private memory is a DRAM attached to an FPGA to provide cost-effective memory resources that cannot be realized on the logic-centric FPGA chip. The private memory attached to the FPGA is used for guaranteed high-speed, low-latency data access that would not be possible using the CPU's system memory.

Computing Architecture Selection

So now we have a very complex computing architecture selection to make, as an example let's use a complex video surveillance system to explore the requirements for development installation and maintenance. Eventually this will apply to larger entertainment and news organizations but for the time being most of these systems are being used for security.

We have a good idea of the high-level network architecture required, and that the components need to be compatible with standard IT procedures and methods.

If cost, power, and form factor were not a problem, we might be tempted to put Intel® Xeon® multi-core processor systems everywhere because of the software and hardware ecosystems that can provide the solution components.

But power and form factor matter. Cost, if we consider the software development and maintenance, might actually be a lesser issue, but both initial and life cycle cost matter, so we can't dismiss it.

Assuming that the preferred solution is a multichannel aggregation point that is one step into the network from the video camera (please see "Network Architecture Impact with Respect the Smart Camera" in Figure B.9), we can make the conclusions outlined in Table B.2.

Table B.2   Deciding on a Computing Architecture for Video Surveillance

Computing Architecture	Comments
CPU + DSP + MSP	Components are available today. This is a fairly complex design, so careful design of the subsystem interfaces is required to allow for evolution of the components. Performance optimizations tend to work against a stable software architecture.
	As each component can be scaled separately, the scalability towards higher multichannel density is fairly obvious.
	Cost and form factor are concerns.
CPU + DSP with MSP	Components are available today. This is a fairly complex design and several of the hardware and software interfaces are given; if these fit the requirements, then it can work fairly well, but otherwise there is a lot of effort required to develop alternatives at extensions.
SOC	Applicable to the smart IP camera. With sufficient volume, this could be the cost effective way to deploy semi-intelligent cameras.
	Limited flexibility and adaptability. The SOC could be used in the multichannel aggregation point, but it would require a complex hardware and software design and integration at the product level.
	The software ecosystem for this approach is a major concern, as is compatibility with IT deployment standards.
CPU + Coprocessor	A more optimal solution in terms of scalability and IT compatibility. This allows solutions to scale to a range of CPUs and platforms.
	Choosing an Intel-based CPU allows us to use the ecosystem to best advantage, while preserving the software investment around a video analytics coprocessor.

Computer Architecture Grading

Use Table B.3 to compare various implementations to determine whether the computer architectural approach makes sense to your products and/or deployment.

Table B.3   Computer Architecture Grading Table

Consideration	Appropriateness						
	CPU	CPU + DSP	CPU + DSP + MSP	CPU + DSP with MSP	Integrated CPU + DSP with MSP	SOC	CPU + Coprocessor
processing elements							
functional partitioning							
compatibility/ authentication/ security							
remote manageability							
operating system							
number distinct processing elements							
power dissipation							
scalability and flexibility							
development time							
maintenance costs							
robustness of hardware and software ecosystems							
compatibility with the users' procedures and policies							
compatibility with emerging technology and deployment							
initial costs							
total cost of ownership							

Network Architecture Impact with Respect the Smart Camera

As the need for systems that can analyze large amounts of video grows it will be necessary to consider how to integrate legacy video post-production and/or security camera systems into a multi-tiered network architecture.

As we discussed in the Informative TV chapter much of the current work in this area is being done with security and surveillance systems. Figure B.9 gives us a good example from the security industry of how legacy video capture systems might be brought into alignment with a new networked architecture. A current trend in some security industries that are using video analytics is to put as much intelligence at the edge of the network as possible, and most people assume this means into the video camera itself.

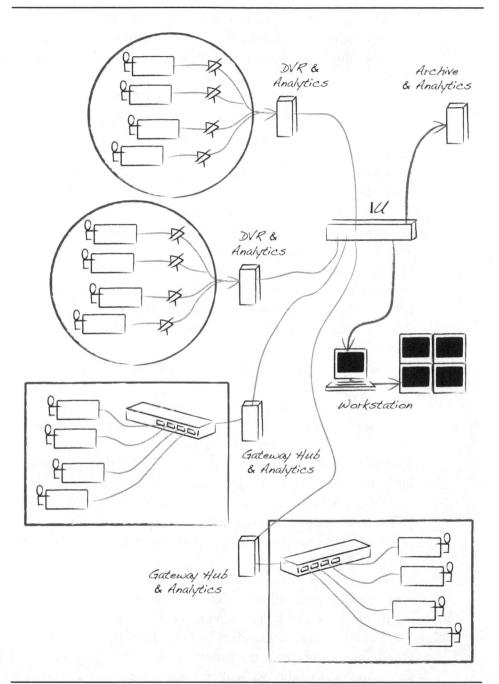

Figure B.9   A simplified diagram of multi-tiered client-server network architecture

There are certainly cases where this is desirable, but there are also many instances where this doesn't make sense, and instead a camera that provides a reliable video stream (analog or digital) is preferred. Consider the following factors:

Form factors for cameras tend to be very small and use passive thermal dissipation (no fans) for the electronic components. This limits the total thermal dissipation within the enclosure because of self-heating of the electronics.

Camera costs tend to be very constrained. Smart cameras have been available for machine vision, but their costs have impeded their adoption.

Increasing resolution of the cameras requires digital encoding. There is no composite video standard(that is, using a single wire) beyond standard definition ("D1"), though a new effort is underway in the industry in the HDcctv Alliance. Without a single-wire interface so higher resolutions must be encoded in H.264 and/or MPEG-4 and/or MPEG-2 and/or Motion JPEG, and possibly proprietary digital encodings. Further, the use of Ethernet (10/100/1000 Mbps) as the transmission media is much better utilized with the digital encoders.

Increased video resolution requires an increase in the processing available to encode the video.

The combination of costs and power dissipation limits impact the total amount of computing that's available for the foreseeable future. Eventually it may be possible to increase the computing ceiling, but by then it's likely the analytics processing requirements will also have risen significantly. This will limit the useful life cycle of the analytics.

The camera is the most exposed part of the surveillance network. Spray paint can ruin a lens. A rock or a baseball bat can ruin the entire camera. This could result in an expensive, short-lived component that will drive up the total cost of ownership.

Because the camera is usually in an awkward placement, remote management and upgradeability become more important, as does compatibility with IT management tools and procedures.

These represent serious drawbacks to the operational feasibility of putting all the intelligence into the camera. One counter argument has been that video analytics quality will suffer when using decoded digital video, which has low quality because of bandwidth constraints. However, all modern

Ethernet deployments are a point-to-point connection between the endpoint and the Ethernet switch sitting in the wiring closet, and there is no shortage of bandwidth over this link in the network.

A better system-level solution is to move the primary analytics processing to the wiring closet next to the Ethernet switch. Simple analytics in the IP camera probably make sense as a fallback, but the interesting analytics is better done one step into the network. Further, the wiring closet fits better with standard IT procedures for deployment and maintenance, and system upgrades are simpler to manage. A multichannel aggregation point with video analytics sitting in the wiring closet and other internal network nodes makes more sense.

Appendix C

Technical Detail: Ubiquitous TV

JEFF FOERSTER, SRINIVASA SOMAYAZULU, BARRY O'MAHONY, OZGUR OYMAN, SRIRAM SRIDHARAM, CHUCK SMITH, ROY WANT

Several technology ingredients are needed to realize the vision for Ubiquitous TV described in Chapter 4. This appendix covers some selected topics related to each of the three pillars of ubiquity shown in Figure C.1, including Device, Spectrum, and Networks, described in Chapter 4, as well as Compression, which spans all the pillars. In particular, this appendix covers:

- The Device pillar: enabling interconnectivity
- The Spectrum pillar: challenges and the need for cooperation
- The Network pillar:
  - Ubiquitous home networks (wired and wireless)
  - Wireless broadband networks
- The role of compression
- Video specific optimizations: a cross-layer approach

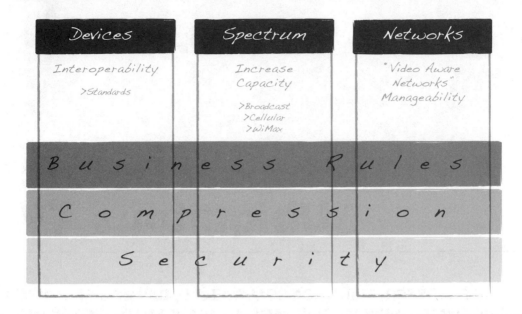

Figure C.1   The three pillars of ubiquity

The intention of this appendix is not to provide an exhaustive summary of all technologies needed to enable Ubiquitous TV, but rather give some technical grounding on just some of the challenges and opportunities that exist.

The Device Pillar: Enabling Interconnectivity

As the TV experience becomes much more interactive in the future, and as people want to access their content on any device they own, there is a need to be able to connect multiple consumer devices to the TV. This could be as simple as using a handheld device, such as an iPhone[†], as the remote control for the TV, to more complex models where a consumer could use the hand-held device to flick various media files to the TV and or "mash up" multiple windows with various content to be viewed on the TV. In order to achieve this interaction between the devices, it will be important to have a reliable wireless link between the TV and the mobile devices, since connecting with a wire may not always be very convenient and impacts the ease of use. So, this wireless connectivity must support low-latency interactivity as well as high speeds for rapid file exchanges.

Due to the ubiquity of Wi-Fi[†], this would be a natural first step for connecting the TV with mobile devices. There is ongoing work in the Wi-Fi Alliance to make a peer-to-peer connection between two Wi-Fi clients seamless and easy to connect. In addition, there is work on the next generation of Wi-Fi within the Very High Throughput (VHT) task groups IEEE 802.11ac, for using the unlicensed bands below 6 GHz, and IEEE 802.11ad for using the unlicensed bands around 60 GHz. Figure C.2 compares the throughputs of the different current and future Wi-Fi technologies with existing cellular and UWB technologies. Clearly, the peak throughput of the short-range technologies, including Wi-Fi, UWB, and 60 GHz, is much greater than the cellular technologies. In addition, the short-range technologies share the available throughput with much fewer number of users, so the throughput is available for more of the time. These high-rate, short-range technologies will become increasingly important both inside the home and outside the home for connecting devices together and exchanging large files, like HD movies.

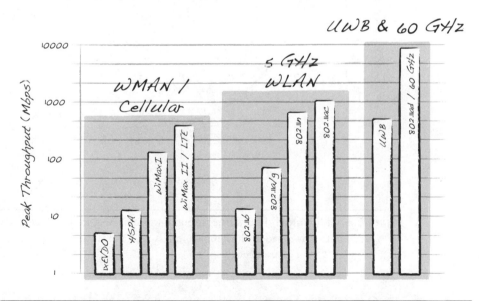

Figure C.2   Peak throughput comparison among different wireless technologies

Having access to a high-speed link opens up many possibilities to connect devices in the home together and with the TV. It enables the opportunity for users to take more content with them on the go. For example, in order to meet acceptable wait times, the throughput needs to be on the order of several Gbps to download an HD movie in less than a minute, as illustrated in Figure C.3. Once this happens, a new business model could emerge where movies could be rented from the set-top box within the home or even devices like the RedBox kiosk or Wi-Fi hot-spots using a wireless link. This could also be a way to easily move content between the home DVR and the car in order to watch movies on the go. Given the limitations of viewing video over broadband wireless or broadcast wireless networks, it will be important to have the ability to download content from local DVRs or kiosks, store them on your mobile device, and watch them on the go.

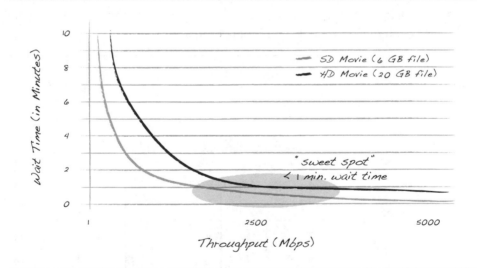

Figure C.3   Download time versus throughput for a short-range wireless link. In order to download an HD movie in less than a minute, wireless data rates above 2.5 Gbps are needed.

One of the biggest hurdles for connecting wireless devices together is making it easy. Much progress has been made over the years to improve this with the Bluetooth Alliance as well as within the Wi-Fi Alliance. In addition, new technologies like near-field communications (NFC) also simplify the linking together of different devices by simply touching them together in the appropriate places. The combination of next generation high-throughput, short-range technologies along with ease-of-use improvements, will help realize the connected TV vision and seamless interaction between devices.

The Spectrum Pillar: Challenges and the Need for Cooperation

Once we move outside the home the networking world becomes vastly more complicated. Even today we have multiple kinds of networks managed by different companies from very different communication sectors and many operating on very different frequency bands or spectrum (such as cell phones, WiMAX, and digital broadcasting).

When outside of the home, consumers can get access to video content in several ways. These include:

1. Real-time streaming content over a wireless network. This could be a cellular or WiMAX network, using unicast or multi-cast streaming; or using a broadcast network like ATSC or DVB-H; or using an unlicensed Wi-Fi hot-spot.

2. Non–real-time streaming. Using any of the above networks, the content could be streamed, but buffered in the device with some delay before viewing could be started. This method adds greater flexibility in delivering the content compared with real-time streaming.

3. Downloading content. Again, this could be accomplished using any of the above mentioned networks, but downloading the files rather than streaming in real-time.

The overall capacity impact on the wireless network is the same for any of these methods, but each has different tradeoffs when trying to optimize the delivery of the content. For example, if a high-speed Wi-Fi network is available, it would be more efficient to download the content at the highest rate so that the video file could be viewed later, and the radio could be turned off after the download to save power. Broadcast networks are good for delivering real-time video content that a large portion of the population might want to view, like sporting events, but it does not allow for providing video-on-demand. Streaming content over a cellular or WiMAX system using a unicast channel allows for different content to be streamed to different people, but this imposes a significant capacity burden on the network. So, it's important to understand how these different wireless networks can be used to deliver video services to mobile users outside of the home, and how the different delivery mechanisms (real-time streaming, non–real-time streaming, and downloading) should be used for different kinds of content.

As discussed earlier, the challenge for realizing the vision for ubiquitous TV on mobile platforms will require significant improvement in capacity for these mobile networks. Table C.1 shows the throughputs required as a function of the level of compression used for different video resolutions.

Table C.1 Uncompressed and compressed throughputs for different screen resolutions

	Col	Row	Bits per Pixel	Frame Rate (Hz)	Uncompressed Throughput (Mbps)	Compressed Throughout (10:1)	Compressed Throughout (20:1)	Compressed Throughput (100:1)	Compressed Throughput (150:1)
QVGA	320	240	24	30	55	5.5	2.8	0.553	0.369
HVGA	480	320	24	30	111	11.1	5.5	1.106	0.737
nHD	640	360	24	30	166	16.6	8.3	1.659	1.106
VGA	640	480	24	30	221	22.1	11.1	2.212	1.475
WVGA	864	480	24	30	299	29.9	14.9	2.986	1.991
SVGA	800	600	24	30	346	34.6	17.3	3.456	2.304
QHD	960	540	24	30	373	37.3	18.7	3.732	2.488
XVGA	1024	768	24	30	566	56.6	28.3	5.662	3.775
720p	1280	720	24	30	664	66.4	33.2	6.636	4.424
1080p	1920	1080	24	30	1493	149.3	74.6	14.930	9.953

To give some perspective to the numbers in Table C.1, Blu-ray[†] discs, which provide HD quality video (720p, 1080p at 60 frames per second) support up to a maximum of 40 Mbps video transfer rate out of the disc (read rates). This is done with compression ratios on the order of 20:1 to 50:1, but requires a substantial amount of complexity in the encoder and decoder to achieve. Compared to current data rates over 3G networks, which support

14.4 Mbps on the downlink and 5.8 Mbps on the uplink for HSPA+, clearly it would not be possible to broadcast even a single Blu-ray quality video channel. In fact, most of the broadcast video solutions, like MediaFlo[†] or DVB-H[†] or ATSC M/H[†], support video data rates on the order to 300 Kbps up to 1 Mbps, depending on the service and quality levels. These data rates result in pretty good quality (always a subjective metric) for small screens on handheld devices. Even these data rates are 50 to 100 times that of voice, which tends to be between 5.6 and 13 kbps. This poses significant business challenges to broadband network providers on how best to monetize their spectrum usage.

In addition to viewing content on your handheld device, people may also want to view video content on a netbook, laptop, or even on a larger screen that may be connected to the netbook or laptop via a docking station or other means. In this case, although the quality delivered to a small screen might be good enough, the quality when viewed on a larger screen may not be acceptable. This kind of usage calls for a more scalable solution supported by the network that can target different devices with different capabilities and attributes. Clearly, the more throughput that could be given to these video channels, the higher the quality. This, in part, is driving the need for higher capacity broadband wireless networks like WiMAX and LTE, since video content accessed by consumers continues to grow. The broadband wireless networks, by themselves, will never be able to match the capacity that can be delivered to the home via fiber or coaxial cable. As such, it will become increasingly important to be able to utilize different wireless networks to deliver these services, including broadband wireless (LTE, WiMAX), broadcast (ATSC, DVB), Wi-Fi, and maybe even new spectrum that recently opened up as part of the TV white space. The use of unlicensed spectrum to offload the main broadband wireless network is becoming an important avenue in order to enable these various mobile video services. For example, companies like AT&T are using Wi-Fi hotspots more and more to offload data applications in order to free up more capacity for services that can generate more revenue for their spectrum, mainly voice and text messaging. The insatiable appetite for video content and staying connected with video (not just voice or text) will continue to drive the need for access to more spectrum over the coming years and will require innovative technologies as well as spectrum regulatory rules.

Even though these challenges are difficult, there is a driving business need to address them. Many wireless operators are going after what's been called a "three screens" strategy as mentioned previously. This refers to the PC, TV, and mobile screens, and reflects the opportunity to send more content and targeted advertisements to each of these screens for additional services and revenue creation. For example, AT&T and Verizon are offering video services over their wireless network, and are combining this with their home Internet and home video service offerings (for example, AT&T U-verse TV[†], Verizon V-cast[†]). However, many of these services are not yet completely integrated in the sense that a user cannot yet get access to the same content that is offered inside the home when the user is outside. There is also a "quad-play" business opportunity to bundle services to offer home video, telephone, Internet, and broadband wireless/cellular services. In Portland, Oregon, Comcast[†] is acting as a mobile virtual network operator (MVNO) by reselling Clearwire[†] broadband wireless services over their WiMAX network in order for Comcast to complete a quad-play. Cox Communications[†], a long time cable provider, is acting as an MVNO by reselling Sprint services, and is also in the process of building its own cellular network. However, the mobile user is not able to get access to all of the cable companies' content over the wireless network yet, due to the many challenges in network capacity that are discussed above. On the other hand, if a single network provider, like Comcast, could deliver all of the various services and content to multiple devices in a seamless manner, it would create a new opportunity for distributing content and more opportunities to show advertisements, potentially with specific targeted ads. Also, by adding the capability of creating a greater personal profile based upon the mobile viewing habits in addition to home viewing habits, companies could learn a lot more about a consumer's likes and dislikes, which could help recommend more relevant content for that user as well as improve the success rate of targeted ads.

One of the challenges for delivering a cohesive experience within the home and outside the home is the fact that there may be different networks and multiple players in the value chain required for enabling these services. For example, a cable company, like Comcast, needs to partner with a wireless network provider, like Clearwire, to provide access to content wirelessly outside the home. However, they may also need to partner with a broadcaster who owns access to broadcast spectrum to allow Comcast to broadcast their content as well. Recently, Sprint called for more cooperation with broadcasters to enable some of these new services. Figure C.4 illustrates the many players involved in the delivery of video content over multiple transport methods.

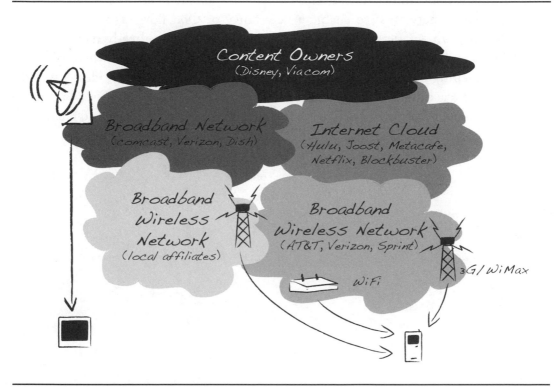

Figure C.4   Multiple video players are involved when delivering video services to the mobile device

In order to create a more ubiquitous experience for users inside and outside the home, it must be possible to allow video content to be delivered across different networks. This is both a technical challenge as well as a business challenge (what's the financial motivation to cooperate?). There need to be more innovative business models and services to enable this kind of cooperation. As an example, as we move towards a more video-on-demand model where people want immediate access to any kind of content wherever they may be, then the traditional broadcast model breaks down. In addition, a more distributed model for delivering video content may be needed in order to handle the network capacity demands of this kind of service. Doing more processing on the edge of the network to ensure a high quality of service and access to a range of quality offerings, which may be possible through the use of a scalable video codec, may be needed. This, in turn, creates a new opportunity for the wireless network providers (broadcast and two-way access networks) to enable a new range of QoS flows as well as a range of payment tiers, while the network providers that already have access to the content could benefit from a distributed architecture where different caching of content could be done by the wireless network nodes. Similarly, this caching of content could be done within the home of a user to create a broader distributed network for video. This kind of model could create new business opportunities for different players in the value chain.

The Network Pillar: Ubiquitous Home Networks

A key ingredient in delivering ubiquitous video content to connected TVs throughout the home is a home network, capable of transporting both user-created and service-provider supplied content from any location within the home to any other, with high quality of service.

While the typical household today has multiple TVs, their connectivity has historically been limited to the simple one-way "push" model of an identical stream of broadcast services being distributed to each individual television, shown in Figure C.5.

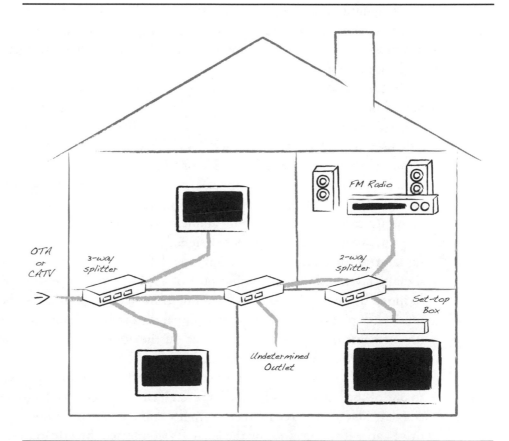

Figure C.5   Typical household TV connectivity today

As shown in Figure C.5, real-time broadcasts of simultaneous programs on multiple channels are received at the house by one or more means; such as with an antenna from *over the air* (OTA) broadcasts, and/or by a coaxial cable feed from a *cable TV multiple system operator* (CATV MSO). The received signal is then delivered from the point of entry to every TV in the household through a series of coaxial cables, typically configured in a branching tree structure. At each cable junction, a signal splitter is used to transfer the signals from the upstream cable to two or more downstream cables, with the ultimate destination being the RF input of a TV or associated set top box (STB). The splitters are hybrid-transformer-based devices that allocate a portion of the input signal to each output port, with minimal overall signal amplitude loss, other than about 0.5 dB loss per port; for example, the signal level at each port of a two output port device is approximately 3.5 dB less than the level supplied to the input port.

Since this type of home coaxial cabling is designed and installed to only deliver broadcast content from a single point of entry and distribute it to each TV, the connectivity options it supports are very limited. Service provider video services are delivered to each TV. This cable configuration also allows signals to travel upstream, from a TV or STB, back up to the service provider: signals pass from an input port of a splitter to its output port just as well as they pass in the downstream direction. This is in fact how the two-way communications needed for cable modems is supported.

This type of wiring was not designed to support end-node-to-end-node signal transmission, such as from one STB to another. Attenuation of signals traveling from one output port of a splitter to another is high, 25 dB or more, by design. Reflections from unterminated outlets (that is, those with no devices plugged into them) cause signal distortions. Taken together, these impairments impose severe limitations on the ability to provide ubiquity of all types of video within the home. For example, a PC or home server storing user-created video content cannot easily use such wiring to send a video clip to one of the home's TVs for display, even if the PC is connected to one of the coaxial cable nodes. As another example, content stored on one STB's hard drive can only be accessed by the local TV connected directly to the STB; the content is unavailable to other TVs in the home.

What is needed to fully realize ubiquitous content is a true network connecting the devices within a home, one that allows transmission of content between any pair of devices residing in a home. The ideal network will cover the entire house including what are now "blind spots," have sufficient throughput to allow multiple simultaneous streams on the network, ensure privacy of user data and activities, ensure protection of content, and enable real-time streaming with sufficient quality of service to achieve a compelling user experience.

Wireless Home Networks

The most common home network technology in today's homes is that based on the IEEE 802.11 suite of standards for wireless LANs, commonly known as Wi-Fi. Wi-Fi networks currently encompass unlicensed operation on the 2.4-GHz and 5-GHz bands. The most popular versions found in homes include the ones based on the 802.11b and 802.11g 2.4-GHz standards, which offer bit rates of up to 11 and 54 Mbps and typical throughput of approximately 5 and 20 Mbps, respectively. The newest version, 802.11n, supports multiple-input multiple-output (MIMO) operation in the 2.4- or 5-GHz bands, at bit rates up to 600 Mbps and typical throughput of approximately 150 Mbps.

The originally defined privacy mechanism in 802.11, Wired Equivalent Protocol or WEP, is now widely considered obsolete, and in fact is easily broken. The current Wi-Fi products use the 802.11i security standard, based on the NIST Advanced Encryption Standard (AES) algorithm, which is considered state of the art.

Most home Wi-Fi networks operate in Infrastructure mode, where all transmissions consist of wireless links between one or more access points (APs), and end node. Another supported mode is Ad Hoc, whereby the intermediate transit through the AP is dispensed with, and transmission occurs directly between pairs of end nodes communicating with each other. A variation of this is mesh networking based on the 802.11s standard, which permits multi-hop communications whereby nodes can act as intermediate relays for communications between node pairs. This is particularly useful for implementing communications between "hidden" nodes, such as, for example, nodes that, due to propagation characteristics, are unable to directly communicate themselves, but are able to communicate with a common set of relay nodes.

The original 802.11 MAC was well-suited for applications insensitive to delay and other QoS concerns, such as data transfer and Web browsing. The 802.11e standard defines MAC enhancements intended to support QoS-dependent applications such as video. It specifies support for both priority-based media access, as well as parameter-based bandwidth reservation.

802.11 and Video

Wireless networks offer the utmost in convenience, supporting connectivity without the need to run wires and offering untethered connectivity to mobile/portable devices. It is largely for this reason that they are by far the most widely deployed home networking technology. By themselves they are not always the ideal basis for networking of video, however.

A key issue that arises is signal propagation. Video cannot be sent between nodes that cannot physically communicate. For example, the 2.4-GHz frequency band used by most home Wi-Fi was originally made available for unlicensed operation because it was thought to be poorly suited for radio communication, and was allocated for industrial, scientific, and medical (ISM) equipment uses, with a secondary allocation for unlicensed radio communications. Innovations in communications technology have steadily improved performance in this and other Wi-Fi bands. In North American homes, the predominant construction techniques use gypsum wallboard ("drywall") for interior partition walls, and wood beams and composite wood sheet goods for flooring. Wi-Fi propagation inside such structures is generally good. Other types of construction such as masonry (especially reinforced concrete) and metal lathe-and plaster, which predominate in other parts of the world but may also be found in North America, form more significant barriers to signal transmission. Recently introduced techniques such as mesh networking and MIMO help to mitigate such effects, although propagation through multiple reinforced concrete walls still proves challenging. In the future, operation at frequencies with better propagation characteristics, such as unoccupied VHF and UHF broadcast TV channels (TV "white space"), may further contribute to enhancing the capabilities of wireless networking in such difficult environments.

Another concern is adequate throughput. While 802.11n networks today deliver approximately 150 Mbps of throughput, this may not be adequate to support the rich range of applications provided by service providers (SPs) and desired by users. Such applications will burden the network with multiple High Definition, trick-mode-enabled real-time video streams, as well as high speed bulk transfers for "sync 'n go" applications. Related to this are concerns with QoS. It is a fundamental challenge to ensure quality of service on communications bands that are unlicensed and where the channel is uncontrolled. For example, home microwave ovens operate in the same 2.4-GHz band as 802.11 devices, and may cause significant interference. Other unlicensed communications devices operating in the same band may also cause interference, such as cordless telephones, wireless toys, and even 802.11 networks in adjacent homes.

Lastly, there are issues regarding security. While 802.11i has solved the concerns regarding WEP's inadequate security, concerns about ease of use and setup must be dealt with. A distressing number of home wireless networks are still operating with security disabled. The Wi-Fi Alliance is addressing this problem with the issuance of the Wi-Fi Protected Setup (WPS), which encourages the use of 802.11i security by making it easier to set up. Aside from user concerns regarding privacy, however, SPs have concerns regarding wireless distribution of high-value video content. In particular, some SPs may be worried that premium content delivered to a subscriber may be shared with the subscriber's neighbors, made easier by the lack of the telltale presence of a wire running between homes (in the past, a coaxial cable running between homes was an indication that theft of service might be occurring).

Wired Home Networks

While nowhere near as convenient or as easy to deploy as wireless networks, wired home networks may offer performance advantages that make them appealing to both users and service providers.

Ethernet

The most widely deployed wired network in business environments is Ethernet, based on IEEE 802.3 standards. Ethernet enjoys significant deployment in home environments as well, especially in newer and higher-end construction. While Ethernet specifies operation up to 10 Gbps over unshielded twisted pair (UTP) cable in the 10GBASE-T IEEE Standard, most home deployments operate at 100 Mbps (100BASE-T), with some 1 Gbps (1GBASE-T) as well.

Ethernet networks use a distinctly different methodology than do wireless home networks such as Wi-Fi. Rather than making use of existing, uncontrolled, non-guaranteed communications channels such as the unlicensed interference-prone radio bands used by 802.11, Ethernet standards specify operation over precisely defined and controlled wired and optical channels. For example, for the Ethernet over UTP standards used in most office environments and in home networks, each Ethernet standard is paired with Telecommunications Industry Association (TIA) standards for the cabling to be used. The Ethernet standards specify the maximum length to be used of this "structured" cabling; the TIA cable standards themselves specify very precisely parameters such as characteristic impedance, inter-pair crosstalk, loss and attenuation, and connector characteristics.

As a result of this methodology, the performance of an Ethernet network is well-specified and guaranteed. For example, the bit rate on a 100BASE-T is always 100 Mbps; there is no variation due to local conditions or channel characteristics. In addition, since both the transceivers and the cabling are specified in the standards, it is possible to trade off complexity and cost in the transceivers versus complexity and cost in the cable. In fact, by tightly controlling cabling characteristics, 802.3 standards permit very high performance with relatively low-cost transceiver implementations (it is often noted that the unofficial motto of the 802.3 committee is "fast and cheap").

The downside of this methodology is that structured cabling must be installed in order to implement an Ethernet network. Routing UTP cabling throughout a home in an unobtrusive manner, while at the same time meeting technical requirements such as minimal bend radius is a challenge, and often a costly undertaking. Cable termination, while not beyond the capability of a knowledgeable and handy do-it-yourselfer, must be done carefully and is prone to error. As a result, most home Ethernet-capable cabling is installed in new homes at the time of construction, when walls are still open and skilled tradespeople are on-site.

"No New Wires" Wired Networks

As an alternative to Ethernet operation on structured wiring dedicated to such use, the concept of "no new wires" networking makes use of wiring already present in a home, wiring that was originally installed for non-networking requirements such as power delivery or telephony. While usually not allowing as high a performance level with as low a transceiver cost as that of Ethernet, such networks may enable whole-home network coverage at performance levels that are difficult to obtain in some home environments by wireless networks alone. Often, one of these networks is used in conjunction with a wireless network installation, combining the range extension capabilities of the wired network with the untethered mobility and convenience of the wireless network.

Phone Lines

Some of the first "no new wires" networks were deployed on household telephone wiring. These devices operate at frequencies above that used by telephone devices, and thus avoid mutual interference with them. Promoted by the Home Phone Line Alliance (HomePNA[†]), an industry group, the first such specification was adopted in 1998, and specified operation at 1.0 Mbps.

Telephone wiring, while not as tightly controlled as Ethernet cabling, still has quite good transmission characteristics, especially over the limited distances (under approximately 70 meters) found in a home. Interference sources are generally not present. As a result, there has been a steady progression in performance, and the latest specification, HomePNA 3.1, specifies operation up to 320 Mbps, using QAM modulation. Both the HomePNA 2.x and HomePNA 3.x generations of specifications have been adopted as international standards by the International Telecommunication Union (ITU); for example, HomePNA 3.1 is ITU-T Recommendation G.9954.

The major downside of phone line networking is the limited number of phone outlets in the typical home, especially their scarcity at locations where video devices are typically deployed. This, and user confusion over the concept of using telephone wire for data transmission, has served to limit its popularity. Related to this is the fact that currently there is only one supplier of HomePNA transceiver ICs.

Coaxial Cable

Unlike phone wiring, it is often the case that coaxial cabling already exists in many if not most of the locations where users wish to locate video devices. As was noted in the introduction, however, such cabling was not designed to permit outlet-to-outlet transmission. For each such signal path, one splitter must be traversed in the "wrong" direction. Splitters are not designed nor characterized for such operation, and as was noted, attenuation is high and very frequency-selective. Reflections may occur off of unterminated, unconnected cable outlets.

Aside from this issue, however, most home coaxial cable is a wonderful communications channel. At the relatively short lengths installed with a home, operation on the cable itself often extends from near DC up to 3 GHz and higher. The cable is inherently well-shielded, with little or no interfering noise sources. Even excluding the frequency bands already on the cable that are used for existing services such as broadcast TV channels and cable modems, there is enough channel capacity available to support communications of 1 Gbps and higher, were it not for the effects of the splitters and the unterminated stubs. With this in mind, an industry group, the Multimedia over Coax Alliance, MOCA[†], was formed in 2004 to promote technology for networking on existing, "ad hoc" home coaxial cabling. By using adaptive orthogonal frequency division modulation (OFDM), the MoCA specification defines a network that allows point-to-point communications in spite of the presence of splitters and stubs, with a throughput of about 100 Mbps.

Downsides of such networks include the fact that currently networks of only up to sixteen nodes are supported, and the 100 Mbps throughput is somewhat less than that of other networks such as HomePNA. In addition, coax outlets may not typically exist at some equipment locations, such as a PC or NAS device that contains user-created content. Perhaps the most serious limitation is that coaxial cabling is relatively rare in homes outside of North America, limiting its potential deployment. Non-U.S. home coaxial cable installations typically take place in newer construction; in such instances, UTP structured cabling is also installed, making the use of Ethernet devices possible and making coaxial cable-based home networks much less compelling. Finally, as is the case with phone line wiring, there are few sources of MoCA ICs (only two at the time of this writing).

Power Lines

Home power lines have been used for data communications since the first crude X-10* devices appeared on the market in the early 1970s. Power lines have the key characteristic of ubiquity: for almost all locations where a video storage or display device is likely to be located, there already exists a power outlet; for example, in the United States, the National Electrical Code mandates that outlets be periodically present along the walls in most rooms in a house.

The key downside is that, in comparison to phone lines and coaxial cables, power lines make for a relatively poor communications channel. Power lines are both unbalanced and unshielded; as a result, regulatory constraints limit the amount of signal power that devices may inject into them in order to avoid interference to licensed radio devices. In addition, interference from switching power supplies and other devices can be severe, resulting in limited signal-to-noise ratio (SNR). While the ubiquity of outlets indicates that power line communications (PLC) offers most potential upside, these channel characteristics ensure that it remains the most challenging of the "no new wires" channels as well.

Another issue that has gained some notoriety is interference of PLC devices with licensed Amateur Radio (HAM) communications. HAM operators use frequency bands overlapped by many PLC devices, and they are the most sensitive radio receivers in operation in residential areas. HAM operators are also technically astute and well-organized. As a result, when instances of interference have occurred, they have tended to garner a lot of attention. However, the frequency bands used by HAM operators in the range used by most PLC devices represent a small percentage of the PLC devices range. Mitigation of interference is usually a straightforward question of notching the HAM frequencies out of the signal transmitted by the PLC device, which can be accomplished with little impact on the performance of the PLC network. In fact, the American Radio Relay League (ARRL), the main representative of HAM operators in the United States, notes that they've never received an interference complaint concerning a PLC device conforming to HomePlug specifications (American Radio Relay League, *CES Not Just for "Consumers"*, QST Magazine, May 2007); such specifications mandate that HAM band notches must always be enabled. It is a bit unfortunate that this issue has generated far more negative attitudes than it appears to deserve, given the apparent ease with it can be resolved.

An unfortunate characteristic of the PLC market segment has been the lack of recognized standards, which has limited its adoption. Three main industry entities have emerged, each promoted their own similar but incompatible approaches.

In Japan, a division of Panasonic has developed a technology known as HD-PLC[†], and established a related industry group, the Consumer Electronics Powerline Communication Alliance (CEPCA[†]). The Universal Powerline Alliance (UPA[†]) promotes a similar but different technology, developed by a company from Spain, DS2. The HomePlug Alliance[†] is promoting yet another technology, with their latest version known as HomePlug AV[†].

Each of these three groups promotes a technology promising PHY bit rates up to 200 Mbps (although point-to-point throughput on some connections can drop to below 20 Mbps). All three use a form of multicarrier modulation like OFDM in the approximate 2–30 MHz region. As is the case with phone line and coax technologies, each of these technologies are currently supported by only one or two suppliers of transceiver ICs At the time of this writing, it does not appear that the battle between the three will be resolved by one of them be picked as a "winner" by an international standards body. While the IEEE P1901 committee is drafting a standard for powerline networking, it specifies that either HD-PLC[†] or HomePlug AV[†] may be supported in order to comply with the standard, thus somewhat perpetuating the current stalemate.

ITU-T G.hn

With the prevalence of single-vendor (or at most, two-vendor) "no new wires" technologies in the marketplace and the regional balkanization of their deployments, there seemed a clear need for a recognized international standards development organization (SDO) to step forward and begin to promote convergence on a single, multivendor, multiregion standard. In April of 2006, the same ITU-T Rapporteur Group that had experience with the HomePNA standards, Question 4 of Study Group 15 (Q4/15), commenced in the G.hn project to do just that. The G.hn project's goal is to specify next-generation home networking transceivers (Physical Layer and Data Link Layer), capable of operating over multiple types of in-place, existing home wiring, including phone lines, coaxial cabling, and power lines.

Progress to date has been final approval of a standard for the PHY layer and overall architecture, known as ITU-T Recommendation G.9960, and first-level approval (known as "Consent" in ITU-T parlance) of a standard for the Data Link (MAC) layer, known as ITU-T Recommendation G.9961. Consent of G.9960 was achieved in December 2008, and G.9961 in January 2010. G.9960 was approved in October of 2009, and approval of G.9961 is expected in June of 2010.

Conclusions for Ubiquitous Home Networks

In summary, the objective of these various home networking technologies and standards is to achieve a simple and ubiquitous way to connect all the devices together in the home. This will enable the delivery of any video based service to any screen in the house, allow for the sharing of information (like viewing preferences) between devices, and provide a means for any device in the home to access stored content either within the home or outside the home.

Outdoor Wireless Broadband Networks

This section reviews technologies for delivery of video services over mobile broadband networks, also referred to as wireless wide-area networks (WWANs) or wireless metropolitan-area networks (WMANs). Relevant mobile broadband technologies in this context are mobile Worldwide Interoperability for Microwave Access (WiMAX) IEEE 802.16e and IEEE 802.16m technologies, and third generation partnership project (3GPP) long-term evolution (LTE) and LTE-Advanced technologies (LTE was introduced in 3GPP Release 8 as the next major step for Universal Mobile Telecommunications System, or UMTS), all of which will provide enhanced user experience, high usability (anytime, anywhere and with any technology), personalization, integrated services and support for multimedia services at low transmission cost and with much richer content, when compared with second-generation (2G) and third-generation (3G) cellular networks.

Motivation: Why Video over Mobile Broadband?

The large base of mobile Internet users, increasing device capabilities and revenue opportunities of wireless multimedia services have been leading to a strong drive by network operators and service providers to provide TV, video, and multimedia services to mobiles. This led to support for video clip and live TV streaming services over second and third generation (2G and 3G) wireless technologies such as GSM, UMTS, HSPA and CDMA2000. As a consequence, traditional broadcasters, wishing to target the base of mobile phones, adopted standards for terrestrial digital TV services such as DVB-H standards. In the meantime, video communication through mobile broadband systems is still a challenging problem due to limitations in bandwidth and difficulties in maintaining high reliability, quality and latency demands imposed by rich multimedia applications.

In 3G networks, mobile video services were first launched as a unicast service using packet-switched streaming (PSS—a standard developed by 3GPP that defines the entire end-to-end streaming and download framework, including streaming and session protocols and media codecs for speech, audio, and video, and is the most commonly used standard today to deliver broadcast services and unicast streaming over cellular networks), since operators realized they could not wait for 3G broadcast due to high user demand on mobile TV, multimedia download, and streaming services. However, since the use of unicast for mobile TV services placed severe demands on network resources, multicast/broadcast service technologies such as multimedia broadcast and multicast services (MBMS) in 3G networks and multicast broadcast services (MBS) in WiMAX networks were developed enabling mobile video services to a large number of users. MBS/MBMS enables mobile broadband networks to distribute, by shared broadcasts a new generation of rich multimedia content in a digital form, sent out simultaneously to all mobile users within each transmitter footprint by a single shared transmission.

The need to deliver mobile video and multimedia content to mobile devices has also given rise to a number of technologies. These technologies for mobile video services are summarized as follows:

1. Satellite technologies, which use high-power spot beams to directly reach mobile phones. Standards for satellite-based services include DMB-S (Korea), DVB-SH (Europe), ISDB-S (Japan) and STiMi (China)

4. Terrestrial broadcasting technologies. Services in this category are provided using formats such as DVB-H, DMB-T, MediaFLO, ATSC, ATSC M/H, and ISDB-T.

5. Cellular mobile networks (such as 3G-UMTS or CDMA) using unicast and multicast/broadcast technologies such as MBMS and MCBCS. The work on adding broadcast/multicast support to 3G networks started back in 2002 when both 3GPP and 3GPP2 created work items for broadcast/multicast services in GSM/WCDMA and CDMA2000, respectively. In 3GPP the work item is called MBMS, while in 3GPP2 it is called Broad-Cast and MultiCast Services (BCMCS).

6. Mobile broadband WWAN and WMAN technologies such as LTE and WiMAX, using the MBS and MBMS technologies as well as unicast-based video delivery solutions.

These different video delivery methods are summarized in Figure C.5. As mentioned previously, Wi-Fi is yet another means for delivering video services, and can be linked with a cellular or broadcast network to offload data or other high-capacity demanding applications.

TV Services	Networks	Unicast/ Multicast
Mobile Netorks MBMS & Unicast Streaming (PSS) MCBCS & Unicast Streaming (PSS)	3GPP #G-UMTS HSDPA HSPA 3GPP2 CDMA2000 EVDO	Unicast, Multicast and Broadcast
Terrestial Broadcasting DVB-H DMB-T MediaFLO	Terrestrial Broadcast	Broadcast
Satellite Broadcasting DMB-S DVB-SH STiMi	Satellite Bradcast	Broadcast
Broadband Wireless MBS / MBMS & Unicast Streaming	WiMax / LTE	Unicast, Multicast and Broadcast

Figure C.6   Overview of mobile video technologies

Among these technologies, mobile broadband technologies WiMAX and 3G LTE have several advantages over the cellular wireless technologies (under the column "Mobile Networks" in Figure C.6) and broadcast technologies (under the columns "Terrestrial Broadcasting" and "Satellite Broadcasting"). Toward usage for mobile video applications, mobile broadband technologies such as WiMAX and LTE have clear advantages over cellular mobile technologies such as HSPA, such as high-speed broadband access, commonality with IP technology and applications, seamless mobility and roaming, and the availability of spectrum surpassing 3G networks. WiMAX networks based on 802.16e can provide city-wide roaming and high data rates up to 75 Mbps with available spectrum of 20 MHz for each operator (latest WiMAX technology based on IEEE 802.16m can support peak data rates up to 300 Mbps in downlink and 135 Mbps in uplink) and 3G LTE networks can support peak data rates of 100 Mbps in downlink and 50 Mbps in uplink over a 20-MHz channel, but 3G (including CDMA2000, 1xEV-DO, HSPA) has much lower data rates (in a 5MHz slot, HSDPA can provide peak downlink speeds up to 14.4 Mbps, while 1xEV-DO operating with a 1.25-MHz carrier can support link rates up to 2.4 Mbps) to support media and internet applications, each with guaranteed QoS. When this is coupled with the end-to-end QoS offered by IPv6 networks, mobile broadband technologies such as WiMAX and LTE can deliver as flawless a quality as it can be achieved over traditional cable or DSL networks. Thus, the connectivity speeds with mobile broadband technologies are good enough to download or upload video in real time, with each user using only a fraction of the cell resources. At the same time, potential costs of mobile broadband technologies can be much lower because of the high-cost 3G spectrum used in cellular networks, which can be overburdened for resources in dense usage environments with limited spectrum and large number of users needing access for voice and data services. As the result of the transition from 3G cellular to mobile broadband, evolved system infrastructures will provide better QoS support and higher data bandwidth, which will lead to more exciting video applications and more innovations in video processing.

While the use of mobile broadband technologies instead of cellular mobile technologies for video delivery can be argued by the clear advantages summarized above, the technology comparison of mobile broadband against broadcasting leads to various pros and cons between these two different paradigms. Here are a number of observations discussing the advantages of mobile broadband technologies over broadcasting technologies for video delivery:

■ Broadcast technologies are unidirectional and strictly downlink, while mobile broadband technologies such as WiMAX and 3G LTE have a two-way architecture allowing them to be coupled with uplink services to enable more personalized and interactive (real-time) applications like video-on-demand without an additional transmitter. Hence, the use of mobile broadband technologies for video/multimedia creates a unique usage environment with respect to traditional broadcast services by simultaneously realizing the advantages of the traditional broadcast and on-demand multimedia, and generates new usage models which include two-way, multi-way and truly interactive new services (possible to support video uploads and video conferencing as well as web services such as multimedia instant messaging, tele-presence or video push to talk).

■ The MBS multicast mode in WiMAX and MBMS multicast mode in 3G LTE can be used to transmit different data streams to each cell, based on user demands. For example, the MBS mode in WiMAX may offer hundreds of video streams in an area, even though it can only transmit a small number of them in each cell. Therefore, mobile broadband technologies seem to be a more appropriate option than broadcasting solutions such as DVB-H for transmitting specialized content to smaller user communities.

■ Multicast/broadcast solutions over mobile broadband systems such as WiMAX MBS and 3G MBMS introduce only minor changes to existing radio and core network protocols. This reduces implementation costs in terminals and in the network, and makes mobile broadcast a relatively inexpensive technology compared to non-mobile broadcast technologies, which require new receiver hardware in the terminal and additional investments in the network infrastructure.

■ Another advantage of mobile broadband is that mobile operators can retain established business models. Current services, such as mobile TV, will greatly benefit from the capacity-boosting effect of mobile broadband. Certainly mobile broadband will also stimulate the development of new, mobile, mass-media services. Likewise, it will enable operators to provide a full triple-play service offering telephony, Internet, and TV for mobile handheld devices in a cost-effective way over a common service and network infrastructure. For instance, as a technology desired for multiple levels of QoS each suited for a different type of service, WiMAX can support a variety of services and not specifically designed to support a particular service. Thus, the range of services that WiMAX can support includes voice, data, video and any of the manifestations including VoIP.

■ Until now, the integration of Web 2.0, VoIP, and broadcasting has been very limited, these have operated as virtually independent networks. The trend towards a unified offering is getting accelerated as the core networks begin to move to all IP and be reorganized as next generation networks (NGNs). Mobile broadband technologies such as WiMAX networks and 3G LTE networks present an important facet for making this transition. As a consequence, an IP-based wireless service provider relying on mobile broadband technologies that can offer all of the Web 2.0 services, offer media broadcasting and also bundle in "on-demand" and "traditional TV" broadcasts, has an obvious advantage over a pure broadcaster. Until recently, this was not possible because of the difficulty of offering live media over the Internet with any degree of reliability or availability on the one hand, and getting interactivity with users in broadcast networks on the other hand.

Unicast versus Multicast/Broadcast in Mobile Broadband

A considerable and growing part of the content distribution services in mobile networks addresses groups of users with similar interests (such as movies, sports clips, and news flashes). As long as the group sizes are small and the densities are low, unicast channels can be used to distribute the content in an efficient fashion. At present mobile video services are offered in 3G networks via unicast streaming technology over point-to-point connections. Unicast also has the advantage that network resources are only consumed when a user is actively using the mobile video service. Further, with unicast, the network can optimize the transmission for each user individually. Particularly, in a unicast mode the transmission can be adapted to the wireless channel conditions by feedback from the receiver (such as channel quality indicator (CQI) feedback or hybrid automatic retransmission request (HARQ) mechanisms in

WiMAX). The main drawback of unicast is its unfavorable scaling behavior if there are many users watching video at the same time, such as in a large-scale market deployment of mass media services like mobile TV. In order to cope with high numbers of simultaneously watching Mobile TV users, broadcast is clearly a more appropriate transport technology.

Figure C.7 depicts mobile TV service with unicast. Ten users are watching three different channels (red, green, and blue) streamed over unicast. Each user requires a separate unicast streaming connection to the server, so the streaming server must handle ten streaming connections, because there are ten mobile TV users. The server, network, and cell load increase with the increasing numbers of users.

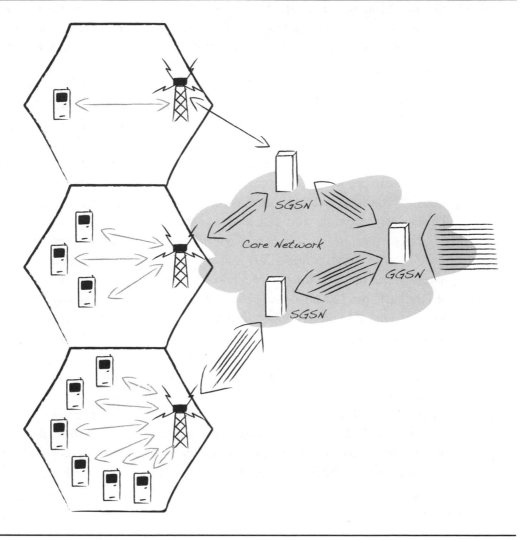

Figure C.7   Mobile TV service with unicast

The basic idea behind multicast/broadcast services (MBS, also known as multimedia broadcast and multicast services, or MBMS, in 3G) is to use IP multicasting in the service layer and core network (instead of point-to-point links for each end device) in order to save on network capacity. In particular, the service content is replicated as close as possible to the radio interface, where a common channel is used to deliver the content to all clients within the same cell. This allows for seamless integration of broadcast/ multicast transmission capabilities into the service and network infrastructure and enables efficient group related one-to-many data distribution services, especially on the radio interface.

Figure C.8 depicts mobile TV service with MBS/MBMS support. The server delivers just one stream per channel to the MBS/MBMS BM-SC, so a total of three streams only. The data flow for each channel in the core and radio network is solely replicated when necessary. In this example, the streaming server must only handle three simultaneous streams. Furthermore, radio resources in the bottommost cell need only be allocated for three parallel broadcast transmissions instead of six separate unicast transmissions. The server, network, and cell load are thus independent of total number of users. Despite its efficiency in consuming network resources, one disadvantage of MBS/MBMS is that it does not allow for adaptation to the wireless channel conditions by feedback from the receiver. In the absence of feedback mechanisms, none of the techniques such as dynamic adaptive modulation and coding, opportunistic multi-user scheduling, power control or automatic repeat transmissions (ARQ) can be effectively deployed. One way to enhance end-to-end reliability in this context is to employ advanced forward error correction (FEC) protocols at the application layer, such as Reed Solomon codes, fountain codes, and Raptor codes (Chen, W.Y., *Home Networking Basis: Transmission Environments and Wired/Wireless Protocols*, Prentice Hall, 2003), where erasure coding across packets provides further protection against channel outages and packet failures. Raptor codes have been adopted in the 3GPP standard's MBMS mode.

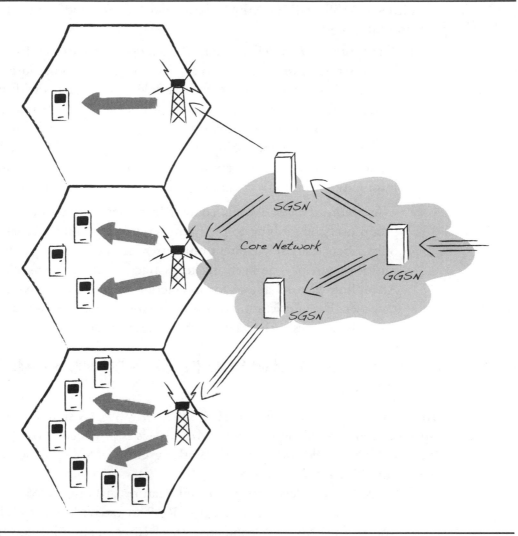

Figure C.8 Mobile TV service with MBS/MBMS support.

WiMAX MBS and 3G MBMS have two modes (unidirectional and point-to-multipoint):

- The *broadcast mode* delivers content from one source to all subscribers in the service area. There is no service-subscription procedure (also known as push-type services, for example, TV programs with mass appeal such as live sporting events, real-time news). Furthermore, no interaction exists between the service and end user; that is, the network does not keep track of individual receiving clients. The broadcast mode is suitable for free or low-cost services such as advertising or information (electronic program guides, news, previews, and so on).

- The *multicast mode* delivers content from one source to a selected group users subscribing to premium services as a multicast service. Subscribers can enjoy content only after joining the corresponding multicast group. The network keeps track of all receiving clients. An uplink channel allows for interaction between the service and end user. The multicast mode is suitable for pay-per-view or pay-per-program services such as television or video on demand.

Overview of Multicast/Broadcast Service (MBS) in the IEEE 802.16 Standard and WiMAX Forum

MBS is an optional feature in the IEEE 802.16e WiMAX standard. Here, a specification only at the PHY and MAC levels is provided. MBS is also a part of WiMAX Forum Network Working Group (NWG) Release 1.5 architecture (referred as MCBCS).

WiMAX MCBCS leverages the airlink features at both the MAC and PHY layers as specified in IEEE 802.16e Rev2 to establish and to release the transport of the MCBCS content(s). Involved companies include Intel, ZTE, Huawei, Nokia, Alvarion, Samsung, Clearwire, UQ/KDDI, and Korea Telecom. In Release 1.5, NWG has specified WiMAX MCBCS network architecture, service initiation, service provisioning procedures, mobility management, power saving support, QoS management, charging/accounting procedures, data transmission, and data synchronization. Finally, MBS has also been proposed as the "enhanced MBS (e-MBS)" mode to the IEEE 802.16m Task Group, with contributions addressing technical challenges such as channel modeling, multi-BS macro-diversity, HARQ, adaptive MCS, feedback channel design, and superposition coding for layered transmission. Among operators, Clearwire, Korea Telecom, and UQ/KDDI have declared interest in deploying the MBS feature for providing video delivery over their WiMAX networks, even though most likely they will support only unicast-based video services in the short term.

The MBS service is supported in IEEE 802.16e at the PHY layer by two mechanisms: (i) dedicating the whole downlink (DL) frame to MBS, (ii) operating a frame as a mixed frame for MBS and unicast services by providing one or more dedicated "MBS Zones" in the DL frame, where MBS Zones are identified in the MAP allocation in the frames. The purpose of defining MBS zones is that once the MS is synchronized, it can access the MBS Zone without having to decode DL MAP in every frame. The MBS zone is identified by the OFDM symbol offset parameter and occurs at the same location in every frame.

The MBS mode in WiMAX has many similarities to the MBMS mode in 3G, as specified in Release 6 of the third generation partnership project (3GPP) standard document. Among these similarities is the possibility for WiMAX MBS to have multiple base station operation for multicasting when base stations operate in the MBS single frequency network (MBSFN) mode such that a common multicast/broadcast data transmission happens from a time-synchronized set of base stations using the same resource block. MBSFN enables over-the-air combining, exploiting the signals from adjacent cells transmitting the same service, thus improving signal quality through macro-diversity gains, especially at cell edge. TDtv, which is an implementation of MBMS over the 3G unpaired spectrum by IPWireless also provides for content which is synchronized over all base stations in the service area. MBMS has also been proposed as the "enhanced MBMS (e-MBMS)" mode in 3G LTE, which supports both single-cell and multi-cell modes. Operators with potential interest in deploying the MBMS feature of the 3G LTE standard includes KDDI, NTT Docomo, Verizon, AT&T Mobile and China Telecom/Unicom.

Multicast/Broadcast Service (MBS) Network Architecture as defined in the WiMAX Forum Specifications

The support of MCBCS services requires modifications in the following components of the WiMAX network architecture depicted in Figure C.9:

- ASN (access service network) to enable MCBCS transport management
- CSN (connectivity services network) to enable MCBCS subscription management

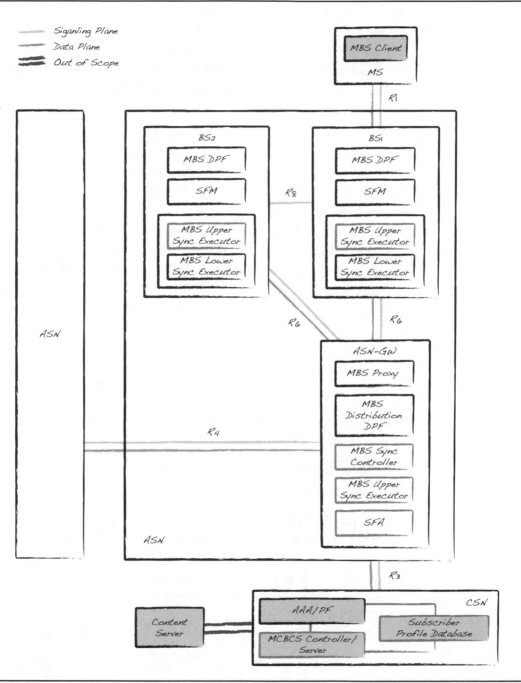

Figure C.9   WiMAX MCBCS network architecture

MCBCS CSN components are as follows:

■ *MCBCS Content Server:* The MCBCS Content Server provides the content for MCBCS services, like multimedia flows and data files. The content provider can be the NSP or can be a third party such as commercial broadcast network servers/video head, outside the WiMAX network.

■ *MCBCS Controller/Server:* The MCBCS Controller/Server is an optional network entity that hosts all the MCBCS specific functional components in the CSN. MCBCS Controller (MBSC) the MBSC provides functions for MCBCS user service provisioning and delivery. It may serve as an entry point for the MCBCS content provider to enable MCBCS content transmissions. MBSC is responsible for coordinating with the MCBCS content network to schedule the reception of the MCBCS contents. MBSC is also responsible for authorizing the incoming contents from the MCBCS content server, and initiating the MCBCS downlink transmission towards the WiMAX access network. It may perform the following functions:

- IP multicast group management

- MCBCS program management

- MCBCS service announcement management, including MCBCS service guide manipulation and distribution

- MCBCS MS and network session management

- Data encryption support

The design of the "optional" MCBCS Controller/Server is based on the assumption that the bearer plane establishment, as well as the service association between the ASN and CSN, is statically configured by default; however, it can also be dynamically established based on some form of event trigger within the ASN associated with the given MCBCS service, and that the given MCBCS service is permanent.

- *AAA/Policy Function (PF):* This entity is responsible for MCBCS authentications, authorizations, and accounting. It accesses the Subscriber Profile Repository to obtain relevant information. This entity is also responsible for providing the MS access authorization for the access of a particular MCBCS service over the corresponding WiMAX access network.

- *Subscriber Profile Database:* This entity stores and manages subscriber profiles. The subscriber profile database may be the same as the one used for unicast services.

MCBCS ASN components are as follows:

- *MBS Proxy:* MBS Proxy is a control plane function for the whole MBS zone, located in the ASN Gateway (ASN-GW) to support MCBCS service, enables functions that manage and control the radio access for a MS with respect to MCBCS functions and provides signaling, establishing, and tearing down bearer channels for MCBCS clients. The MBS Proxy may responsible for the following functions:

  - Interact with the ASN and CSN MCBCS functions to support MCBCS network session management.

  - Assign the MCBCS access parameters such as MCIDs, MBS Zone IDs, and so on for a given MBS Zone

  - MBS service policy enforcement for multicast transport (such as QoS, accounting, and radio resource management,

  - MCBCS Transmission Zone to MBS Zone mappings, and so on) to enable the MCBCS service over the WiMAX system.

- *Anchor SFA:* Anchor Service Flow Authorization (SFA) is a logical entity in the ASN, which is located in the ASN-GW/ASN. The anchor SFA is responsible for managing the MCBCS service request for a given MS according to its corresponding user's service profile if the user's service profile is downloaded to the anchor SFA. It assigns a service flow ID for a given MCBCS service flow for the MS once the MCBCS service is authorized by the AAA/PF for the MS. It may interact with MBS Proxy to support the MCBCS service flow establishment, modification and release.

- *MBS Distribution Data Path Function (DPF):* The MBS Distribution DPF function is a bearer plane entity in the ASN, which is located at the ASN-GW for the MBS bearer control management and data distribution for one or more MBS Zones. It receives the downlink transmission of a MCBCS content, sent from the CSN, classifies the incoming SDUs into the appropriate MCBCS Service Flow and applies the corresponding WiMAX Convergence Sublayer rules. After classification and CS processing, the MBS traffic is delivered to the Sync Controller and the Sync Executer functional entities.

- *MBS DPF:* The MBS DPF includes the collection of MBS bearer control management specific functions of ASN, which are located at the BS. The data path for the MCBCS is established between the MCBCS Controller/Server and the ASN-GW, and between the ASN-GW and BSs.

- *SFM:* SFM is a service flow management logical entity in the ASN and is located at the BS. The SFM is responsible for creation, modification or deletion of service flow for a given IP multicast address and the associated airlink service parameters assignment for an MS using the IEEE 802.16Rev2 based DSx airlink signaling. This entity is responsible for organizing the local Base Station (BS) resource management function to coordinate the system resource allocation and airlink scheduling support for the MCBCS transport.

- *MBS Sync function:* The MBS Sync Function is designed to coordinate the MCBCS content downlink transmission over a single frequency or multi-frequency WiMAX networks in one or more MBS zones. The MBS Synch function consists of two sub-functions:

- *MBS Sync Controller Function:* A centralized control entity that is responsible for interacting with the MBS Distribution DPF in order to specify the synchronization rules, including time stamp to support the downlink frame level coordination or macro diversity.

- *MBS Sync Executer Function:* MBS Sync Executer is responsible for executing the MBS synchronization rules that are instructed by MBS Sync Controller in support of data synchronization. It is further divided into two sub-functions:

- MBS Upper Sync Executer: MBS Upper Sync Executer is responsible for constructing the MAC PDU and package them into a MAC burst based on the sync rule received from the MBS Sync controller.

- MBS Lower Sync Executer: MBS Lower Sync Executer is responsible for constructing the final PHY burst which is corresponding to the MCID(s) in the given MBS permutation zone that is corresponding to an MBS Zone based on the sync rules that it received from MBS Sync Controller. It delivers the mapping information of the MCID's to the corresponding MBS zone IDs, and so on, and broadcasts the MBS_MAP_IE, MBS_MAP and MBS_DATA_IE including the MBS zone ID and MCID.

MBS Client: The MBS Client represents functionality required by the MS to support the MCBCS service delivery.

The Role of Compression

Compression is a fundamental technology that is key to enabling Ubiquitous Video Services. From Table C.1 and Figure C.9, it's clear that uncompressed streaming of high-definition video content is not feasible over existing wired or wireless networks. The bitrate for video content must therefore be reduced substantially in order to make the transmission over wireless networks feasible and cost-effective. However, bitrate is only one important consideration when it comes to which compression technology should be used. Several other characteristics of compression to support these ubiquitous video services are:

1. Low cost and low power: Since compression is primarily a digital signal processing technique, it benefits from Moore's Law and the scaling of low cost silicon. As such, it should get cheaper and lower power over time. However, using this technology in smaller and smaller devices still poses a significant challenge.

2. Low latency: For applications such as video conferencing and gaming, it's important to be able to do rapid encoding and decoding in order to minimize end-to-end latency which may be visible to the end user.

3. Efficiency: Compression must be able to provide the optimal tradeoff needed to deliver high-quality video content within the available wireless bandwidth. This means compressing the content down to ~1 Mbps rates or lower for moderate resolutions like VGA. Higher throughputs may be needed for higher resolutions and/or higher frame rates.

4. Scalability: It's important for the codec to provide a bit stream that scales in several different ways:

   a. Quality. The codec must support both high quality and lower quality content, which may be part of a tiered service contract offering.

   b. Resolution. The codec must support multiple resolutions, from handheld devices to netbooks to laptops to larger screens which may be connected to the mobile devices (in-car monitor, external monitor connected to a dock).

   c. Bit rate. Wireless inherently experiences changing channel conditions, and so the codec must be able to adapt to these changes in throughput while still delivering an acceptable quality experience.

5. Standardized: It's important that a compression scheme be broadly adopted within the industry, including the mobile, consumer electronic, and PC industries. This enables ubiquity and low cost implementations of the compression technology in order to allow the same content be viewed on these different devices.

The latest generation video compression standard is known as ITU-T H.264 AVC. It provides powerful techniques for compressing the video content to very low bit rate ranges while maintaining high quality. A recent extension of this standard, completed in 2007, is H.264 SVC (Scalable Video Coding), which provides many of the scaling features above, and so becomes a key ingredient for supporting ubiquitous video services. Therefore, we focus primarily on this codec and aspects of which can be exploited for mobile devices and wireless channels.

A scalable video encoder produces a bit stream that has a layering property—such that some of the component substreams of the coded bit stream can be removed and the remaining substreams can still lead to a valid reconstruction of the original sequence, albeit with a lower quality.

The substream decomposition can be performed in different ways to offer spatial, temporal, or quality scalability, depending on the actual characteristics. Spatial scalability refers to the case when the nested substreams represent the original video sequence at a series of progressively increasing spatial resolution levels. Temporal scalability similarly refers to the case when the substreams represent the original content at a series of progressively increasing frame rates. Quality scalability, also known as SNR scalability, provides for different substreams that offer progressively higher quality (PSNR) reconstruction of the original content (but are all at the same spatiotemporal resolution level as the original bit stream).

One of the main considerations for the development of the H.264 SVC standard was to design it as an extension of the H.264 AVC standard. It was additionally required that the layered SVC codec deliver good coding efficiency and limited increase in decoding complexity when compared to single layer H.264 AVC coding — these being key shortcomings of previous efforts to develop scalable video codec standards. The other key system level requirement was that H.264 SVC should enable post-encode bit rate adaptation, which is an important feature to enable distributed adaptation to changing network or wireless link conditions. In the following section, we describe the key features of H.264 SVC that build upon the H.264 AVC tools.

Basic Concepts of H.264/SVC Encoding and Decoding

As mentioned previously, the H.264 SVC standard enables temporal, spatial, and quality (or SNR) scalability. The first feature we examine is how temporal scalability is enabled. The way in which a temporal scalable bit stream is defined is that for a bit stream with N temporal layers $\{T_i, i=1, \ldots, N\}$ (where larger values of the suffix i represent layers with higher frame rates) any substream formed by removing all access units from temporal layers T_i, $i>k$ should be a valid bit stream for a H.264 SVC decoder. In fact, since H.264 AVC provides a great degree of flexibility through the multiple reference frames and reference picture memory control, it is easy to construct the bit stream with a hierarchical structure for the motion compensated temporal prediction as shown in the example in Figure C.10. In this example, with three temporal scalability layers T_0, T_1, and T_2, it can be seen that the access units of layer T_1 only depend upon temporal layer T_0, and can be decoded independently of the access units in T_2. It should be noted that the full flexibility of H.264 AVC reference picture list management can be used for providing temporal scalability of this kind—and in fact the only additional provision in the H.264 SVC bit stream is the signaling of temporal layers. Also, the flexibility in prediction structures enables different requirements to be met—such as improved coding efficiency, or low delay, and so on.

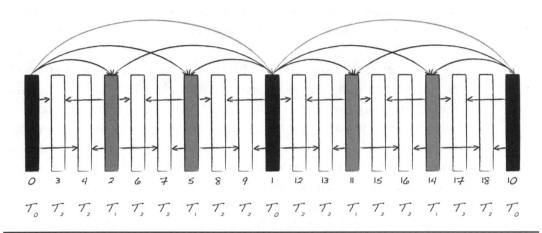

| 0 | 3 | 4 | 2 | 6 | 7 | 5 | 8 | 9 | 1 | 12 | 13 | 11 | 15 | 16 | 14 | 17 | 18 | 10 |

T_0 T_2 T_2 T_1 T_2 T_2 T_1 T_2 T_2 T_0 T_2 T_2 T_1 T_2 T_2 T_1 T_2 T_2 T_0

Figure C.10   Example of a hierarchical prediction frame structure for enabling temporal scalability

The second feature we examine is spatial scalability, in which the H.264 SVC coded bit stream has multiple layers or substreams, each enabling a particular spatial resolution, identified by a spatial layer identifier D. In each spatial layer, the H.264 AVC tools of intra-frame prediction and motion-compensated inter-frame prediction are used. In addition, predictions from lower spatiotemporal layers are also defined for H.264 SVC. Thus if D_0 represents the base layer, in coding the higher resolution spatial layer identified by D_1 the encoder would consider intra-frame and inter-frame predictions within the layer and also inter-layer predictions from corresponding access units in the D_0 layer as shown in the example in Figure C.11.

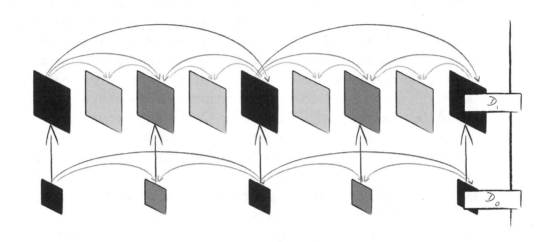

Figure C.11   Improved coding efficiency for spatial scalability mode employing inter-layer prediction

In particular, in H.264 SVC inter-layer prediction is employed to help in prediction of the macroblock modes and motion parameters, and in prediction of the residual signal. The prediction mode and the partitioning of a macroblock in the D_1 layer is determined by that of the corresponding 8x8 block in the D_0 layer (assuming dyadic spatial scalability). In addition, if the encoder determines that the scaled motion vectors from a 8x8 block in an immediately lower spatial layer are to be used for a macroblock partition at the enhancement spatial layer, it will set the *motion prediction flag* to 1, and not signal the reference picture list and motion vectors in the enhancement layer. In this case, the decoder will use the reference indices of the co-located 8x8 block from the lower layer, along with the scaled motion vectors.

Inter-layer prediction is also available to refine the enhancement layer residual signal, both for inter-frame and intra-frame coded macroblocks. The use of this is signaled by the use of *residual prediction flag* in the macroblock syntax for the enhancement layers. When this flag is set to 1, the residual signal from the corresponding 8x8 block in the lower (reference) layer is block-wise upsampled and used as the prediction for the residual signal for the enhancement layer macroblock. For inter-frame coded macroblocks, the upsampling is done on a transform block basis and no filtering across block boundaries is performed. For intra-frame coded macroblocks, however, if the neighboring blocks are also intra-coded, upsampling is performed by filtering across submacroblock boundaries (the H.264 AVC in-loop deblocking filter is applied first). If the neighboring blocks are inter-frame coded, the required samples for filtering across the block boundaries are obtained by algorithms to extend the border samples. This is combined with a restriction on the usage of inter-layer intra prediction to only those enhancement layer macroblocks for which the co-located reference layer block is intra-coded. The net effect of all this is to enable *single-loop decoding*—the decoder does not need multiple motion compensation loops for the decoding of a given macroblock. This is a major achievement for H.264 SVC since it leads to a smaller overhead for multiple layer decoding over single layer H.264 AVC decoding (when compared with previous coding standards that attempted to enable multi-layer coding).

The third dimension of scalability we shall describe is called quality (or SNR) scalability. The coarse grain scalability (CGS) mode in particular uses all the inter-layer coding mechanisms defined for use in the spatial scalability mode. It can be understood in the context of spatial scalability where the base layer and enhancement layer have the same dimensions; that is, no up- or down-sampling is performed in the coding of the multiple layers. Because of this, a further simplification results in the implementation of the encoder and decoder, where the inter-layer predictions for the residuals are performed in the transform domain directly, with the enhancement layer employing a smaller quantization step size compared with that used in the lower CGS layer.

In addition, an even more efficient medium grain scalability (MGS) mode is defined, which provides more flexibility in the bit rate adaptation compared with CGS. With MGS, the encoder enables switching between different quality layers in any access unit; any enhancement layer NAL unit can be discarded, enabling rate scalability down to the packet level. Also, the enhancement layer transform coefficients can be partitioned and signaled in different slices. This distributes the quality refinement layer for a given quantization step size across several packets that can be prioritized differently by the transport mechanism. The MGS mode also defines the concept of *key pictures* to control drift, which can occur at the decoder when some packets are lost or dropped in transmission. To signal key pictures, for each picture a flag indicates whether the base/enhancement layer is employed for motion compensated prediction. These key pictures serve as resynchronization points and limit encoder-decoder drift propagation to higher temporal layers. They enable good optimization between coding efficiency and drift.

Figure C.12 shows the general block diagram for a H.264 SVC encoder that enables all three dimensions of scalability as described here.

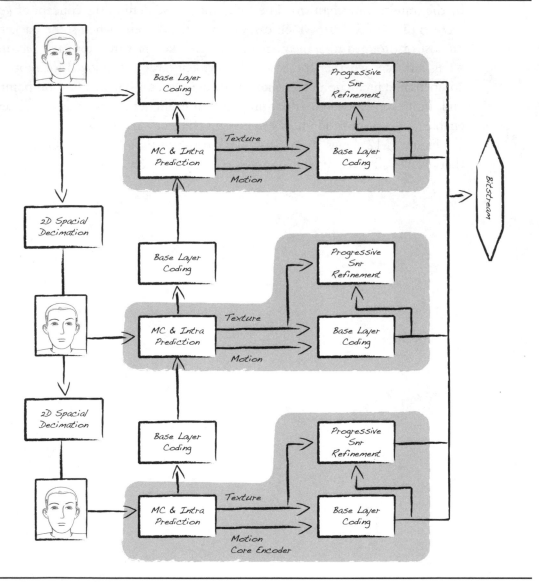

Figure C.12   Structure of the H.264 SVC encoder

H.264 SVC System Interface

One of the key requirements for the H.264 standard was to enable easy packet level adaptations in order to extract substreams matching given quality/spatial/ temporal requirements. The 1-byte NAL unit header for H.264 AVC NALUs is augmented by providing an additional 3-byte extension with the identifiers T (temporal), D (spatial), and Q (quality) as shown in Figure C.17.

The first byte of the H.264 SVC NAL unit header replicates the syntax for H.264 AVC NAL unit headers. Some of the key parameters to note in bytes 2 to 4 are: *priority_id* (PID, 6 bits) and the three scalability dimensions *dependency_id* (DID, 3 bits), *quality_id* (QID, 4 bits), and *temporal_id* (TID, 3 bits).

0	1	2	3	4	5	6	7	0	1	2	3	4	5	6	7	0	1	2	3	4	5	6	7	0	1	2	3	4	5	6	7
F	NRI		NUT					R	I	PID						N	DID			QID				TID			U	D	O	R2	

Figure C.13 Four-byte NAL unit header defined in H.264 SVC

The NAL units may be grouped in different ways to form logical entities. As an example, a coded video sequence would consist of a base layer and different scalable layers, which can be grouped into dependency layers (see the example in Figure C.14).

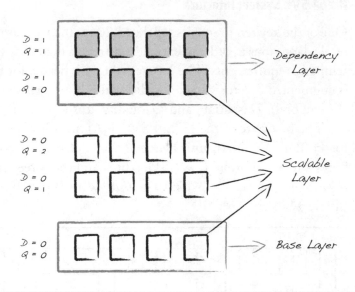

Figure C.14 A coded video sequence with 2 dependency layers (D=0, 1) and 20 scalable layers

The encoder may assign priorities in the PID field to each NAL unit to help the process of extracting a substream to match a given average rate constraint with the best possible quality. The network node performing the rate adaptation would then start by discarding the NAL units with the lowest PID value first, and would continue this process with the next lowest priority NAL units until the available bit rate is achieved (alternatively, the scheduler can transmit packets starting from the highest priority NAL units and continue until the available bandwidth is used up, at which point it discards the remaining lower priority NAL units until the next transmission slot and resumes transmission with a new access unit).

H.264 SVC Standard Profiles

The H.264 SVC standard specifies three profiles: Scalable Baseline, Scalable High, and Scalable High Intra. Table C.2 summarizes the key features of these profiles, which are targeted for different applications.

Table C.2 Summary of H.264 SVC profile definitions

	Scalable Baseline Profile	Scalable High Profile	Scalable High Intra Profile
Targeted applications	Conversational, mobile, surveillance	Broadcast, streaming, videoconferencing	Professional
Base layer	H.264 AVC Baseline Profile	H.264 AVC High Profile	H.264 AVC High Profile with only IDR pictures
Enhancement layer	B slices CABAC coding, 8x8 transform	Supports all tools in H.264 SVC	Supports all tools in H.264 SVC
Other	Spatial resolution ratios restricted to 1.5–2 between successive spatial layers Quality, temporal scalability not restricted	No restrictions	Only IDR pictures allowed in any layer

In summary, the H.264 SVC standard provides the best effort towards a scalable, layered coding standard that minimizes both the loss in coding efficiency and decoder complexity relative to a single-layer codec, and keeps base layer compatibility with the H.264 AVC decoders.

Video Specific Optimizations: A Cross-layer approach

Wireless communication technology has entered a new era, having evolved from a system offering mainly voice service to one that provides services with rich multimedia content. Recent advances in mobile computing and hardware technology enable transmission of rich multimedia content over wireless networks. With the high demand for such services, it becomes crucial to identify the system limitations, define the appropriate performance metrics, and to design wireless systems that are capable of achieving the best performance by overcoming the challenges posed by the system requirements and the wireless environment.

Most communication systems today involve the transmission of a continuous source over a noisy channel. In such communication systems, the source is encoded into a finite stream of bits and the bit stream is then communicated over the noisy channel. Source coding is done to convert the continuous source into a finite stream of bits and channel coding is performed to mitigate the errors in the bit stream introduced by the noisy channel. As source coding and channel coding are usually performed across separate layers of the communication systems, most practical systems perform the coding operations in a separate manner. That is, source coding is done without taking into account the channel and channel coding is performed without considering the nature of the source. We depict a separate source-channel coding implementation in Figure C.15.

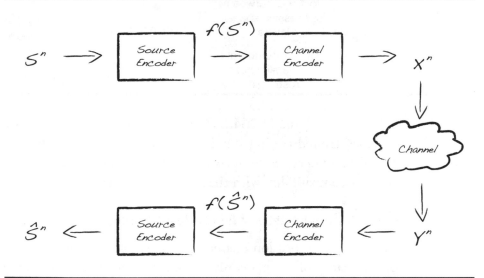

Figure C.15 Separate source-channel coding

The increased demand for different services at the application layer results in higher transmission rate and reliability requirements at the physical layer. However, high data rate and high reliability are two conflicting design parameters. Accordingly, an end-to-end performance measure is necessary for the overall system.

In general, multimedia wireless communication requires transmitting analog sources over fading channels while satisfying the end-to-end average distortion and delay requirements (delay-limitedness accounts for the presence of stringent latency and buffer constraints, typical for real-time video streaming applications) of the application within the power limitations of the mobile terminal. In this context, separation of source and channel coding may no longer be optimal, for instance when the channel state information (CSI) is not available at the transmitter since the channel is not ergodic. On the other end of the spectrum is the joint source-channel coding (JSCC) scheme where the source and channel coding is performed together. That is, the source coding and channel coding blocks depend on each other. Figure C.16 depicts joint source-channel coding operation.

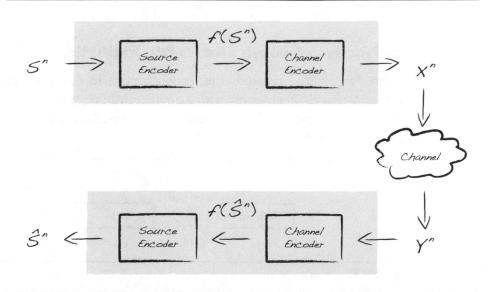

Figure C.16 Joint source-channel coding

It can be quantitatively shown that JSCC has advantages over other coding techniques, which separate source coding and channel coding processes. To show this, the performance measure is average end-to-end distortion between the source and its reconstruction at the destination (which can be used to also compute PSNR). We analyze different transmission strategies from the perspective of minimizing the end-to-end distortion of the source. Distortion is an important metric to consider in communication systems and is a better metric of performance than rate of transmission when continuous source is involved. Based on a simple information-theoretic framework that accounts for the impact of both quantization errors and channel-induced errors, the end-to-end distortion formulation allows us to analyze the role of source compression and channel coding jointly in the JSCC framework. In addition to single-layer transmission, it is possible to capture in the average end-to-end distortion metric the impact of layered source coding techniques with unequal error protection (UEP) and successive refinement, including progressive coding and broadcast coding strategies. Furthermore, one can easily characterize the average end-to-end distortion when using advanced network architectures with features relevant for future mobile broadband systems, such as multi-hop relaying, cooperative communications and femto-cells.

JSCC Performance Gains over a Point-to-Point Wireless Link

System Model: We first study the theoretic gains in distortion possible in a point-to-point channel setting with a single transmitter and receiver. Here, we describe the system model we investigate. We first look at the point-to-point channel model depicted in Figure C.17.

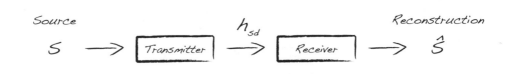

Figure C.17   Point-to-point channel Model

In this channel setup, the channel attempts to communicate a source S to the destination over a Gaussian channel. We assume that the transmitter encodes the source n-length source sequence S^n to codeword X^n. The receiver receives Y^n, which is decoded to $\widehat{S}^n$. The channel gain from the transmitter to the receiver is denoted by h_{sd} and is drawn from a complex Gaussian distribution with unit variance. The channel can be summarized by the following equation:

$$Y = h_{sd}X + Z$$

In the above equation, Z denotes the additive white Gaussian noise with zero mean and unit variance at the receiver. The source S is assumed to be i.i.d complex Gaussian with mean zero and unit variance. Note that in this section, we have normalized the variance of the source to 1 and the results are readily extended to any variance. In reconstructing the source as $\widehat{S}^n$ at the receiver, we observe a distortion which is given by the distortion metric $d(S,\widehat{S})$. The expected distortion suffered is given by

$$ED = \frac{1}{n}\sum_{i=1}^{n}d(S_i,\widehat{S}_i)$$

In this analysis, we assume a squared error distortion metric given by

$$d(s,\widehat{s}) = (s - \widehat{s})^2$$

For a complex Gaussian source with unit variance transmitted at rate R, it is well known that the expected distortion is given by the distortion rate function

$$D(R) = 2^{(-R)}$$

Transmission Strategies: Here, we discuss the transmission strategies that we will investigate. The transmission strategies differ in the way in which the rate of transmission is chosen by the source and channel encoder. We investigate the open loop scenario, where source and channel encoder do not know the actual channel values, but know only the channel distribution and the closed loop scenario, where the channel encoder knows the actual channel values, but the source encoder knows only the channel distribution.

1. Separate Source Channel Coding (SSCC) (Open Loop): In this the rate of transmission is chosen to maximize the throughput of the channel. The rate adaptation is performed at the channel encoder and the source encoder basically adjusts its source coding rate in order to match the rate determined at the channel encoder. The average end-to-end distortion is dictated by this selected rate at the channel encoder, and is computed from the distortion-rate function (for Gaussian sources). In this delay-limited scenario, where there is no instantaneous CSI but only long-term CSI at the transmitter (for example, average link SNR), the rate chosen is given by

$$\widehat{R} = \arg\max_R P_{out}(R) + (1 - P_{out}(R))2^{-R}$$

where Pout(R) denote the probability of outage when rate of transmission equals R, that is, the probability that the transmitted packet cannot be recovered at the receiver since the actual channel capacity falls below the code rate R.

The expected distortion experienced by this scheme is given by

$$ED(R_1, R_2) = P_{out}(R_1) + (P_{out}(R_2) - P_{out}(R_1))2^{-R_1/2} + (1 - P_{out}(R_2))2^{-(R_1+R_2)/2}$$

This scheme is called separate source-channel coding (SSCC) because the rate of transmission is chosen without regards to minimizing the expected distortion. This often happens when the channel coder is not aware of the nature of the source or the distortion rate function. Hence, the transmitter here only focuses on minimizing the negative impact of channel induced errors (that is, channel outages, or packet decoding errors), without trying to mitigate quantization errors.

2. Joint Source Channel Coding (JSCC) (Open Loop): In this, we assume that the source and channel encoder do not have the true channel state information. At a fixed average link SNR, there is a tradeoff between reliable transmission over the channel (through the outage probability or packet error rate (PER), favoring the choice of a lower rate) and an

increased fidelity in the source reconstruction (through the distortion-rate function, favoring the choice of a higher rate). This suggests that there is an optimal rate that minimizes the average end-to-end distortion, hence the source and channel encoder should choose the rate of transmission in a joint manner so as to minimize the end-to-end distortion. Thus, in our framework, even though source compression and channel coding are done separately, the rate adaptation is performed jointly at the source encoder and channel encoder in such an end-to-end optimal way that minimizes average end-to-end distortion (computed from the distortion-rate function (for Gaussian sources)). Here, it is important to note that since the transmitter does not have the instantaneous CSI but only the long-term CSI (that is, the average link SNR), the rate adaptation at the transmitter (that is, at the source encoder and channel encoder) is only from a statistical optimization standpoint. The rate of transmission is given by

$$\widehat{R} = \arg\max{}_R \, P_{out}(R) + (1 - P_{out}(R))2^{-R}$$

In this transmission scheme it is assumed that the source encoder has full knowledge about the nature of the channel and the channel encoder knows about the source and the distortion rate function. Hence, they optimize the rate of transmission to minimize the expected distortion.

3. Layered Joint Source Channel Coding (Open Loop): In this the source is communicated over two different layers, the base layer and the enhancement layer, with unequal error protection (UEP). The base layer is encoded at a lower rate and stronger codes while the enhancement layer is encoded at a higher rate. The main drawback of communicating at a higher rate is that it leads to more outages and larger expected distortion. By sending two different layers at different rates, we attempt to communicate just the base layer when the channel is heavily faded and both the layers when the channel is strong. The base layer has to be decoded before the enhancement layer can be decoded. We assume that R_1 and R_2 ($R_1 \leq R_2$) are the rates at which the two layers are communicated. If the two layers are sent in a time-division multiplexed (TDM) manner, then the expected distortion incurred is given by

$$ED(R_1,R_2) = P_{out}(R_1) + (P_{out}(R_2) - P_{out}(R_1))2^{-R_1/2} + (1 - P_{out}(R_2)2^{-(R_1+R_2)/2}$$

If the layers are superimposed on each other before transmission, the expected distortion achieved is lower than that achieved by transmitting the layers in a TDM manner. To compute the expected distortion, we also need to optimize over the powers allocated to the two layers. In either case, the rates R_1 and R_2 are chosen jointly by the source and channel encoder to minimize the expected distortion.

4. Joint Source-Channel Coding (Closed Loop): In this, we assume that the channel encoder completely knows the channel gains which allows for it to perform dynamic rate adaptation, but the source encoder knows only the long term channel statistics. In this setting, there is no concern about channel outage due to dynamic rate adaptation at the channel encoder based on the instantaneous channel realization. The performance of this scheme is similar to the performance of the open loop scenario when only a single layer is transmitted. This is because the source encoder, not knowing the channel gains, transmits at a rate R, which may be higher than the channel capacity. If the rate of transmission is higher than the channel capacity, the channel encoder cannot do anything as it has access to only 1 layer. The only possible advantage in this scenario is that the channel encoder can stop transmitting data if the rate of transmission exceeds channel capacity (as it will definitely result in outage) leading to power savings.

In this scenario, when the source is encoded at two or more different rates using multiple description source coding techniques, the closed loop scenario leads to significantly lower distortion values. For instance, the source encoder may encode the data using two different compression levels at rates R1, and R2, where R2 is greater than R1. Depending on the channel value, the channel encoder chooses to either send the high-rate data stream or the low-rate data stream. The expected distortion based on this approach is given by

$$ED(R_1,R_2) = P_{out}(R_1) + (P_{out}(R_2) - P_{out}(R_1))2^{-R_1} + (1 - P_{out}(R_2)2^{-R_2}$$

If the two streams are sent in a broadcast manner (superimposed), then again, we see significant improvement in distortion values.

In our theoretical analysis, capacity and end-to-end distortion calculations are based on the assumption of large coding block-lengths over the channel (as well as the source), which make sure that decoding errors caused by AWGN noise (which arise due to finite coding block-lengths) are kept negligibly small and the only cause of packet loss is link failure due to a poor channel fading state (Shannon's capacity theorem ensures that as long as the channel code rate is selected below the capacity, decoding errors due to channel noise can be kept at negligibly small levels via coding over large enough block-lengths). More realistically, even in a closed loop setting with perfect transmit CSI, the dynamic rate adaptation would have to be done subject to a target PER or end-to-end distortion constraint to account for the decoding errors caused by finite coding block-lengths. This may have additional implications on the selection procedures for source and channel code rates, but our presented theoretical analysis does not account for any decoding errors due to finite coding block-lengths. The impact of finite coding block-lengths can easily be incorporated via a simulation-based approach, that will generate lookup table that ensures that any possible target PER or end-to-end distortion constraints will met by the dynamic rate adaptation policy in our closed-loop JSCC framework. In particular, it is possible to achieve a joint optimization for JSCC by imposing an end-to-end distortion constraint (along with a latency constraint to account for delay-limitedness) and dynamically adapting the source and channel rates to the channel variations in a similar way as in the closed-loop approach.

JSCC with Advanced FEC: One way to enhance the end-to-end reliability for multimedia communications is to employ advanced forward error correction (FEC) protocols at the application layer, such as erasure codes, fountain codes and Raptor codes, where erasure coding across packets provides further protection against channel outages and packet failures. In other words, an outer erasure code is concatenated with the inner channel code to correct the errors due to outages (here, one can view the channel as a symbol erasure channel, where each symbol refers to a channel codeword or a packet transmitted over the channel). The application of erasure codes in this context treats the event of packet reception failure (channel outage) as an erasure, and adds extra coding protection to mitigate these types of channel-induced errors by coding across packets. For instance, in the 3GPP standard's MBMS mode, Raptor codes (a practical implementation of rateless erasure codes, also known as fountain codes) developed by Digital Fountain were adopted for this purpose.

JSCC may also be integrated with erasure coding techniques (such as fountain codes, and Raptor codes). In particular, the end-to-end distortion minimization framework and the consequent source and channel coding rate selection procedures can be extended for demonstrating the benefits of JSCC, so that it can also be used in conjunction with erasure coding, and shown that erasure coding leads to further performance gains in addition to those provided by JSCC. Here, the JSCC-based end-to-end optimization framework jointly optimizes erasure code rate in conjunction with source and channel code rates. Additionally, the JSCC optimization framework may be applicable together with other outer coding and advanced FEC techniques such as Bose-Chaudhuri-Hocquenghem (BCH) codes, Reed-Solomon (RS) codes, and rate-compatible punctured convolutional (RCPC) codes.

Simulation Results: As described in the system model, we consider a complex Gaussian source with zero mean and unit variance communicated across a Gaussian channel where the channel gain is drawn from a complex Gaussian distribution with unit variance. The power constraint at the transmitter is assumed to be equal to P, while the noise level at the receiver is normalized to unity. We compare the performance of different transmission strategies from the peak SNR (PSNR) perspective. PSNR is related to the average distortion ED in the following manner (assuming a pixel representation with 8 bits per sample):

$$PSNR = 10 * \log(255^2 / ED)$$

In Figure C.18, we plot PSNR versus SNR (dB) for the different transmission strategies considered. As seen here, the JSCC techniques lead to an advantage in performance over the classical rate control scheme with separate source and channel coding due to a rate adaptation policy that aims to mitigate quantization errors and channel-induced errors simultaneously. The reduction in distortion from JSCC would be even higher if source coding and channel coding were done completely separately. Furthermore, we observe that closed-loop JSCC can achieve a lower end-to-end distortion with respect to open-loop approaches, but this scheme may not be feasible in many delay-limited communication settings where reliable feedback mechanisms are not available.

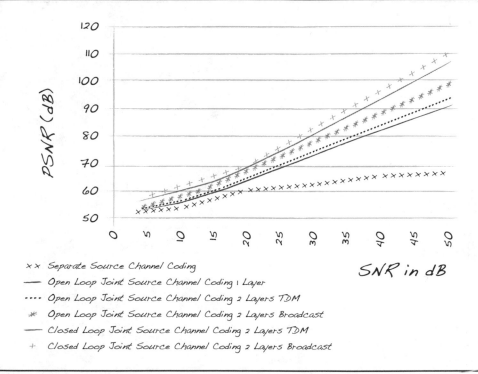

Figure C.18   Plot of PSNR versus SNR (dB) for Point-to-Point Channel Model

As seen in the plot in Figure C.19, erasure coding in conjunction with JSCC further helps to reduce end-to-end distortion for both separate source and channel coding schemes (black curve without erasure coding, cyan curve with erasure coding) and JSCC schemes (blue curve without erasure coding, red curve with erasure coding).

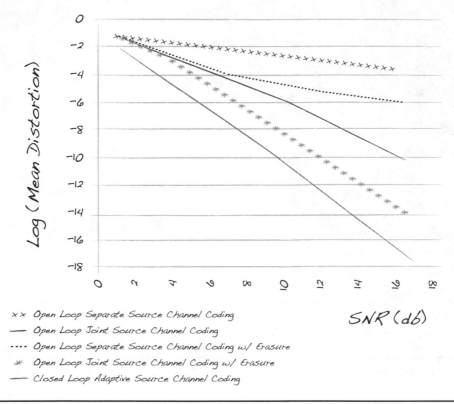

Figure C.19   End-to-end distortion performance of JSCC in conjunction with erasure codes

Validation of JSCC Gains over the Multicellular WiMAX Network

In this section, we analyze the benefits of joint source-channel coding for a WiMAX cellular network. Next, we describe the system model for the WiMAX cellular network.

System Model: We study a multicellular network with the center cell surrounded by neighboring interfering cells. The radius of each cell is assumed to be D. At the center of each cell is the base station and the mobile users are distributed uniformly within the cell. We assume global frequency reuse across all cells. During each scheduling interval, each base station chooses a mobile user to serve. The choice of mobile user is done in a greedy manner. That is, the base station chooses the mobile user with the best channel gain. We assume that there is a minimum radius W around the base station where no mobile users can exist. The system is described in Figure C.20.

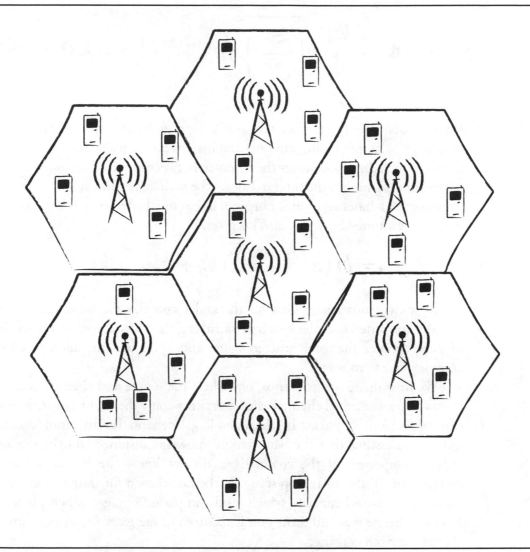

Figure C.20   Cellular Network System Model

In the multicellular network, we consider the broadband channel model. Using OFDMA turns the frequency selective fading channel into a set of parallel frequency-flat fading channels. We define the frequency response over a given link by

$$H(e^{j2\pi\theta}) = \sum_{l=0}^{L-1} \sqrt{\left(\frac{\xi}{d^p}\right)} \, h_l \, e^{-j2\pi \, l\theta} \qquad 0 \le \theta \le 2\pi$$

where L denotes the number of channel taps, h_l denotes the lth tap of the frequency selective fading channel impulse response realization, ξ denotes the shadow fading, d denotes the distance between the base station and the corresponding mobile user and p denotes the path loss exponent. The discrete time complex-baseband input-output relation for the frequency flat channel over the kth tone ($k = 1, 2, \ldots, K$) is given by

$$y_k = H(e^{j2\pi \, (k/K)})x_k + z_k$$

In the above equation, x_k denotes the scalar complex Gaussian data input signal transmitted over the k-th tone satisfying the transmit power constraint of P, y_k denotes the reconstructed signal and z_k denotes the additive white complex Gaussian noise.

We investigate two scenarios, one where the source and channel encoder do not know the actual channel values, but know only the channel distribution (the open-loop) scenario. In the open-loop scenario for the multicellular model, we assume that the base station know the distance and the shadow fading component of the channel but do not know the Rayleigh fading component. In the open loop scenario, the rate chosen for transmission may exceed the channel capacity which results in packet outage. When packet is lost, we assume that full distortion is incurred as the receiver has to estimate the source from nothing.

In the second scenario, we assume that the channel encoder has complete knowledge of the channel, however the source encoder knows only the channel statistics, this setting is referred as the closed loop scenario.

We assume that the source encoder sends different independent streams of data at certain fixed rates, and depending on the channel values, the channel encoder selects the streams of data to send.

Transmission Strategies: We consider the same transmission strategies for the multicellular network. The only difference is the way in which the user is selected in each cell. In the open-loop scenario, the base station chooses the user with the best combination of shadow fading and path loss component of the channel. This is because, the Rayleigh fading follows the same distribution for each user and hence, the user with higher shadow and path loss fading is more likely to have a higher overall channel gain. Moreover, the same user is assigned to all the frequency bands, since the path loss and the shadow fading component of the channel is the same for all the frequency bands. In the closed-loop scenario, the base station chooses the user with best channel gain, and users are assigned to frequency bands in a greedy manner. That is, for each frequency band, the user with the best channel gain is allotted. Note that in both the cases, the base station looks only at the direct channel and does not consider the interfering links in selecting the best user.

Simulation Results: Here, we present simulation results for the multicellular WiMAX system model. We present the system parameter values in Table C.3.

Table C.3   System Parameters Used in the Simulation Study

Parameter	Value
Transmit Power (dBM)	36
Transmitter Gain (dBi)	6
Noise PSD (dBM/Hz)	-167
Bandwidth (MHz)	20
Path Loss Model	EG
Shadowing std (dB)	8
Tx Antenna Height (m)	25
Rx Antenna Height (m)	2
Carrier Frequency (GHz)	3.5
Cell Radius (km)	1.5

We generate users randomly in four discs around the base station and generate users randomly in each disc. The first disc is between 100–500 m, the second disc from 500–800 m, third disc from 800–1000 m, and fourth disc from 1000–1200 m. This is done to show the gains of joint source channel coding as average SINR increases (closer the user to the base station, higher the average SINR). The simulation results are presented in Figure C.25, where we plot PSNR as a function of distance between the mobile station (MS) and base station (BS) for SSCC and various types of JSCC techniques in the open-loop and closed-loop scenarios. We observe that JSCC can significantly reduce end-to-end distortion with respect to SSCC and improve end-to-end robustness of multimedia delivery, particularly for cell-center users closer to the base station, by yielding PSNR gains up to 10-15 dB.

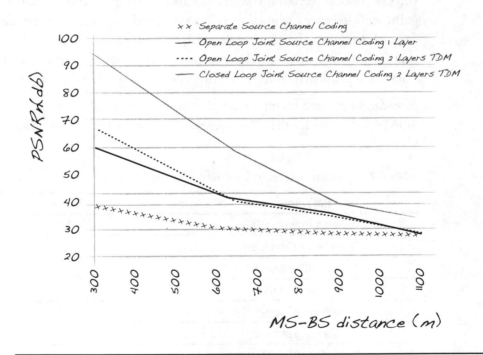

Figure C.21 Simulation results for multicellular WiMAX system model

To summarize this section, we analyzed the benefits of joint source channel coding in terms of minimizing end to end distortion in communicating a continuous source. We showed that joint source channel coding performs significantly better than separate source channel coding for a point to point channel. The joint source channel coding schemes considered were also simple from the point of view of implementation. The only cooperation needed between the source and channel encoder is for the source encoder to know the nature of the channel and for the channel encoder to know the distortion rate function of the source. We also validated that the benefits of joint source-channel coding extend to more practical system models such as the multicellular WiMAX system we considered with realistic broadband frequency-selective channel models. From our WiMAX simulation study, we observed that nearby users gain significant distortion reduction by using joint source-channel coding schemes. We also showed that knowledge of channel gains at the channel encoder can also lead to significant performance benefits with layered coding approaches.

Index